Unity Game Development Essentials

Build fully functional, professional 3D games
with realistic environments, sound, dynamic effects,
and more!

Will Goldstone

BIRMINGHAM - MUMBAI

Unity Game Development Essentials

Copyright © 2009 Packt Publishing

First published: October 2009

Production Reference: 1250909

Published by Packt Publishing Ltd.
32 Lincoln Road
Olton
Birmingham, B27 6PA, UK.

ISBN 978-1-847198-18-1

www.packtpub.com

Cover Image by Charles Hinshaw (charles@unity3d.com)

Credits

Author
Will Goldstone

Reviewers
Aaron Cross
Emil E. Johansen
Clifford Peters
Jonathan Sykes

Acquisition Editor
James Lumsden

Development Editor
Amey Kanse

Technical Editors
Shadab Khan
Smita Solanki

Copy Editor
Leonard D'Silva

Indexer
Monica Ajmera

Editorial Team Leader
Akshara Aware

Project Team Leader
Priya Mukherji

Project Coordinator
Zainab Bagasrawala

Proofreader
Sandra Hopper

Graphics
Nilesh R. Mohite

Production Coordinators
Adline Swetha Jesuthas
Aparna Bhagat

Cover Work
Adline Swetha Jesuthas

About the Author

Will Goldstone is an interactive designer and tutor based in the south west of England. Spending much of his time online, he focuses on web design and game development, specializing in online tutoring of many interactive disciplines.

Having discovered Unity in its first version, he has been working to promote its 'game development for everyone' ethic ever since and works with Unity to produce online games and games for the Apple-iPhone platform.

Will is reachable through his blog at www.willgoldstone.com, where you can find links to his various other online activities. He spends his free time on graphics designing, photography, writing loud music, and playing frisbee on the beach.

I would like to thank my fantastic family and friends for supporting me during the production of this book—it wouldn't be here without you! Massive thanks also to the members of the Unity Technologies team and Unity IRC channel whose tireless patience got me started in Unity development back when; big thanks especially to Dan Blacker, Joachim Ante, Emil Johansen, Cliff Peters, Tom Higgins, Charles Hinshaw, Neil Carter, ToreTank, Mike Mac, Duckets, Joe Robins, Daniel Brauer, Dock, oPless, Thomas Lund, Digitalos and anyone else I've neglectfully forgotten. A massive cheers to all of you; you guys rock.

About the Reviewers

Aaron Cross is a freelance video game developer based in New Zealand. A successful musician and music producer, film-maker, and 3D artist, he switched his focus to game development in 2006. Since then he has produced three video game titles, and has provided art and programming solutions to Unity developers across the globe. He is based in Wellington, New Zealand.

In addition to commercial games, he has developed simulations for medical training, architectural visualization, science and research, conservation, and visual reconstructions for evidence used in court cases, using the Unity game engine.

I would like to acknowledge the creators of this amazing program, this amazing tool that allows the ultimate digital experience in creative expression. I've done a lot of things in my life, but only when I found the gateway to real-time development through Unity did I finally realize that I could be really passionate and successful at the same time. My imagination has turned into a tangible reality with this tool, and it's become a foundation to my professional success. I can't thank you enough. I'd also like to thank my clients for being part of the fun! Many of you have become good friends over the code and polygons, late nights, and creative successes. And finally, I'd like to thank Gavin Hewitt, who taught me all the hard stuff, but also taught me how to love pencils and paper, and got me on good firm ground right from the start...

Enjoy your work my friends!

Emil E. Johansen is a freelance game development consultant living in Copenhagen, Denmark. Having worked professionally with engines, such as Renderware, CryEngine, and UnrealEngine 3, Emil joined the Unity community when going freelance and has been very active there by the alias AngryAnt.

In the Unity community, Emil has actively promoted and participated in the Wiki and IRC channels, while developing AI middleware solutions for Unity.

When not hooked up to the internet, Emil enjoys biking, sailing, and concert going. Online he can be found on the Unity forums, Wiki, and IRC channel as AngryAnt, on Twitter by the same name, and at AngryAnt.com.

Clifford Peters is 19 years old and has recently graduated from high school. A few years ago, Clifford decided to make his own web site. He learned about HTML and started to hand code his own web site. Later, he rewrote his web site after learning about XHTML and CSS. Later, after getting bored with making a web site, Clifford decided that he would instead make a computer game. He tried a bunch of different game engines but did not like using them very much. Clifford then found out about Unity, and after using it for a few weeks, he realized that he liked it because it was easy to use. He liked it so much that he went and bought it, and now he often spends hours a day programming with Unity and developing games.

Jonathan Sykes is a senior play researcher, skilled in the design and evaluation of the play experience. He is the director of eMotionLab, a premier research facility, which offers both consultancy and development services in the area of game production and play-testing. His particular research focus is the application of play technologies to serious endeavors, such as health, education, and business.

Both a psychologist and usability engineer, Jonathan's work is very much player-centered, and focused on the player experience. He has worked with Microsoft's Game User Research group to develop player-centered approaches to game design and evaluation and written academic papers and textbook chapters on the subject. He also works as a senior lecturer at Glasgow Caledonian University where he delivers undergraduate courses in player-centered game development.

Table of Contents

Preface

Unity is a 3D game authoring tool for Mac and PC. Game engines are the nuts and bolts that sit behind the scenes of every video game. From the artwork right down to the mathematics that decide every frame on screen, the "engine" makes the decisions. Starting out with rendering—the method of displaying graphics on screen, and integrating a control method and a set of rules for the game to follow—the engine is what a developer builds to "house" the game. Modern 3D game engines are a deluge of meticulously written code, and as such, once used for their intended purpose (which is the production of a game they are made for), these engines are often sold, modified, and reused. An obvious example of this is the Epic Games Unreal Engine. Originally developed in the late 90s for Unreal—a PC First Person Shooter—the engine has gone on to see massive success in its more recent incarnations, being licensed by other developers for literally hundreds of commercial games and simulations.

Due to the level of complexity and cost of such commercial game engines, the game development industry is a difficult area of interest for potential fresh talent to break into, without studying programming languages such as C++ extensively. Modern console and computer games are built around C++ as it is currently the most efficient language in terms of computational speed, and as such, the structure and commands of commercial games engines require thousands upon thousands of such lines of code to function. This code is delivered in Unity with the help of just-in-time compilation (known as JIT), using the open source C++ library Mono. By using JIT compilation, engines such as Unity can take advantage of high-speed compilation, whereby the code you will write for Unity is compiled to Mono just before it is executed. This is crucial for games that must execute code at specific moments during runtime. In addition to the Mono library, Unity also takes advantage of other software libraries in its functionality, such as Nvidia's PhysX physics engine, OpenGL, and DirectX for 3D rendering and OpenAL for audio. All these libraries are built into the application, so you will not need to worry about learning how to use them individually. So, simply sit back and enjoy them working for you seamlessly within Unity.

The developers of engines also build tools with which to command the functional coding they have created. For example, the creation of an outdoor terrain is held in a set of instructions which define its shape (or topography), visual appearance, and even how it responds to deformation in game. But this set of instructions would be inefficient as a part of the game engine were it not attached to a visual tool to control the aforementioned properties. This is where a Graphical User Interface (GUI) comes in. Game engine developers will often build an interface of tools to aid their team in manipulating parts of the engine in order to save time in the development process and make the engine accessible to potential buyers, post production. This is also true of Unity, as it has a very strong community of users that share their tools in the form of plugins for the package. Visit the Unify community wiki at http://www.unifycommunity.com/wiki for more information.

For many new potential developers, the steep learning curve required to pick up programming languages such as C++, or the engines that utilize it, is simply too great a task to attempt. Without completing degree-level studies in programming or computer animation, it is difficult for many enthusiasts to get started in learning the concepts, methods, and design principles involved in game production. Unity Technologies is one such company that has set out to rectify this. Starting with their own game engine in 2001, the Danish-based game development company endeavoured to strip down their complex game development tools and make a simple, user-driven package that anyone could pick up and begin experimenting with. The team resolved to keep the source code that drives the engine behind the scenes, instead providing a complete GUI (Graphical User Interface) that allows the user to control the powerful engine source code without ever having to create parts of it themselves. This factor has made Unity highly popular with new developers, and is likely one of the key reasons you're reading this book. By establishing logical concepts and categorizing common methods involved in game production, Unity puts the power of its engine into the user's hands, allowing maximum results with minimal effort, thereby encouraging experimentation with the most crucial factor of all—gameplay.

Having appealed to many games developers, Unity has filled a gap in the games development market that few others can fully claim to cater to. Having the ability to produce professional standard games, publish 3D to both Mac and PC, as well as having its own Web Player, Unity is one of the fastest growing game engines in its sector. The engine also has its own Nintendo Wii and Apple iPhone developing versions, meaning that once you have mastered the basics, a pipeline to not only home computer, but also to console and mobile development lies ahead of you.

The fast pace of the entertainment and marketing industries requires a quick turnaround of gaming media. Also, many companies are now looking to packages such as Unity to enable their creatives to produce better products with the greatest of ease. With 2009 seeing the release of Unity version 2.5, and its first steps onto PC format, its usage looks set to skyrocket. But what is Unity? How does it work? What can it do? And most importantly, how can it get you get started on the path to 3D game development in just a few weeks?

What this book covers

This book is designed to cover a set of easy-to-follow examples, which culminate in the production of a First-Person-viewed 3D game, complete with an interactive island environment. By introducing common concepts of game and 3D production, we'll explore the use of Unity to make a player character interact with the game world, and build puzzles for the player to solve in order to complete the game.

Here's a quick chapter-by-chapter overview of what will be covered:

Chapter 1—Welcome to the Third Dimension

This chapter covers the key concepts we'll need to understand and complete the exercise in this book. It takes a brief look at 3D concepts and the processes used by Unity to create games.

Chapter 2—Environments

Our game world is but an empty void! We'll kick off with this chapter by taking a look at the various ways to incorporate terrains, externally produced 3D models, and other Unity engine features such as sound and lighting to get your game environment up and running.

Chapter 3—Player Characters

Every game needs a hero, right? In this chapter, we'll be taking a look at every element that goes into making the first-person player character from input controls to cameras and colliders. Once you've learnt what goes into making him, you'll introduce the player character to your island and take a stroll around.

Chapter 4—Interactions

Games are all about interacting with a virtual world, so where would our character be without some in-game actions? In this chapter, I'll introduce you to collision detection and ray casting. We'll look at how we can combine these techniques with scripting and animation to transform our static building into one that responds to our player.

Chapter 5—Prefabs, Collection, and HUD

Giving your player a sense of achievement in your game is essential. To help with this, you'll need to remind them of actions they've taken so far in the game, and give them something to aim for. In this fifth chapter, we will construct what is often referred to as a Heads Up Display (HUD) with text and graphical displays that change dynamically as the user plays.

Having created a simple HUD, you'll create a short object-collection game, which will allow the player character to pick up batteries in order to gain access to the building on the island.

Chapter 6—Instantiation and Rigidbodies

Almost every game scenario that you can imagine will involve creating or "spawning" objects in your environment. Known in programming terms as **Instantiation**, the creation of objects during the game's runtime is a crucial concept for every beginner developer to get to grips with.

Having created our collection game and building interaction in previous chapters, we'll be building upon the interactivity in our game by creating a basic target game, which will involve throwing objects at targets to unlock a part of our environment. This will not only teach you about instantiation, but also the crucial concept of using rigid body physics objects in your games.

Chapter 7— Particle Systems

What's a 3D game these days without some fancy graphic effects to wow the player? In this chapter, you'll be creating a log fire to keep our player warm—using two particle systems, one for flames and the other for smoke.

Using a Particle System, we'll look at how we can mimic the behavior of fire and utilize images for each particle to add realism; we'll finish by disabling the fire, giving the player something to aim for—getting it lit to keep warm!

Chapter 8—Menu Design

Creating a professional, easy-to-navigate menu is a crucial part of making an enjoyable game product. What user is going to want to play your game if he or she can't even find the Start button? In this chapter, we look at the various ways of creating menus and other user interfaces for the player to interact with.

You will create menus using both GUI textures and the GUI class in order to create scalable interfaces that can be deployed on the desktop or the Web.

Chapter 9—Finishing Touches

In game production, especially in Unity, you will reach a point at which you have just created some piece of interaction in your game that you're so pleased with, you want to add that extra polish to make it really stand out to the player.

In this chapter we'll take a look at further uses of sound, lighting effects, trail rendering, and other dynamic effects that are easy to implement, and make the difference between a simple working game and a polished final product.

Chapter 10—Building and sharing

In this chapter, we will look at how we can export your game for the Web and as a standalone project. We'll look at various different settings you will need to consider when you are preparing your finished product for your audience, such as graphical quality, control input, and more.

Chapter 11—Testing and further study

In this chapter, we will discuss the ways in which you should move on from this book, and how you can gather information from test users to improve your game. This will help you prepare your project to be tested by a wider audience to get feedback and make even better games!

What you need for this book

- An installed copy of the Unity software—a trial version is available from Unity3D.com

- Internet connection in order to download supplied 3D models and other assets, available from PacktPub.com

- An available 3D modelling package, although this is not essential. All materials used are provided as per above. If you are new to modelling, you may wish to download one of a few free applications that work well with Unity, such as Blender from Blender.org.

Who this book is for

Having worked with Unity for the past few years as a tutor, I've found the main complaint that its users encounter is not with the software itself, but rather that there is a lack of introductory material for new users coming from a non-programming based background.

In the existing climate, this is, of course, rare; but with a tool such as Unity allowing such ease of production as it does, the importance of such a tutorial guide has become ever more pressing.

If you're a designer or animator who wishes to make their first steps into game development, or if you've simply spent many hours seated in front of video games, with ideas bubbling away in the back of your mind, Unity and this book could be your ideal starting point. I will assume no prior knowledge of game production and start completely from scratch, inviting you to simply bring with you a passion for making great games.

Conventions

In this book, you will find a number of styles of text that distinguish between different kinds of information. Here are some examples of these styles, and an explanation of their meaning.

Code words in text are shown as follows: "We can include other contexts through the use of the include directive."

A block of code will be set as follows:

```
if(collisionInfo.gameObject.name == "matchbox"){
    Destroy(collisionInfo.gameObject);
        haveMatches=true;
        audio.PlayOneShot(batteryCollect);
```

New terms and **important words** are shown in bold. Words that you see on the screen, in menus or dialog boxes for example, appear in our text like this: "clicking the **Next** button moves you to the next screen."

Warnings or important notes appear in a box like this.

 Tips and tricks appear like this.

Reader feedback

Feedback from our readers is always welcome. Let us know what you think about this book—what you liked or may have disliked. Reader feedback is important for us to develop titles that you really get the most out of.

To send us general feedback, simply drop an email to feedback@packtpub.com, and mention the book title in the subject of your message.

If there is a book that you need and would like to see us publish, please send us a note in the **SUGGEST A TITLE** form on www.packtpub.com or email suggest@packtpub.com.

If there is a topic that you have expertise in and you are interested in either writing or contributing to a book, see our author guide on www.packtpub.com/authors.

Customer support

Now that you are the proud owner of a Packt book, we have a number of things to help you to get the most from your purchase.

Downloading the necessary assets for the book

Visit http://www.packtpub.com/files/code/8181_Code.zip to directly download the asset packages you will need to use to complete this book.

The package also contains example code for the programming parts of the book.

Errata

Although we have taken every care to ensure the accuracy of our contents, mistakes do happen. If you find a mistake in one of our books—maybe a mistake in text or code—we would be grateful if you would report this to us. By doing so, you can save other readers from frustration, and help us to improve subsequent versions of this book. If you find any errata, please report them by visiting http://www.packtpub.com/support, selecting your book, clicking on the **let us know** link, and entering the details of your errata. Once your errata are verified, your submission will be accepted and the errata added to any list of existing errata. Any existing errata can be viewed by selecting your title from http://www.packtpub.com/support.

Piracy

Piracy of copyright material on the Internet is an ongoing problem across all media. At Packt, we take the protection of our copyright and licenses very seriously. If you come across any illegal copies of our works in any form on the Internet, please provide us with the location address or web site name immediately so that we can pursue a remedy.

Please contact us at copyright@packtpub.com with a link to the suspected pirated material.

We appreciate your help in protecting our authors, and our ability to bring you valuable content.

Questions

You can contact us at questions@packtpub.com if you are having a problem with any aspect of the book, and we will do our best to address it.

1
Welcome to the Third Dimension

Before getting started with any 3D package, it is crucial to understand the environment you'll be working in. As **Unity** is primarily a 3D-based development tool, many concepts throughout this book will assume a certain level of understanding of 3D development and game engines. It is crucial that you equip yourself with an understanding of these concepts before diving into the practical elements of the rest of this book.

Getting to grips with 3D

Let's take a look at the crucial elements of 3D worlds, and how Unity lets you develop games in the third dimension.

Coordinates

If you have worked with any 3D artworking application before, you'll likely be familiar with the concept of the **Z-axis**. The Z-axis, in addition to the existing X for horizontal and Y for vertical, represents depth. In 3D applications, you'll see information on objects laid out in X, Y, Z format—this is known as the **Cartesian coordinate** method. Dimensions, rotational values, and positions in the 3D world can all be described in this way. In this book, like in other documentation of 3D, you'll see such information written with parenthesis, shown as follows:

(10, 15, 10)

This is mostly for neatness, and also due to the fact that in programming, these values must be written in this way. Regardless of their presentation, you can assume that any sets of three values separated by commas will be in X, Y, Z order.

Local space versus World space

A crucial concept to begin looking at is the difference between **Local space** and **World space**. In any 3D package, the world you will work in is technically infinite, and it can be difficult to keep track of the location of objects within it. In every 3D world, there is a point of origin, often referred to as zero, as it is represented by the position (0,0,0).

All world positions of objects in 3D are relative to world zero. However, to make things simpler, we also use Local space (also known as **Object space**) to define object positions in relation to one another. Local space assumes that every object has its own zero point, which is the point from which its axis handles emerge. This is usually the center of the object, and by creating relationships between objects, we can compare their positions in relation to one another. Such relationships, known as **parent-child relationships**, mean that we can calculate distances from other objects using Local space, with the parent object's position becoming the new zero point for any of its child objects. For more information on parent-child relationships, see Chapter 3.

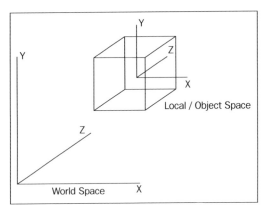

Vectors

You'll also see 3D vectors described in Cartesian coordinates. Like their 2D counterparts, 3D vectors are simply lines drawn in the 3D world that have a direction and a length. Vectors can be moved in world space, but remain unchanged themselves. Vectors are useful in a game engine context, as they allow us to calculate distances, relative angles between objects, and the direction of objects.

Cameras

Cameras are essential in the 3D world, as they act as the viewport for the screen. Having a pyramid-shaped field of vision, cameras can be placed at any point in the world, animated, or attached to characters or objects as part of a game scenario.

With adjustable **Field of Vision** (FOV), 3D cameras are your viewport on the 3D world. In game engines, you'll notice that effects such as lighting, motion blurs, and other effects are applied to the camera to help with game simulation of a person's eye view of the world—you can even add a few cinematic effects that the human eye will never experience, such as lens flares when looking at the sun!

Most modern 3D games utilize multiple cameras to show parts of the game world that the character camera is not currently looking at—like a 'cutaway' in cinematic terms. Unity does this with ease by allowing many cameras in a single scene, which can be scripted to act as the main camera at any point during runtime. Multiple cameras can also be used in a game to control the rendering of particular 2D and 3D elements separately as part of the optimization process. For example, objects may be grouped in layers, and cameras may be assigned to render objects in particular layers. This gives us more control over individual renders of certain elements in the game.

Polygons, edges, vertices, and meshes

In constructing 3D shapes, all objects are ultimately made up of interconnected 2D shapes known as **polygons**. On importing models from a modelling application, Unity converts all polygons to **polygon triangles**. Polygon triangles (also referred to as **faces**) are in turn made up of three connected **edges**. The locations at which these vertices meet are known as **points** or **vertices**. By knowing these locations, game engines are able to make calculations regarding the points of impact, known as **collisions**, when using complex collision detection with **Mesh** Colliders, such as in shooting games to detect the exact location at which a bullet has hit another object. By combining many linked polygons, 3D modelling applications allow us to build complex shapes, known as **meshes**. In addition to building 3D shapes, the data stored in meshes can have many other uses. For example, it can be used as surface navigational data by making objects in a game, by following the vertices.

In game projects, it is crucial for the developer to understand the importance of polygon count. The polygon count is the total number of polygons, often in reference to a model, but also in reference to an entire game level. The higher the number of polygons, the more work your computer must do to render the objects onscreen. This is why, in the past decade or so, we've seen an increase in the level of detail from early 3D games to those of today—simply compare the visual detail in a game, such as Id's *Quake* (1996) with the details seen in a game, such as Epic's *Gears Of War* (2006). As a result of faster technology, game developers are now able to model 3D characters and worlds for games that contain a much higher polygon count and this trend will inevitably continue.

Materials, textures, and shaders

Materials are a common concept to all 3D applications, as they provide the means to set the visual appearance of a 3D model. From basic colors to reflective image-based surfaces, materials handle everything.

Starting with a simple color and the option of using one or more images — known as **textures** — in a single material, the material works with the **shader**, which is a script in charge of the style of rendering. For example, in a reflective shader, the material will render reflections of surrounding objects, but maintain its color or the look of the image applied as its texture.

In Unity, the use of materials is easy. Any materials created in your 3D modelling package will be imported and recreated automatically by the engine and created as assets to use later. You can also create your own materials from scratch, assigning images as texture files, and selecting a shader from a large library that comes built-in. You may also write your own shader scripts, or implement those written by members of the Unity community, giving you more freedom for expansion beyond the included set.

Crucially, when creating textures for a game in a graphics package such as Photoshop, you must be aware of the resolution. Game textures are expected to be square, and sized to a power of 2. This means that numbers should run as follows:

- 128 x 128
- 256 x 256
- 512 x 512
- 1024 x 1024

Creating textures of these sizes will mean that they can be tiled successfully by the game engine. You should also be aware that the larger the texture file you use, the more processing power you'll be demanding from the player's computer. Therefore, always remember to try resizing your graphics to the smallest power of 2 dimensions possible, without sacrificing too much in the way of quality.

Rigid Body physics

For developers working with game engines, **physics engines** provide an accompanying way of simulating real-world responses for objects in games. In Unity, the game engine uses Nvidia's *PhysX* engine, a popular and highly accurate commercial physics engine.

In game engines, there is no assumption that an object should be affected by physics—firstly because it requires a lot of processing power, and secondly because it simply doesn't make sense. For example, in a 3D driving game, it makes sense for the cars to be under the influence of the physics engine, but not the track or surrounding objects, such as trees, walls, and so on—they simply don't need to be. For this reason, when making games, a **Rigid Body** component is given to any object you want under the control of the physics engine.

Physics engines for games use the Rigid Body dynamics system of creating realistic motion. This simply means that instead of objects being static in the 3D world, they can have the following properties:

- Mass
- Gravity
- Velocity
- Friction

As the power of hardware and software increases, rigid body physics is becoming more widely applied in games, as it offers the potential for more varied and realistic simulation. We'll be utilizing rigid body dynamics as part of our game in Chapter 6.

Collision detection

While more crucial in game engines than in 3D animation, collision detection is the way we analyze our 3D world for inter-object collisions. By giving an object a **Collider** component, we are effectively placing an invisible net around it. This net mimics its shape and is in charge of reporting any collisions with other colliders, making the game engine respond accordingly. For example, in a ten-pin bowling game, a simple spherical collider will surround the ball, while the pins themselves will have either a simple capsule collider, or for a more realistic collision, employ a Mesh collider. On impact, the colliders of any affected objects will report to the physics engine, which will dictate their reaction, based on the direction of impact, speed, and other factors.

In this example, employing a mesh collider to fit exactly to the shape of the pin model would be more accurate but is more **expensive** in processing terms. This simply means that it demands more processing power from the computer, the cost of which is reflected in slower performance—hence the term *expensive*.

Essential Unity concepts

Unity makes the game production process simple by giving you a set of logical steps to build any conceivable game scenario. Renowned for being non-game-type specific, Unity offers you a blank canvas and a set of consistent procedures to let your imagination be the limit of your creativity. By establishing its use of the **Game Object (GO)** concept, you are able to break down parts of your game into easily manageable objects, which are made of many individual **Component** parts. By making individual objects within the game and introducing functionality to them with each component you add, you are able to infinitely expand your game in a logical progressive manner. Component parts in turn have variables—essentially settings to control them with. By adjusting these variables, you'll have complete control over the effect that Component has on your object. Let's take a look at a simple example.

The Unity way

If I wished to have a bouncing ball as part of a game, then I'd begin with a sphere. This can quickly be created from the Unity menus, and will give you a new Game Object with a sphere mesh (a net of a 3D shape), and a **Renderer** component to make it visible. Having created this, I can then add a Rigid body. A Rigidbody (Unity refers to most two-word phrases as a single word term) is a component which tells Unity to apply its physics engine to an object. With this comes mass, gravity, and the ability to apply forces to the object, either when the player commands it or simply when it collides with another object. Our sphere will now fall to the ground when the game runs, but how do we make it bounce? This is simple! The collider component has a variable called **Physic Material**—this is a setting for the Rigidbody, defining how it will react to other objects' surfaces. Here we can select **Bouncy**, an available preset, and voila! Our bouncing ball is complete, in only a few clicks.

This streamlined approach for the most basic of tasks, such as the previous example, seems pedestrian at first. However, you'll soon find that by applying this approach to more complex tasks, they become very simple to achieve. Here is an overview of those key Unity concepts plus a few more.

Assets

These are the building blocks of all Unity projects. From graphics in the form of image files, through 3D models and sound files, Unity refers to the files you'll use to create your game as assets. This is why in any Unity project folder all files used are stored in a child folder named Assets.

 This book consists of code files and assets uploaded on our web site (www.packtpub.com/files/code/8181_Code.zip) and available for extraction here. Please extract the files from the already mentioned link to take advantage of the asset codes, an integral part of unity game development.

Scenes

In Unity, you should think of **scenes** as individual levels, or areas of game content (such as menus). By constructing your game with many scenes, you'll be able to distribute loading times and test different parts of your game individually.

Game Objects

When an asset is used in a game scene, it becomes a new Game Object—referred to in Unity terms—especially in scripting—using the contracted term "GameObject". All GameObjects contain at least one component to begin with, that is, the **Transform** component. Transform simply tells the Unity engine the position, rotation, and scale of an object—all described in X, Y, Z coordinate (or in the case of scale, dimensional) order. In turn, the component can then be addressed in scripting in order to set an object's position, rotation, or scale. From this initial component, you will build upon game objects with further components adding required functionality to build every part of any game scenario you can imagine.

Components

Components come in various forms. They can be for creating behavior, defining appearance, and influencing other aspects of an object's function in the game. By 'attaching' components to an object, you can immediately apply new parts of the game engine to your object. Common components of game production come built-in with Unity, such as the Rigidbody component mentioned earlier, down to simpler elements such as lights, cameras, particle emitters, and more. To build further interactive elements of the game, you'll write scripts, which are treated as components in Unity.

Scripts

While being considered by Unity to be Components, **scripts** are an essential part of game production, and deserve a mention as a key concept. In this book, we'll write our scripts in JavaScript, but you should be aware that Unity offers you the opportunity to write in C# and Boo (a derivative of the Python language) also. I've chosen to demonstrate Unity with JavaScript, as it is a functional programming language, with a simple to follow syntax that some of you may already have encountered in other endeavors such as Adobe Flash development in ActionScript or in using JavaScript itself for web development.

Unity does not require you to learn how the coding of its own engine works or how to modify it, but you will be utilizing scripting in almost every game scenario you develop. The beauty of using Unity scripting is that any script you write for your game will be straightforward enough after a few examples, as Unity has its own built-in Behavior class—a set of scripting instructions for you to call upon. For many new developers, getting to grips with scripting can be a daunting prospect, and one that threatens to put off new Unity users who are simply accustomed to design only. I will introduce scripting one step at a time, with a mind to showing you not only the importance, but also the power of effective scripting for your Unity games.

To write scripts, you'll use Unity's standalone script editor. On Mac, this is an application called **Unitron**, and on PC, **Uniscite**. These separate applications can be found in the Unity application folder on your PC or Mac and will be launched any time you edit a new script or an existing one. Amending and saving scripts in the script editor will immediately update the script in Unity. You may also designate your own script editor in the Unity preferences if you wish.

Prefabs

Unity's development approach hinges around the GameObject concept, but it also has a clever way to store objects as assets to be reused in different parts of your game, and then 'spawned' or 'cloned' at any time. By creating complex objects with various components and settings, you'll be effectively building a template for something you may want to spawn multiple instances of, with each instance then being individually modifiable. Consider a crate as an example—you may have given the object in the game a mass, and written scripted behaviors for its destruction; chances are you'll want to use this object more than once in a game, and perhaps even in games other than the one it was designed for.

Prefabs allow you to store the object, complete with components and current configuration. Comparable to the *MovieClip* concept in Adobe Flash, think of prefabs simply as empty containers that you can fill with objects to form a data template you'll likely recycle.

The interface

The Unity interface, like many other working environments, has a customizable layout. Consisting of several dockable spaces, you can pick which parts of the interface appear where. Let's take a look at a typical Unity layout:

As the previous image demonstrates (PC version shown), there are five different elements you'll be dealing with:

- **Scene** [1] — where the game is constructed
- **Hierarchy** [2] — a list of GameObjects in the scene
- **Inspector** [3] — settings for currently selected asset/object
- **Game** [4] — the preview window, active only in play mode
- **Project** [5] — a list of your project's assets, acts as a library

The Scene window and Hierarchy

The **Scene** window is where you will build the entirety of your game project in Unity. This window offers a perspective (full 3D) view, which is switchable to orthographic (top down, side on, and front on) views. This acts as a fully rendered 'Editor' view of the game world you build. Dragging an asset to this window will make it an active game object. The **Scene** view is tied to the **Hierarchy**, which lists all active objects in the currently open scene in ascending alphabetical order.

The **Scene** window is also accompanied by four useful control buttons, as shown in the previous image. Accessible from the keyboard using keys *Q*, *W*, *E*, and *R*, these keys perform the following operations:

- **The Hand tool** [*Q*]: This tools allows navigation of the **Scene** window. By itself, it allows you to drag around in the **Scene** window to pan your view. Holding down *Alt* with this tool selected will allow you to rotate your view, and holding the *Command* key (Apple) or *Ctrl* key (PC) will allow you to zoom. Holding the *Shift* key down also will speed up both of these functions.
- **The Translate tool** [*W*]: This is your active selection tool. As you can completely interact with the **Scene** window, selecting objects either in the **Hierarchy** or **Scene** means you'll be able to drag the object's axis handles in order to reposition them.
- **The Rotate tool** [*E*]: This works in the same way as Translate, using visual 'handles' to allow you to rotate your object around each axis.
- **The Scale tool** [*R*]: Again, this tool works as the Translate and Rotate tools do. It adjusts the size or scale of an object using visual handles.

Having selected objects in either the **Scene** or **Hierarchy**, they immediately get selected in both. Selection of objects in this way will also show the properties of the object in the **Inspector**. Given that you may not be able to see an object you've selected in the **Hierarchy** in the **Scene** window, Unity also provides the use of the *F* key, to focus your **Scene** view on that object. Simply select an object from the **Hierarchy**, hover your mouse cursor over the **Scene** window, and press *F*.

The Inspector

Think of the **Inspector** as your personal toolkit to adjust every element of any game object or asset in your project. Much like the *Property Inspector* concept utilized by Adobe in Flash and Dreamweaver, this is a context-sensitive window. All this means is that whatever you select, the **Inspector** will change to show its relevant properties—it is sensitive to the context in which you are working.

The **Inspector** will show every component part of anything you select, and allow you to adjust the variables of these components, using simple form elements such as text input boxes, slider scales, buttons, and drop-down menus. Many of these variables are tied into Unity's drag-and-drop system, which means that rather than selecting from a drop-down menu, if it is more convenient, you can drag-and-drop to choose settings.

This window is not only for inspecting objects. It will also change to show the various options for your project when choosing them from the **Edit** menu, as it acts as an ideal space to show you preferences—changing back to showing component properties as soon as you reselect an object or asset.

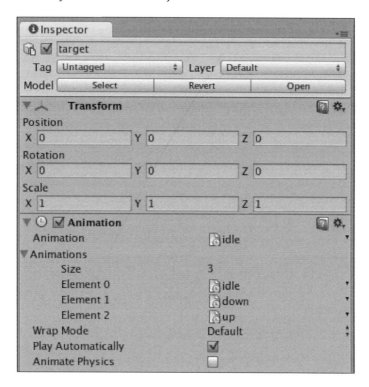

In this screenshot, the **Inspector** is showing properties for a target object in the game. The object itself features two components—**Transform** and **Animation**. The **Inspector** will allow you to make changes to settings in either of them. Also notice that to temporarily disable any component at any time—which will become very useful for testing and experimentation—you can simply deselect the box to the left of the component's name. Likewise, if you wish to switch off an entire object at a time, then you may deselect the box next to its name at the top of the **Inspector** window.

The Project window

The **Project** window is a direct view of the `Assets` folder of your project. Every Unity project is made up of a parent folder, containing three subfolders—`Assets`, `Library`, and while the Unity Editor is running, a `Temp` folder. Placing assets into the **Assets** folder means you'll immediately be able to see them in the **Project** window, and they'll also be automatically imported into your Unity project. Likewise, changing any asset located in the `Assets` folder, and resaving it from a third-party application, such as Photoshop, will cause Unity to reimport the asset, reflecting your changes immediately in your project and any active scenes that use that particular asset.

> It is important to remember that you should only alter asset locations and names using the **Project** window—using Finder (Mac) or Windows Explorer (PC) to do so may break connections in your Unity project. Therefore, to relocate or rename objects in your `Assets` folder, use Unity's **Project** window instead.

The **Project** window is accompanied by a **Create** button. This allows the creation of any assets that can be made within Unity, for example, scripts, prefabs, and materials.

The Game window

The **Game** window is invoked by pressing the **Play** button and acts as a realistic test of your game. It also has settings for screen ratio, which will come in handy when testing how much of the player's view will be restricted in certain ratios, such as 4:3 (as opposed to wide) screen resolutions. Having pressed **Play**, it is crucial that you bear in mind the following advice:

> In play mode, the adjustments you make to any parts of your game scene are merely temporary—it is meant as a testing mode only, and when you press **Play** again to stop the game, all changes made during play mode will be undone. This can often trip up new users, so don't forget about it!

The **Game** window can also be set to **Maximize** when you invoke play mode, giving you a better view of the game at nearly fullscreen—the window expands to fill the interface. It is worth noting that you can expand any part of the interface in this way, simply by hovering over the part you wish to expand and pressing the *Space bar*.

Summary

Here we have looked at the key concepts, you'll need to understand and complete the exercises in this book. Due to space constraints, I cannot cover everything in depth, as 3D development is a vast area of study. With this in mind, I strongly recommend you to continue to read more on the topics discussed in this chapter, in order to supplement your study of 3D development. Each individual piece of software you encounter will have its own dedicated tutorials and resources dedicated to learning it. If you wish to learn 3D artwork to complement your work in Unity, I recommend that you familiarize yourself with your chosen package, after researching the list of tools that work with the Unity pipeline (see list in Chapter 2) and choosing which one suits you best.

Now that we've taken a brief look at 3D concepts and the processes used by Unity to create games, we'll begin using the software by creating the environment for our game.

In the following chapter, we'll get to grips with the terrain editor. With a physical height painting approach, the terrain editor is an easy to use starting point for any game with an outdoor environment. We'll use this to build an island, and in the ensuing chapters we'll add features to the island to create a minigame, in which the user must light a campfire by retrieving matches from a locked outpost. Let's get started!

2
Environments

When building your 3D world, you'll be utilizing two different types of environment—buildings and scenery built in a third-party 3D modelling application and terrains created using the Unity **terrain editor**.

In this chapter, we'll look at the use of both, while giving an overview of the necessary import settings for externally created models, but focusing mainly on using Unity's own tools for creating terrains. We shall specifically be looking at:

- Creating your first Unity project
- Creating and configuring terrains
- Using the terrain toolset to build an island
- Lighting scenes
- Using sound
- Importing Packaged Assets
- Introducing External 3D Models

External modellers

Given that 3D design is an intensive discipline in itself, I recommend that you invest in a similar tutorial guide for your application of choice. If you're new to 3D modelling, then here is a list of 3D modelling packages currently supported by Unity:

- Maya
- 3D Studio Max
- Cheetah 3D
- Cinema 4D
- Blender

- Carara
- Lightwave
- XSI

These are the eight most suited modelling applications as recommended by Unity Technologies. The main reason for this is that they export models in a format that can be automatically read and imported by Unity, once saved into your project's `Assets` folder. These eight application formats will carry their meshes, textures, animations, and bones (a form of skeletal rigging for characters) across to Unity, whereas some smaller packages may not support animation using bones upon import to Unity. For a full view of the latest compatibility chart, visit: http://unity3d.com/unity/features/asset-importing.

Resources

Models in this book will be provided online in a `.fbx` format (a native format for Unity use, which is common to most 3D modelling applications).

When downloading content to use as part of the exercises in this book, you'll need to utilize Unity's **package** system. Accessible from the **Assets** top menu, importing and exporting Unity packages gives you the ability to transfer assets between projects while including **dependencies**. A dependency is simply another asset related to the one you are importing/exporting. For example, when exporting a 3D model as part of a Unity package—when transferring to a collaborator, or simply between your own Unity projects—you would need to transfer the relevant materials and textures associated with the models, and these associated assets would be referred to as the model's dependencies.

When prompted throughout the book, you'll download the assets provided in the Unity package format and add them to your assets by using **Assets | Import Package**.

Your first Unity project

As Unity comes in two different forms—an Indie and Pro developer license, we'll stick to using features that the beginner, and therefore a likely Indie license holder, will have access to.

Having installed Unity, your first launch will present you with the *Island Demo* project. This is effectively a showcase project to demonstrate Unity's abilities and also to help new users pick apart certain features by observing and deconstructing the creations of its developers.

In this book, you will be starting from scratch, and you will need a new project to work with, so go to **File | New Project**. This will close the currently opened project and present you with the **Project Wizard**, a dialog window allowing you to select an existing project to open. You can also start a new one by selecting from several **Asset Packages** to start with.

 Be aware that if at any time you wish to launch Unity and be taken directly to the **Project Wizard**, then simply hold the *Alt* key (Mac and PC) while launching the Unity Editor.

To begin making your Unity project, choose a location to save your new project folder by either specifying a file path in the **Project Directory** field or by choosing the **Set** button and specifying a location in the dialog window that appears. I'm naming mine **Project 1**, but feel free to name yours as you please. Now select the box next to **Standard Assets**. This will give you a set of free assets provided by Unity Technologies to get started with. When you're happy with where you want to store your work, click on **Create Project**.

Using the terrain editor

In building any game that involves an outdoor environment, a terrain editor is a must-have for any game developer. Unity has featured a built-in terrain editor since version 2.0, and this makes building complete environments quick and easy.

In Unity terms, think of a terrain as simply a game object that has a terrain toolkit component applied to it. Beginning as a **Plane**—a flat, single-sided 3D shape— the terrain you'll create shortly can be transformed into a complete set of realistic geometry, with additional details such as trees, rocks, foliage, and even atmospheric effects such as wind speed.

Terrain menu features

In order to take a look at the features outlined below, you will need to create a terrain. So let's begin by introducing a new terrain object to the game—this is an Asset that can be created within Unity, so simply go to **Terrain | Create Terrain** from the top menu.

Before you can begin to modify your terrain, you should set up various settings for size and detail. The **Terrain** menu at the top of Unity allows you to not only create a terrain for your game, but also perform the following operations:

Importing and exporting heightmaps

Heightmaps are 2D graphics with light and dark areas to represent terrain topography and can be imported as an alternative to using Unity's height painting tools.

Created in an art package such as Photoshop and saved in a `.RAW` format, heightmaps are often used in game development, as they can be easily exported and transferred between art packages and development environments such as Unity.

As we will be using the Unity Terrain tools to create our environment, we will not be utilizing externally created heightmaps as part of this book.

Set Heightmap resolution

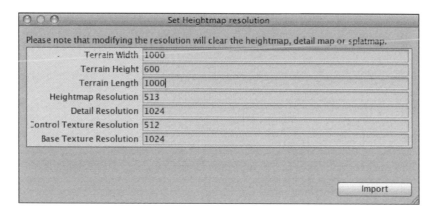

The given dialog window allows you to set a number of properties for the new terrain you have made. These settings should always be adjusted before the topography of the terrain is created, as adjusting them later can cause work on the terrain to be reset.

- **Terrain Width**, **Height** and **Length**: Measured in meters. Note that *Height* here sets the maximum height that the terrain's topography can feature.

- **Heightmap Resolution**: The resolution of the texture that Unity stores to represent the topography in pixels. Note that although most textures in Unity must be a power of two dimension—128, 256, 512 and so on, heightmap resolutions always add an extra pixel because each pixel defines a vertex point; so in the example of a 4 x 4 terrain, four vertices would be present along each section of the grid, but the points at which they meet—including their endpoints—would equal five.

- **Detail resolution:** The resolution of the graphic, known as a **Detail resolution map**, that Unity stores. This defines how precisely you can place **details** on the terrain. Details are additional terrain features such as plants, rocks, and bushes. The larger the value, the more precisely you can place details on the terrain in terms of positioning.

- **Control Texture Resolution**: The resolution of textures when painted onto the terrain. Known as **Splatmap** textures in Unity, the **Control Texture Resolution** value controls the size and, therefore, the detail of any textures you paint on. As with all texture resolutions, it is advisable to keep this figure lower to increase performance. With this in mind, it is a good practice to leave this value set to its default of 512.

- **Base Texture Resolution:** The resolution of the texture used by Unity to render terrain areas in the distance that are further from the in-game camera or on older performance hardware.

Creating the lightmap

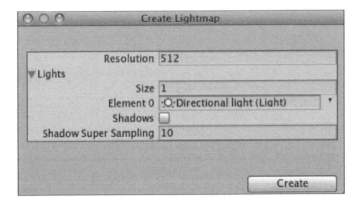

This dialog is used to bake (semi-permanently render) the lighting of topography onto the textures that make up its appearance. For example, if we created a small hilly terrain and then wished to include a mountain in the middle, then we would use the terrain tools to create the mountain. However, given the shadow cast on the terrain by this new mountain, we would need to re-create the lightmap to render the dark areas onto the textures in the newly shaded area of our terrain.

Utilizing the **lights** area of this dialog allows you to increase the number of lights used to render the lightmap. For example, our scene may be lit mostly by a **Directional light**, which acts as sunlight from a certain direction. Some **Point lights** may be included also, such as those representing outdoor lamps or fires.

As you create new topography when using the terrain tools, the `create lightmap` function is an example of one you may need to revisit as your landscape changes. By creating a lightmap to map light and dark areas on the terrain, you are also saving on processing power when the game runs, as you have already calculated part of the lighting. This is in opposition to dynamic lighting for the terrain, which is more expensive in processing terms.

Mass Place Trees

This function does exactly what its name says — placing a specified number of trees onto the terrain, with specific tree and associated parameters specified in the **Place Trees** area of the terrain script component in the `Inspector`.

This function is not recommended for general use, as it gives you no control over the position of the trees. I recommend that you use the `Place Trees` part of the terrain script instead, in order to manually paint a more realistic placement.

Flatten Heightmap

Flatten Heightmap is present to allow you to flatten the entire terrain at a certain height. By default, your terrain height begins at zero, so if you wish to make a terrain with a default height above this, such as we do for our island, then you can specify the height value here.

Refresh Tree and Detail Prototypes

If you make changes to the assets that make up any trees and details that have already been painted onto the terrain, then you'll need to select **Refresh Tree and Detail Prototypes** to update them on the terrain.

The terrain toolset

Before we begin to use them to build our island, let's take a look at the terrain tools so that you can familiarize yourself with their functions.

As you have just created your terrain, it should be selected in the **Hierarchy** window. If it is not selected, then select it now in order to show its properties in the `Inspector`.

Terrain Script

On the **Inspector**, the terrain toolset is referred to in component terms as the **Terrain (Script).** The **Terrain (Script)** component gives you the ability to utilize the various tools and specify settings for the terrain in addition to the functions available in the terrain menu outlined above.

In the following screenshot, you can see that this is the second of three components on the Terrain game object (the others being **Transform** and **Terrain Collider**).

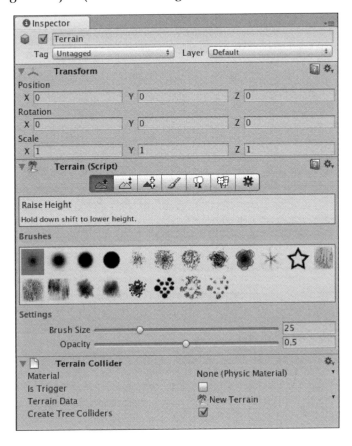

The **Terrain (Script)** component has seven sections to it, which are easily accessible from the icon buttons at the top of the component. Before we begin, here is a quick overview of their purpose in building terrains.

Raise Height

This tool allows you to raise areas by painting with the **Transform tool** (*Shortcut – W key*).

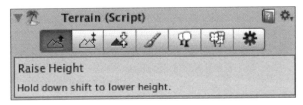

You also have the ability to specify **Brush** styles, **Size,** and **Opacity** (effectiveness) for the deformation you make. Holding the *Shift* key while using this tool causes the opposite effect—lowering height.

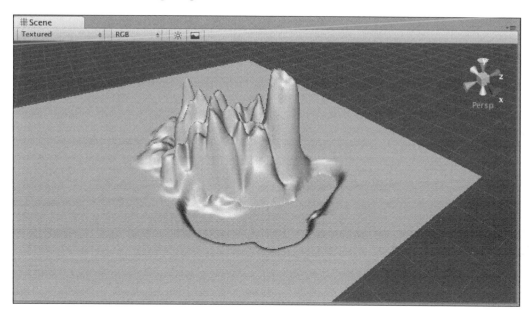

Paint height

This tool works similarly to the **Raise Height** tool, but gives you an additional setting—height.

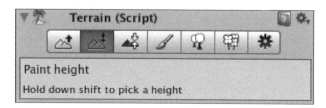

This means that you can specify a height to paint towards, which means that when the area of the terrain that you are raising reaches the specified height, it will flatten out, allowing you to create plateaus, as shown in the following screenshot:

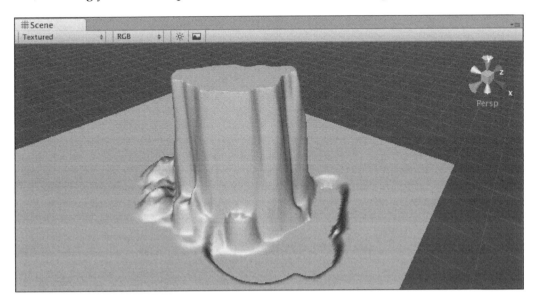

Smooth height

This tool is used mostly to complement other tools such as Paint Height in order to soften harsh areas of topography.

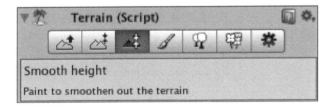

For example, in the previous plateau, the land goes straight up, and should I wish to soften the edges of the raised area, I would use this tool to round off the harsh edges, creating the result shown in the following screenshot:

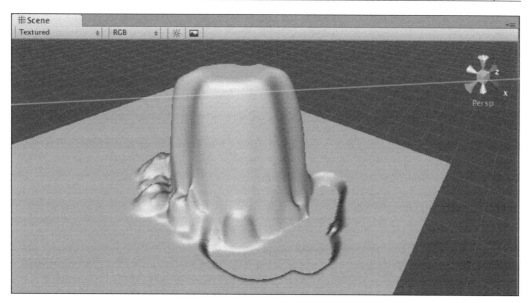

Paint Texture

Paint Texture is the tool used to brush textures—referred to as **Splats** in Unity terrain terms—onto the surface of the terrain

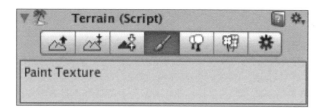

In order to paint with textures, the textures must first be added to the palette in the **Textures** area of this tool. Textures can be added by clicking on the **Edit Textures** button and selecting **Add Texture**, which will allow you to choose any texture file currently in your project, along with parameters for tiling the chosen texture.

The next screenshot is an example of this tool with three textures in the palette. The first texture you add to the palette will be painted over the entire terrain by default. Then, by combining several textures at varying opacities and painting manually onto the terrain, you can get some realistic areas of whatever kind of surface you're hoping to get.

To choose a texture to paint with, simply click on its preview in the palette. The currently chosen texture is highlighted with a blue outline.

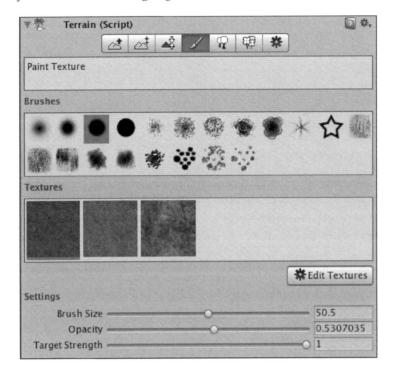

Place Trees

This is another tool that does what its name suggests. By brushing with the mouse, or using single clicks, **Place Trees** can be used to paint trees onto the terrain, having specified which asset to use when painting.

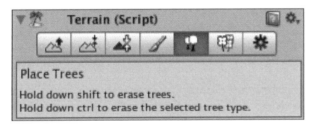

In the same way as specifying textures for the **Paint Texture** tool, this tool gives you an **Edit Trees** button to add, edit, and remove assets from the palette.

In its **Settings**, you can specify:

- **Brush Size**: The amount of trees to paint per click
- **Tree Density**: The proximity of trees placed when painting
- **Color Variation**: Applies random color variation to trees when painting several at once
- **Tree Width/Height**: Sizes the tree asset you are painting with
- **Tree Width/Height Variation**: Gives you random variation in sizing to create more realistically forested areas

This tool also utilizes the *Shift* key to reverse its effects. In this instance, using *Shift* erases painted trees and can be used in conjunction with the *Ctrl* key to only erase trees of the type selected in the palette.

Paint Details

This tool works in a similar manner to the **Place Trees** tool but is designed to work with detail objects such as flowers, plants, rocks, and other foliage.

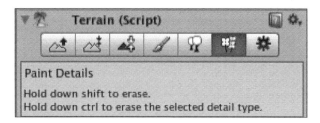

Terrain Settings

The **Terrain Settings** area of the **Terrain (Script)** contains various settings for the drawing of the terrain by the computer's GPU (graphical processing unit).

Here you can specify various settings that affect the **Level of Detail (LOD)**.

Level of Detail in game development defines the amount of detail specified within a certain range of a player. In this example—a terrain—we need to be able to adjust settings such as **Draw Distance**, which is a common 3D game concept that renders less detail after a certain distance from the player in order to improve performance.

In **Terrain Settings**, for example, you can adjust **Base Map Distance** in order to specify how far away until the terrain replaces high resolution graphics for lower resolution ones, making objects in the distance less expensive to render.

The following screenshot is an example of a low **Base Map Distance** of around 10 meters. As you can see, the textures further than the specified distance are drawn at far lower detail.

We'll look at the Terrain script's settings further as we begin to build our terrain.

Sun, Sea, Sand—creating the island

Step 1—Terrain setup

Now that we have looked at the tools available to create our terrain, let's get started by setting up our terrain using the **Terrain** top menu. Ensure that your Terrain is still selected in the **Hierarchy**, and go to **Terrain | Set Resolution**.

As we don't want to make too large an island for our first project, set the terrain **width** and **length** both to **1000**. Remember to press *Enter* after typing these values in so that you've effectively confirmed them before clicking on **Import**.

Next, our island's height needs to begin at its ground level, rather than at zero, which is the default for new terrains. If you consider that the terrain height of zero should be the sea bed, then we can say that our ground level should be raised to be the surface height of the island. Go to **Terrain | Flatten Heightmap**.

Click inside the **Height** box, and place in a value of **30** meters, and then press *Enter* to confirm. Click on **Flatten** to finish.

This change is a *blink-and-you'll-miss-it* difference in the **Scene** view, as all we've done is shift the terrain upward slightly. However, the reason we've done this is that it is a great time saver—as we can now flatten around the edges of the terrain using inverse **Raise Height** to leave a raised island in the centre of the terrain. This is a more time-efficient method than beginning with a flat island and raising the height in the centre.

Step 2—Island outline

On the **Inspector** for the Terrain object's **Terrain (Script)** component, choose the **Raise Height** tool—the first of the seven buttons.

Select the first brush in the palette, and set its **Brush Size** to **75**. Set **Opacity** for the brush to **0.5**.

Change your view in the **Scene** panel to a top-down view by clicking on the Y-axis (green spoke) of the view gizmo in the top-right.

Using the *Shift* key to **lower height**, paint around the outline of the terrain, creating a coastline that descends to zero height—you will know it has reached zero as the terrain will flatten out at this minimum height.

While there is no need to match the outline of the island I have created, try not to make a wildly different shape either, as you will need a flat expanse of land later. Once you have painted around the entire outline, it should look something like this:

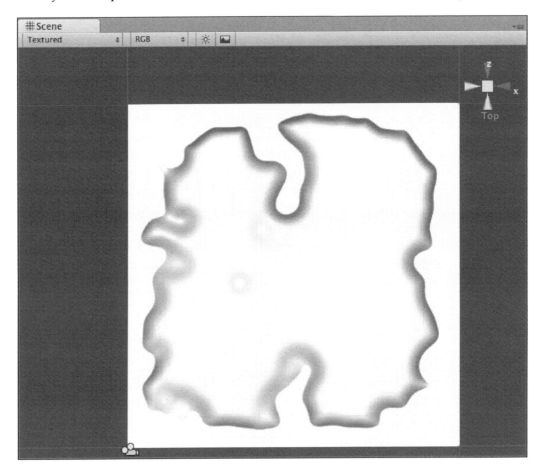

Now switch back to a perspective (3D) view of your **Scene** by clicking on the center cube of the view gizmo in the top-right of the **Scene** window and admire your handiwork. If you are unsure, here is what mine looks like:

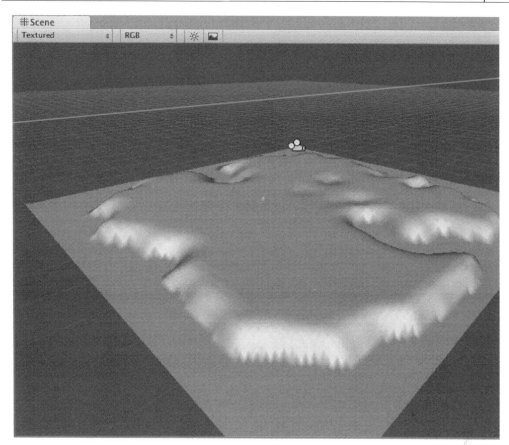

Now spend some time going over the island, using the **Raise Height** tool to create some further topographical detail, and perhaps using Lower Height (with the *Shift* key) to add an inlet or lake. Leave a flat area in the center of your terrain and one free corner of your map in which we are going to add a volcano!

Step 3—Volcano!

Now to create our volcano! For this we will combine the use of the **Paint Height**, **Raise Height**, and **Smooth Height** tools. First, select the **Paint Height** tool.

Choose the first brush in the palette, and set the **Brush Size** to **75**, **Opacity** to **0.5**. and **Height** to **200**. Select the **Top** view again using the **view gizmo**, and paint on a plateau in the corner that you left free on your terrain. Remember that this tool will stop affecting the terrain once it reaches the specified height of **200**.

Your island should now look like this in the perspective view:

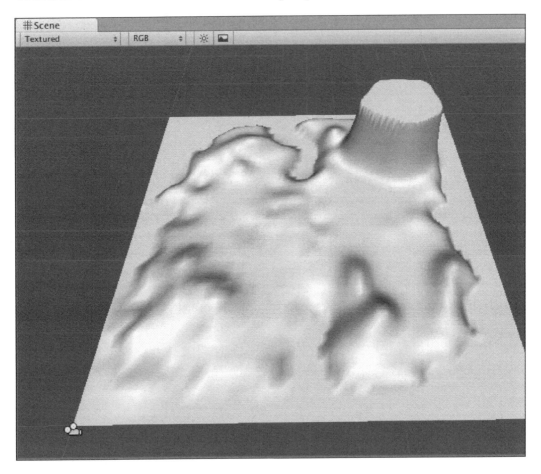

Now this plateau may look clunky — we'll rectify this with smoothing shortly, but first we need to create the volcano mouth. So now with the **Paint Height** tool still selected, change the **Height** setting to **20** and the **Brush Size** to **30**.

Now hold down the mouse and start painting from the center of the plateau outwards towards its edge in every direction, until you have effectively hollowed out the plateau, leaving a narrow ridge around its circumference, as shown in the following screenshot:

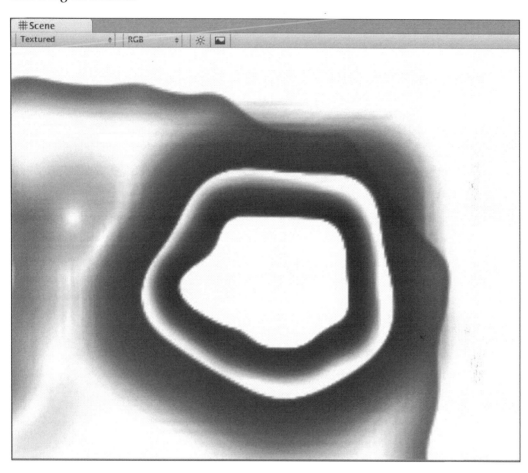

We still have a fairly solid edge to this ridge, and when switching to the perspective view, you'll see that it still doesn't look quite right. This is where the **Smooth Height** tool comes in. Select the **Smooth Height** tool and set the **Brush Size** to **30** and **Opacity** to **1**. Using this tool, paint around the edge of the ridge with your mouse, softening its height until you have created a rounded soft ridge, as shown in the following screenshot:

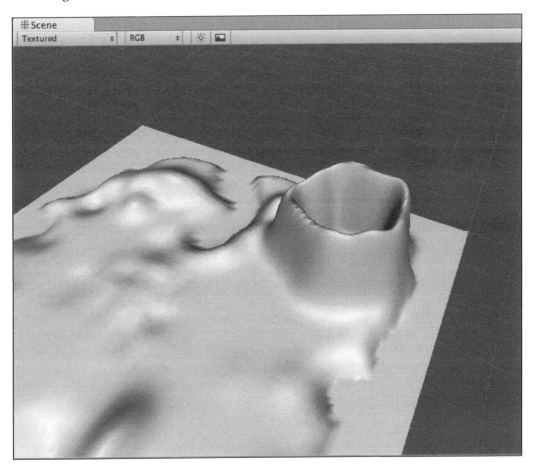

Now that our volcano has started to take shape, we can begin to texture the island to add realism to our terrain.

Step 4—Adding textures

When texturing your terrain, it is crucial to remember that the first texture you add will cover the terrain entirely. With this in mind, you should ensure that the first texture you add to your texture palette is the texture which represents the majority of your terrain.

In the **Standard Assets Package** we included when we started the project, we are given various assets with a variety of game features to get started with. As such, you'll find a folder called **Standard Assets** in your **Project** panel. Expand this down by clicking on the gray arrow to the left of it, and then expand the subfolder called **Terrain Textures**.

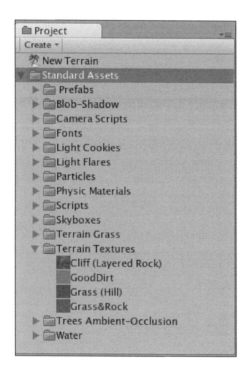

These are the four textures we'll use to paint our island terrain, so we'll begin by adding them to our palette. Ensure that the **Terrain** game object is still selected in the screenshot, and then select the **Paint Texture** tool from the **Terrain (Script)** component in the **Inspector**.

Painting procedure

To introduce the four textures for our terrain, begin by clicking on the **Edit Textures** button, and select **Add Textures** from the menu that pops out. This will launch the **Add Textures** dialog window in which you can select any texture currently in your project. Click on the down arrow to the right of the **Splat** setting to choose from a list of all available textures, and select the texture called **Grass (Hill)**.

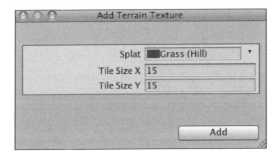

Leave the **Tile Size X** and **Y** values on **15** here, as this texture will cover the entire map, and this small value will give us a more detailed-looking grass. Click on **Add** to finish. This will cover your terrain with the grass texture, as it is the first one we have added. Any future textures added to the palette will need to be painted on manually.

Repeat the previous step to add three further textures to the palette, choosing the textures named **Grass&Rock**, **Cliff (Layered Rock)**, and **GoodDirt**—while leaving the **Tile Size** settings unchanged for all except the **Cliff (Layered Rock)** texture, which should have an **X** and **Y Tile Size** of **70**, as it will be applied to a stretched area of the map and will look distorted unless tiled at a larger scale.

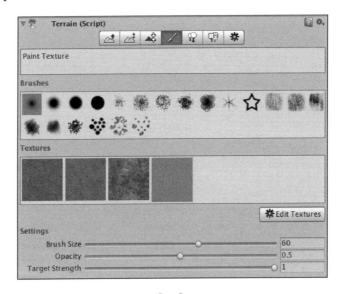

Sandy areas

You should now have all four textures available in your palette. Matching the above settings, choose the last texture added—**GoodDirt**—and it should become highlighted by a blue underline as shown. Set the **Brush Size** to **60**, **Opacity** to **0.5**, and **Target Strength** to **1**. You can now paint around the coast of the island using either the **Top** or **Perspective** view.

If you are using the **Perspective** view to paint textures, it will help to remember that you can use the *Alt* key while dragging the mouse, with either the **Hand** (Shortcut – *Q*) or **Transform** (Shortcut – *W*) tools selected, in order to rotate your view.

When finished, you should have something like this:

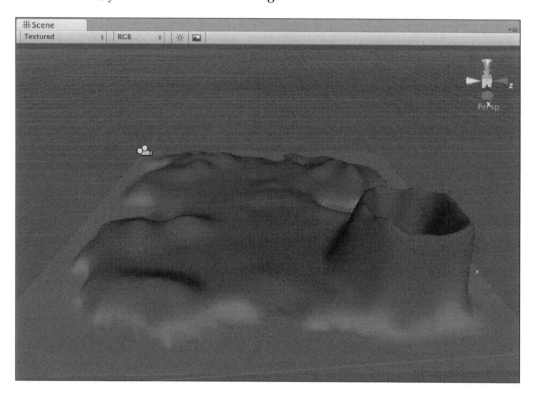

If you make a mistake while painting, you can either use **Edit | Undo** to step back one brush stroke, that is, a single-0.held mouse click, or select the texture from the palette that you do want to be where you accidentally painted, and re-paint with that.

Grass & Rock

Next select the **Grass & Rock** texture by clicking on the second thumbnail added. Set the **Brush Size** to **25**, **Opacity** to **0.3**, and **Target Strength** to **0.5**. Now brush over any hilly areas on your terrain and around the top half of the volcano until you have created something like this:

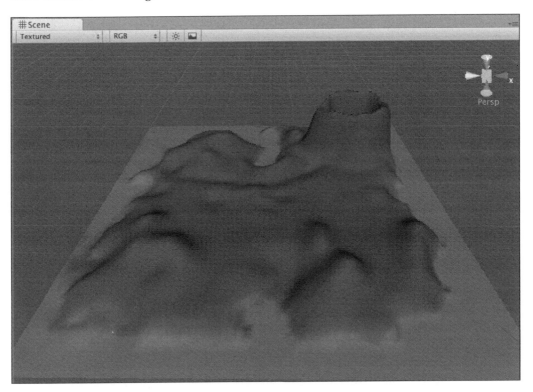

Volcanoes Rock!

Now we need to make our volcano look more realistic by adding the **Cliff (Layered Rock)** texture to it. Select the cliff texture from the palette, and set the **Brush Size** to **25** and both **Opacity** and **Target Strength** to **1**.

Paint over the top outer half and the entire inner with these settings and then slowly decrease the **Opacity** and **Brush Size** values as you work your way down the outside of the volcano so that this texture is applied more subtly towards the ground. With a lower opacity, you may also want to paint over the tops of some of your taller hilled areas on the terrain.

While this will take some experimentation, when finished, your volcano should look something like this:

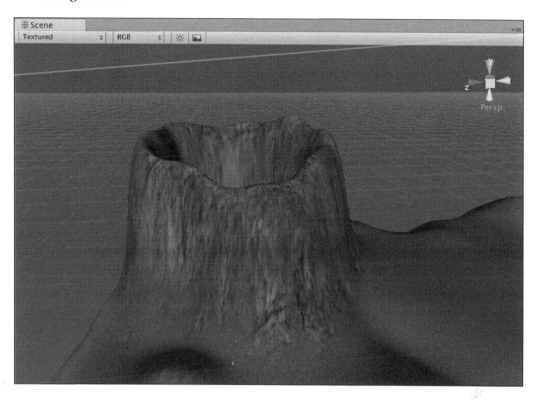

Step 5—Tree time

Now that we have a fully textured island, we need to spruce up the place a little with some trees. In our Standard Assets package, there is a tree provided to get us started with the terrain editor, and thankfully for us, it is a palm tree asset.

Select the **Place Trees** section of the **Terrain (Script)** component, and click on the **Edit Trees** button. From the drop-down menu that appears, choose **Add Tree**.

The **Add Tree** dialog window appears. As with some of the other terrain tools, this *Add* dialog allows us to select from any object of an appropriate type from our Assets folder.

This is not restricted to trees provided in **Standard Assets**, which means that you can model your own trees by saving them into the Assets folder of your project in order to use them with this tool. However, we are going to use the Standard Assets provided palm tree. So select the **Palm** asset by clicking on the down arrow to the right of the **Tree** setting.

Bend Factor here allows our trees to sway in the wind. This effect is computationally expensive, so we'll simply use a low number. Type in a value of **2** and press *Enter* to confirm. If you find that this is causing low performance later in development, then you can always return to this setting and set it back to zero. Click on the **Add** button to finish.

With your palm tree in the palette, you should see a small preview of the tree with a blue background to show that it is selected as the tree to place.

Set the **Brush Size** to **15** (painting 15 trees at a time) and the **Tree Density** to **0** (giving us a wide spread of trees). Set **Color Variation** to **0.4** to give us a varied set of trees and **Tree Height / Width** to **1.5** with their Variation settings to **0.3**.

Using single-clicks, place trees around the coast of the island, near the sandy areas that you would expect to see them. Then to complement the island's terrain, place a few more palm trees at random locations inland.

Remember that if you paint trees incorrectly at any time, you can hold the *Shift key* and click, or paint (drag) with the mouse to erase trees from the terrain.

Step 6—Grassed up

Now that we have some trees on our island, we'll add a small amount of grass to complement the grass textures we covered the terrain with.

Select the **Paint Details** section of the **Terrain (Script)** component and click on the **Edit Details** button. Select **Add Grass Texture** from the pop-up menu.

The Standard Assets package provides us with a grass texture to use, so from the drop-down menu to the right of the **Detail Texture** setting, select the texture simply called **Grass**.

Having chosen the **Grass** texture, leave the **Width** and **Height** values at their default and ensure that **Billboard** is selected at the bottom of this dialog. As our grass detail textures are 2D, we can employ *billboarding*, a technique in game development that rotates the grass texture to face the camera during game play in order to make the grass seem less two-dimensional.

Using the color-picker boxes, ensure that the **Healthy** and **Dry** colors are of a similar shade of green to the textures we have painted onto the terrain, because leaving them on the default bright green will look out of place.

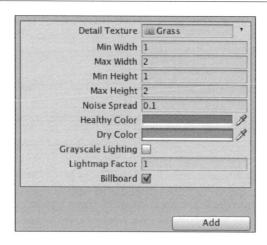

Click on the **Add** button at the bottom of the dialog window to confirm adding this texture to your palette.

To paint grass onto our map, we can yet again use mouse-based brushing in a similar way to the other terrain tools. Firstly, we'll need to choose a brush and settings in order to ensure a wide and disparate painting of grass detail onto our map. Given that rendering grass is another expensive feature for the computer to render, we'll keep the grass to a minimum by setting the **Brush Size** to **100**, but **Opacity** to **0.05**, and **Target Strength** to **0.6**. This will give a wide spread with very little grass, and by choosing a stipple brush (see the next screenshot) we can paint on patchy areas of grass.

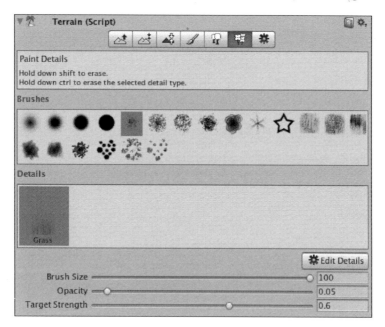

Now zoom into the terrain surface by selecting the **Hand** tool, and holding the *Command* key (Mac) or the *Ctrl* key (PC) while dragging the mouse to the right. Once at a close level of zoom, you'll be able to click the mouse to paint on areas of grass. Move around the island painting on a few grassy areas—do this sparingly for performance reasons—and later you can always come back and add more grass if the game performs well.

It is crucial to zoom in on your terrain while painting details as the Unity Editor's Scene view does not render them visibly when zoomed out in order to save memory—so often it'll seem that when you have zoomed out, your grass and other details will disappear—do not worry, this is not the case.

Step 7—Let there be lights!

Now that our island terrain is ready to explore, we'll need to add lighting to our scene. When first approaching lighting in Unity, it's best to be aware of what the three different light types are used for:

- **Directional light**: Used as the main source of light, often as sunlight, a Directional light does not emanate from a single point, but instead simply travels in a single direction.
- **Point light**: These lights emanate from a single point in the 3D world and are used for any other source of light, such as indoor lighting, fires, glowing objects, and so on.
- **Spot light**: Exactly what it sounds like, this light shines in a single direction but has a *radius* value that can be set, much like focusing a flashlight.

Creating sunlight

To introduce our main source of light, we'll add a Directional light. Go to **GameObject | Create Other | Directional Light**. This adds the light as an object in our scene, and you will see that it is now listed in the **Hierarchy**.

As the Directional light does not emanate from a point, its position is ordinarily irrelevant as it cannot be *seen* by the player—only the light it casts is seen. However, in this tutorial, we're going to use the Directional light to represent the sun, by applying a light **Flare** to the light.

In order to represent the sun, we'll position the light high above the island, and to ensure that it is consistent with the direction of the light it casts, we'll position the light away from the island in the Z-axis.

Position the light at **(0, 500, -200)** by typing in the Inspector **Transform** boxes and pressing *Enter* to confirm each value set. Set the **X rotation** to **8** in order to tilt the light downward in the X-axis, and this will cast more light onto our terrain.

Finally, we'll need to make the light visible. To do this, choose a light flare by clicking on the drop-down arrow to the right of the **Flare** setting in the **Light** component—it will currently be set to **None**, but instead, choose **Sun**.

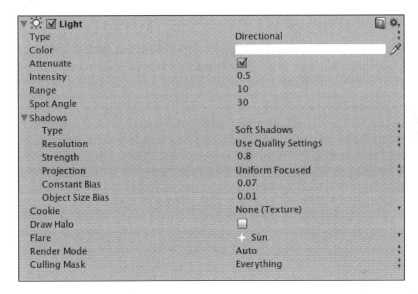

Step 8—What's that sound?

An oft-overlooked area of game development is sound. For a truly immersive experience, your player needs to not only see the environment you've made, but hear it too.

Sound in Unity is handled through 2 components, the **Audio Source**, and the **Audio Listener.** Think of the **Source** as a speaker in your game world, and the **Listener** as a microphone or the player's ear. By default, camera game objects in Unity have an audio listener component. So given that you always have a camera in your game, chances are you'll only ever have to set up sound sources. It is also worth noting that the **Audio Listener** component has no properties to adjust—it just works—and that Unity will inform you with an error if you accidentally remove the only listener in any scene.

Stereo versus Mono

Unity handles the behavior of sound by utilizing Stereo (two-channel) sound as constant volume, and Mono (single channel) sound as variable volume, based upon its source's proximity to the listener in the 3D world.

For example, for the following purposes:

- In game music: Stereo sound would be best, as it would remain constant no matter where the player's listener goes in the game.

- Sound effect of a Hi-Fi inside a building: Mono sound would be best—although you may be playing music as your sound effect, using mono sound files would allow the sound source to become louder, the closer the player gets to it.

Formats

Unity will accept the most common audio formats—**WAV, MP3, AIFF,** and **OGG.** Upon encountering a compressed format such as MP3, Unity converts your audio file to the **Ogg Vorbis** file format, while leaving uncompressed sounds such as WAVs unconverted.

As with other assets you import, audio files simply get converted as soon as you switch between another program and Unity, as Unity scans the contents of the Assets folder each time you switch to it to look for new files.

The hills are alive!

To make our island feel more realistic, we'll add a sound source playing outdoor ambience using a stereo sound.

Begin by selecting the **Terrain** object in the **Hierarchy**. Go to **Component | Audio | Audio Source** from the top menu. This adds an **Audio Source** component to the terrain. As the volume remains constant when using stereo sounds, and position is irrelevant, we could place the ambience sound source on any object—it simply makes logical sense that ambient sound of the terrain should be attached to that game object.

In the **Inspector** of the terrain, you will now see the **Audio Source** component with which you may either choose a file to play or leave blank if you are planning to play sounds through scripting.

Importing your first package

For this step, you'll need to download the first of several asset packages from the Packt publishing web site, `www.packtpub.com/files/8181_Code.zip`. Locate the file called `Sound1.unitypackage` from the list of files associated with this book and then return to Unity and go to **Assets | Import Package**.

You will be presented with a file selection **Import Package** dialog, from which you should navigate to the location on your hard drive that you saved the downloaded file. Select it, and then click on **Open** to choose it. Unity will then present you with a list of assets that are contained in the package—by default it assumes that the user wants to import all assets in the package, but the ability to only import certain assets is useful when extracting single files from larger packages.

In our Sound1 package, there is simply a single MP3 format sound file called `hillside.mp3`—along with a folder called `Sound` to keep it in—so you will only see those two files.

Click on **Import** to confirm adding these files to your project and after a short conversion progress bar, you should see them in your project panel—you'll need to open the **Sound** folder you've added by clicking on the gray arrow to the left of it in order to see the **hillside** sound file. Sound files are represented in your **Project** panel by the speaker icon, as shown in the following screenshot:

The **hillside** file is now ready to be applied to the **Audio Source** component of the terrain.

Click on the down arrow to the right of the **Audio Clip** setting in the **Audio Source** component of the terrain game object. This will show you a list of all available audio files in your project. As we only have the **hillside** audio file in ours, that is all you will see on this drop-down menu, so select it now.

Further audio settings

The **Audio Source** component has various settings to control how the audio clip sounds, as well as how it plays back. For our ambient hillside sound, simply ensure that the checkboxes for **Play On Awake** and **Loop** are selected.

This will play the ambience sound clip when the player enters the scene (or *level*) and continually loop the clip until the scene is exited.

Your **Audio Source** component should look like this:

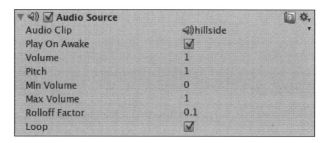

As our sound is in Stereo, and therefore not affected by distance, the **Min / Max Volume** and **Rolloff Factor** settings do not apply. However, when using Mono sound, they do the following:

- **Minimum/Maximum Volume**: The quietest/loudest the sound can be regardless of audio listener proximity
- **Rolloff Factor**: How quickly the audio fades as the audio listener moves towards/away from the source

Step 9—Look to the skybox!

In creating 3D environments, the horizon or distance is represented by the addition of a **skybox**. A skybox is a **cubemap**—a series of six textures placed inside a cube and rendered seamlessly to appear as a surrounding sky and horizon. This cubemap sits around the 3D world at all times, and much like the actual horizon, it is not an object the player can ever *get to*.

To apply a skybox to your scene, go to **Edit | Render Settings**. The **Inspector** area of the interface will now change to show the preferences for the rendering of this scene. To the right of the **Skybox Material** setting, click on the drop-down arrow, and select **Sunset**. This will apply the skybox, but it is crucial to understand that any skybox you add will only be shown in the **Game View** panel by default.

As with many skyboxes, the **Sunset** skybox provided with Standard Assets features a drawn on Sun. The problem here is that we have our sun visually represented by the flare of the directional light, so we'll need to reposition the light to match the skybox. But first, we'll add our **First Person Controller** player character, so that you can see this issue first hand.

Step 10—Open water

As we have constructed an island terrain, it follows that our land mass should be surrounded by water. Water in Unity is created using an animated material applied to a surface. While it is possible to create further dynamic water effects by utilizing particles, the best way to add a large expanse of water is to use one of the water materials provided by Unity.

The Standard Assets package gives us two readymade surfaces with the water material applied. Readily saved as prefabs, these objects can be introduced easily from the **Project** Panel. Simply open the **Standard Assets | Water** folder.

Drag the **Daylight Simple Water** prefab into the scene and position it at **(500, 4, 500)** by filling in the X, Y and Z values for **Position** in the **Transform** component in the **Inspector**. In order to expand the scale of the water prefab to form a sea around the island, simply increase both the **X** and **Z** values under **Scale** to **1600**.

This places the water in the center of the map and four meters above the sea bed. This will cover up the corners of your island, and mask the terrain's true square-based nature. It should look like this:

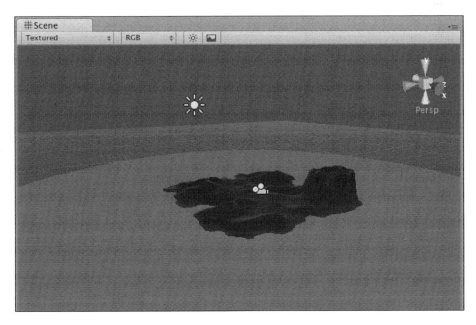

Step 11—Island walkabout

In the **Project** panel, expand the subfolder of **Standard Assets** called **Prefabs**. In here you will find a single prefab – a readymade **First Person Controller** object. This can be dropped into your scene, and will allow you to walk around your terrain using the keyboard and mouse.

Drag this prefab from the **Project** panel onto the **Scene** view—remember you will not be able to accurately position this object when you initially drop it into the scene, as this should be done afterwards.

Now that your **First Person Controller** object is an active game object, you can see it listed in the **Hierarchy** and its component parts listed in the **Inspector**.

Reposition the **First Person Controller** object to **(500, 35, 500)** by typing the values in the **Transform** component in the **Inspector**. This position places the character directly in the centre of the map in the X and Z axes, because we have created a terrain with a width and length of 1000 meters. The **Y** value of **35** ensures that the player is above ground level—if it is not, then the character will fall through the map upon play. If you happen to have made a hill at this position when sculpting your terrain, simply increase the **Y** value to place the character above the hill at game start.

To see where your character object is positioned more easily, ensure that it is selected in the **Hierarchy**. Then hover the mouse cursor over the **Scene** window and press *F* on the keyboard. This focuses the **Scene** view on the selected object.

Now press the **Play** button to test the game, and you should be able to walk around on your island terrain!

The default controls for the character are as follows:

- Up/*W*: Walk forward
- Down/*S*: Walk backward
- Left/*A*: Sidestep left (also known as *Strafing*)
- Right/*D*: Sidestep right
- Mouse: Look around/turn the player while walking

Walk to the top of a hill and turn until you can see the flare of the Sun. Then look to the right of the flare, and you will see that the skybox also has a lit area to represent the sun, so we need to reposition the **Directional Light** object to correspond to the sun in the skybox, as mentioned earlier.

Stop the game testing by pressing the **Play** button again. It is crucial to stop the game when you continue editing. If you leave it playing or on pause, then any edits you make to the scene will only be temporary—lasting until you press **Play** again or **quit** Unity.

Step 12—Sun alignment and final tweaks

Select the **Directional Light** object in the **Hierarchy**, and in the **Transform** component in the **Inspector**, reposition the object to (**-500, 500, 500**). This will place the light on the side of the map which the skybox's sun is on. **Rotate** the object by **120** in the Y axis (center box) and your **Directional light's** position will now match the light in the skybox.

Finally, as we have added the **First Person Controller** object, we no longer need the object that our scene came with by default—**Main Camera**. Unity reminds us of this by showing an info message in the **console** preview area at the bottom of the screen:

There are 2 audio listeners in the scene (Main Camera). Please ensure there is always one audio listener in the scene.

To rectify this, simply remove the **Main Camera** object, as we no longer need it. To do this, select it in the **Hierarchy**, and on Mac, press *Command+Backspace*, on PC use *Shift+Delete*, or on either platform, go to **Edit | Delete**.

Now that this object is gone, your island terrain is complete. Save your scene so that you do not lose any work—go to **File | Save Scene** and name your scene **Island Level**—Unity will assume you want to save in the Assets folder of your project, and will choose that folder as the save location automatically because all assets must be in this folder. To keep things neat, you can make a **Levels** subfolder now and save in there if you like.

Congratulations, your island terrain is ready for exploration, so hit the **Play** button again and have a wander! Just remember to press **Play** again when you are finished.

Take Me Home! Introducing models

Now that our island terrain is ready for populating with gameplay, the first key concept to explore is the introduction of models from external applications. As we have provided you with models for the exercises in this book, you'll need to download and import another Unity package to add the first model asset—an outpost—to your project.

Importing the model package

Go to www.packtpub.com/files/8181_Code.zip and locate the asset package from the files available in the code bundle for this book titled Outpost.unitypackage.

Next, return to Unity and go to **Assets | Import Package**.

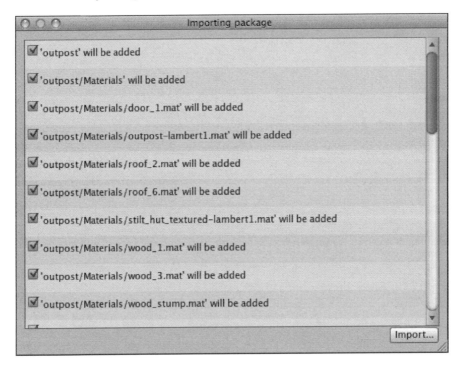

Leave all files here selected, and click on the **Import** button to confirm. Now that you have imported the contents of the package, you'll see a new folder of assets called **outpost** inside your **Project** panel, and therefore in the **Assets** folder of your project in your operating system. Expand this folder by clicking on the gray arrow next to its name on the **Project** panel in order to view its contents.

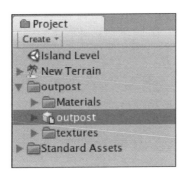

The imported folder contains the model itself and two subfolders, one with its **Materials**, the other containing the images that make up the **Textures** for those materials. You can spot a 3D model asset in Unity by its icon—a small cube icon with an accompanying page icon, differentiating it from Unity's prefab icon, which, as you'll discover, is simply a cube icon by itself.

Common settings for models

Before you introduce any model to the active scene, you should always ensure that its settings are as you require them to be in the Inspector. When Unity imports new models to your project, it is interpreting them with its **FBX file format** Importer.

By using the **FBX Importer** component in the **Inspector**, you can select your model file in the **Project** window and adjust settings for its **Meshes**, **Materials**, and **Animations** before your model becomes part of your game.

Meshes

In the **Meshes** section of **FBX Importer**, you can specify:

- **Scale Factor**: Typically set to a value of 1, this setting states that 1 unit should equal 1 meter in the game world. If you wish your models to be scaled differently, then you can adjust them here before you add the model to the scene. However, you can always scale objects once they are in your scene using the **Transform** component's **Scale** settings.

- **Generate Colliders**: This checkbox will find every individual component part of the model and assign a mesh collider to it. A mesh collider is a complex collider that can fit to complex geometric shapes and, as a result, is the usual type of collider you would expect to want to apply to all parts of a map or 3D model of a building.

- **Calculate Normals**: The *normal* is the forward facing surface of each mesh in your 3D model, and therefore the side which is rendered as visible. By enabling this checkbox, you allow Unity to ensure that all surfaces are correctly set up to render in the game.

- **Smoothing Angle**: When using the **Calculate Normals** function, smoothing allows you to specify how detailed an edge must be to be considered a hard edge by the game engine.

- **Split Tangents**: This setting allows corrections by the engine for models imported with incorrect Bump Mapped lighting. Bump Mapping is a system of utilizing two textures, one a graphic to represent a model's appearance and the other a heightmap. By combining these two textures, the bump map method allows the rendering engine to display flat surfaces of polygons as if they have 3D deformations. When creating such effects in third-party applications and transferring to Unity, sometimes lighting can appear incorrectly, and this checkbox is designed to fix that by interpreting their materials differently.

- **Swap UVs**: This setting allows the correction of import errors on lighting shaders introduced from third-party applications.

Materials

The **Materials** section allows you to choose how to interpret the materials created in your third-party 3D modelling application. The user can choose either **Per Texture** (creates a Unity material for each texture image file found) or **Per Material** (creates Materials only for existing materials in the original file) from the **Generation** drop-down menu.

Animations

The **Animations** section of the Importer allows you to interpret the animations created in your modelling application in a number of ways. From the **Generation** drop-down menu, you can choose the following methods:

- **Don't Import**: Set the model to feature no animation.

- **Store in Original Roots**: Set the model to feature animations on individual parent objects, as the parent or root objects may import differently in Unity.

- **Store in Nodes**: Set the model to feature animations on individual child objects throughout the model, allowing more script control of the animation of each part.

- **Store in Root**: Set the model to only feature animation on the parent object of the entire group.

The **Animations** section then features three further checkboxes:

- **Bake Animations**: Tell Unity to interpret joints in models with IK (Inverse Kinematics) skeletal animation.

- **Reduce Keyframes**: This removes unnecessary keyframes in exported models from modelling applications. This should always be selected as Unity does not need the keyframes and doing so will improve performance of the animated model.

- **Split Animations**: When creating models to be used with Unity, animators create timeline-based animation, and by noting their frame ranges, they can add each area of animation in their timeline by specifying a name and the frames in which each animation takes place. The advantage of this is that it allows you to call individual animations by name when scripting.

Setting up the outpost model

With the outpost model you have imported and selected in the **Project view**, we'll use the **FBX Importer component** in the **Inspector** to adjust settings for the outpost. Ensure that:

- Under **Meshes**: **Scale Factor** is set to **1**, and **Generate Colliders/Calculate Normals** are selected
- Under **Materials**: **Generation** is set to **Per Texture**
- Under **Animations**: **Reduce Keyframes** and **Split Animations** are selected

Now using the table based area at the bottom, add three animation clips by clicking on the **+** (Add symbol) button to the right.

The first animation is automatically named idle, which is fine, but you'll need to specify the frame range. Therefore, under **Start**, place a value of **1** to tell Unity to start on frame **1**, and under **End**, specify a value of **2**.

Repeat this step to add two further animations:

- **dooropen**—from frames 3 to 12
- **doorshut**—from frames 13 to 24

 Bear in mind that these animation names are case sensitive when it comes to calling them with scripting, so ensure that you write yours literally as shown throughout this book.

The **Loop** field of the Animations table can be misleading for new users. It is not designed to loop the particular animation you are setting up—this is handled by the animation's **Wrap Mode** once it is in the scene. Instead, this feature adds a single additional frame to animations that will be looped, but the start and end frames of which do not match up in Unity after importing them from modelling applications.

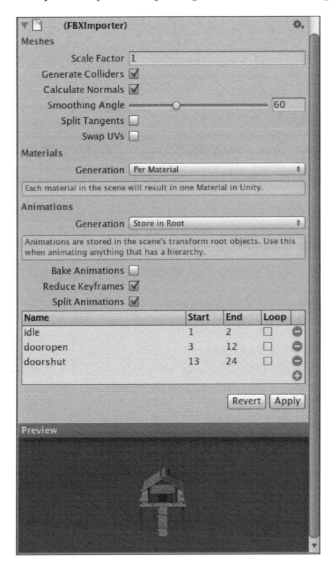

Provided that your outpost model is set up as described above, click on the **Apply** button to confirm these import settings, and you're all done—the model should be ready to be placed into the scene and used in our game.

Summary

In this chapter, we've explored the basics of developing your first environment. Beginning with nothing but a flat plane, you have now created a completely explorative island terrain in a short space of time. We've also looked at lighting and sound, two core principles that you'll apply in every kind of game project you encounter.

Remember, you can always return to the terrain tools covered in this chapter at any time in order to add more detail to your terrain, and once you feel more confident with sound, we'll return to adding further audio sources to the island later in the book.

As you continue to work through this book, you'll discover all types of additional nuances you can bring to environments in order to further suspend disbelief in the player.

We'll be looking at adding a dynamic feel to our island when we look at the use of particles, adding camp fires, and even a plume of smoke and ash from our volcano!

In the next chapter, we'll take the outpost building into our scene, and look at how we can trigger its animations when the player approaches the door. To do this, I'll introduce you to writing JavaScript for Unity, and we'll take our first leap into developing real game interactions.

3
Player Characters

In this chapter, we'll expand the island scenario we created in the previous chapter by taking a look at the construction of the player character that you have already added to the scene. Stored as a prefab (a data template object) provided by Unity Technologies as part of the Standard Assets package, this object is an example of a first person perspective player character. But how does its combination of objects and components achieve this effect?

In this chapter, we'll take a look under the hood of this prefab, while looking at how each of the components work together to create our player character. You'll get your first look at scripting in Unity JavaScript. As we have already added our prefab to the game scene, it would be all too easy to continue with the development and accept that this object just works. Whenever you are implementing any externally created assets, you should make sure you understand how they work. Otherwise, if anything needs adjusting or goes wrong, you'll be in the dark.

With this in mind, we'll take a look at the following in order to help you understand how combining just a few objects and components can create a fully-fledged character:

- Tags, layers, and prefabs in the **Inspector**
- Parent-child relationships in objects
- JavaScript basics
- Scripting for player movement
- Public member variable adjustment in the **Inspector**
- Using cameras to create the viewpoint

Working with the Inspector

As it is our first time dissecting an object in the **Inspector**, let's begin by looking at the features of the **Inspector** that are common to all of the objects.

At the top of the **Inspector**, you will see the name of the object that you have currently selected, along with a game object or prefab icon (red, green, and blue-sided cube or light blue cube respectively) and a checkbox to allow you to temporarily or permanently deactivate the object.

For example, when newly creating a game object (not from an existing prefab) with our **Directional light**, the top of the **Inspector** looks as follows:

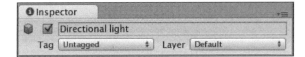

Here, you can see the red, green, and blue icon, which represents a standard game object. It is also worth noting that the name box of this part of the **Inspector** can be used to rename an object simply by clicking and typing.

Below the icon, the active checkbox, and the name, you will see the **Tag** and **Layer** settings.

Tags

Tags are simply keywords that can be assigned to a game object. By assigning a tag, you can use the chosen word or phrase to address the game object (or objects) to which it is assigned within your game scripting (one tag can be used many times). If you have worked with Adobe Flash before, then you could liken tags to the *instance name* concept in Flash—in that they are keywords used to represent objects in a scene.

Adding a tag to a game object is a two-step procedure—firstly your tag must be added to a list within the **Tag Manager**, and then applied to your chosen object.

To help you get used to using tags, let's make and apply our first tag to the **Directional light** object. With this object selected in the **Hierarchy** panel, click on the **Tag** drop-down menu where it currently says **Untagged**.

You will now see a list of existing tags. You can either choose one of these or make a new one. Select **Add Tag** at the bottom in order to add a tag to the list in the **Tag Manager**.

The **Inspector** panel will now switch to displaying the **Tag Manager**, rather than the components of the object that you previously had selected.

The **Tag Manager** shows both **Tags** and **Layers**. To add a new tag, you'll need to click on the gray arrow to the left of **Tags** in order to see the **Size** and **Element** fields. Once you have done this, you will be able to type in the space to the right of **Element 0**.

Type in the name **Sunlight** (bearing in mind that tags may be named whatever you please), and press *Enter* to confirm. Note that as soon as you press *Enter*, the **Size** value increments to the next number, and adds a new **Element** field—you need not fill this in, as it's simply available for the next tag you wish to add.

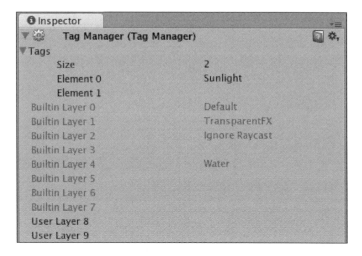

The **Size** parameter here is simply the amount of tags currently set up. Unity uses the **Size** and **Element** system for many different menus, and you'll encounter it as we continue to work with the **Inspector**.

You have added a tag to the list. However, it has not yet been added to the **Directional light** object. Therefore, reselect this object in the **Hierarchy** panel, and then click again on **Untagged** next to **Tag** at the top of the **Inspector**. You will now see your newly created tag called **Sunlight** at the bottom of your tag list. To apply it, simply select it from the drop-down menu, as shown in the following screenshot:

Layers

Layers are an additional way of grouping objects in order to apply specific rules to them. They are mostly used to group-apply rendering rules for lighting and cameras. However, they can also be used with a physics technique called **Ray casting** in order to selectively ignore certain objects.

By placing objects on a layer, for example, they can be deselected from a light's **Culling Mask** parameter, which would exclude them from being affected by the light. Layers are created in the same manner as tags, and are accessible from the **Tag Manager**, seen listed below the list of **Tags**.

Prefabs and the Inspector

If the active game object you select from the **Hierarchy** panel originates from a prefab, then you will be shown some additional settings, as shown in the following example:

Beneath the **Tag** and **Layer** fields, you can see three additional buttons for interacting with the object's originating **Prefab**.

- **Select**: This simply locates and highlights the prefab this object belongs to in the **Project** panel.

- **Revert**: Reverts any settings for components in the active object back to the settings used in the prefab in the **Project** panel.

- **Apply**: Changes the settings of the prefab to those used in the currently selected instance of that prefab. This will update any other copies of this prefab currently in the active scene.

Now that you are aware of the additional settings available on the **Inspector**, let's start using it to inspect our player character.

Deconstructing the First Person Controller object

Let's begin by looking at the objects that make up our **First Person Controller** (FPC) before we look into the components that make it work.

Click on the gray arrow to the left of **First Person Controller** in the **Hierarchy** in order to reveal the objects nested underneath. When objects are nested in this way, we say that there is a parent-child relationship. In this example, **First Person Controller** is the *parent*, while **Graphics** and **Main Camera** are its *child* objects. In the **Hierarchy**, child objects are indented to show their parenting, as shown in the following screenshot:

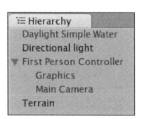

Parent-child issues

When considering nested or *child* objects, you should note that there are some key rules to remember.

A child object's position and rotation values are relative to their parent. This is referred to as the **local position and local rotation**. For example, you may consider your parent object to exist at (500, 35, 500) in world coordinates, but when selecting a child, you'll notice that while its position is (0,0,0), it still appears to be in the same position as the parent. This is what we mean by *relative to*—by placing a child object at (0,0,0), we are telling it to be at the origin of its parent, or relative to the parent's position.

In the **Hierarchy** panel, click on **Graphics** beneath the FPC parent object, and you'll see this in action—the FPC is in the center of the island, yet our **Graphics** object has transform position values of (0,0,0).

As a result of this relativity, you should also be aware that whenever the parent object is moved, its children will follow, while maintaining their local positions and rotations according to the parent's position and rotation in the game world.

First Person Controller objects

The three parts of this object are as follows:

1. **First Person Controller**: The FPC object, or parent of the group, which has the main scripting and collider applied to it and is in control of how it behaves. This object has a script applied for movement using the keyboard and another allowing rotation when moving the mouse left and right.

2. **Graphics**: Simply a Capsule primitive shape (shown in the following screenshot), which allows you as a developer to see where you have placed the FPC.

3. **Main Camera**: Positioned at where you would expect the player's eye level to be. The **Main Camera** is there to provide the viewpoint, and has scripting applied, allowing us to look up and down.

Bearing in mind the parent-child relationship, we can say that wherever the FPC object moves or rotates to, the **Graphics** and **Main Camera** will follow.

Select the **First Person Controller** in the **Hierarchy** panel, and with your mouse cursor over the **Scene** window, press the *F* key to focus the view on that object. You should now see the FPC, as shown in the following screenshot:

Now press the **Play** button, click anywhere on the **Game** window, and start to move the character while watching it in the **Scene** window. You should notice that as you move the character with the keys and rotate it with your mouse, the child objects also move.

Object 1: First Person Controller (parent)

With the **First Person Controller** still selected in the **Hierarchy** window, take a look at the components attached to it in the **Inspector**.

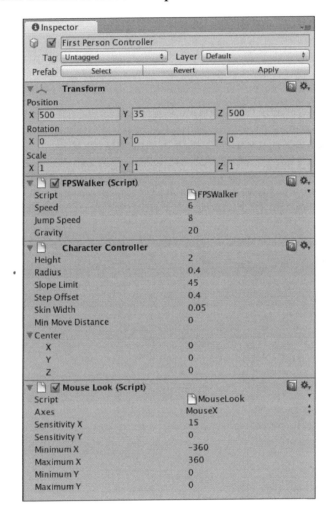

As shown in the previous screenshot, you will see that there are four components making up the FPC parent object—**Transform**, **FPSWalker (Script)**, **Character Controller**, and **Mouse Look (Script)**.

Transform

As with all active game objects, the FPC has a **Transform** component, which shows, and allows adjustment of its position, rotation, and scale parameters.

FPSWalker (Script)

This script, written in JavaScript, is in charge of allowing the character to move backward and forward using our **vertical axis keys** (Up arrow/Down arrow or *W/S*), and to move side-to-side (known as **strafing** in video gaming terms) with the **horizontal axis keys** (Left arrow/Right arrow or *A/D*), and to jump using the **jump** key, which, by default, is the *Space* bar.

The script has three **public member variables** exposed in the **Inspector**, allowing us to adjust elements of the script without even opening it. These are **Speed**, **Jump Speed**, and **Gravity**.

While Unity's physics engine can control objects with a Rigidbody component, our character does not feature one. It must have its own gravity-creating part of the script — this variable allows us to increase its effect, as a result making us fall more quickly.

> With any script type component, the first parameter before its public member variables is **Script**. This is a setting that allows you to swap it for a different script without removing the component and adding a new one.
>
> This is useful enough, but it comes into its own when you begin to write scripts that are incremental improvements on your existing scripts — you can simply start duplicating scripts, amend them, and swap them by selecting a different one from the drop-down menu to the right of the script name. By doing this, you will retain your existing settings for the public member variables in the **Inspector**.

Character Controller

This object acts as a Collider (a component giving our object a physical presence that can interact with other objects) and is specifically designed to cater to character movement and control within the world. It features the following parameters:

- **Height**: The height of the character, which defines how tall the capsule-shaped character collider will be.

- **Radius**: How wide the capsule-shaped collider will be — this has a default radius that matches the radius of the **Graphics** child object. However, if you wish to make your character wider, either to restrict movement or in order to detect collisions with a larger space, then you could increase the value of this parameter.

- **Slope Limit**: Taking into account uphill movement, this parameter allows you to specify how steep an incline can be before the character can no longer walk up the particular incline. By including this parameter, the **Character Controller** stops the player from simply walking up vertical walls or steep areas of land, which would of course seem unrealistic.

- **Step Offset**: As your game world may well feature stairs, this parameter allows you to specify how far from the ground the character can step up —the higher the value, the larger the distance they can step up.

- **Skin Width**: As the character will collide with other game objects in the scene, often at speed, this parameter is provided to let you specify how deeply other colliders may intersect with the character's collider without reacting. This is designed to help reduce conflicts with objects, the result of which can be a jittering (a slight but constant character shake) or the character getting stuck in walls. This occurs when two colliders suddenly intersect, without allowing the game engine time to react accordingly —rather than crashing, the engine will switch off colliders to halt control or force the colliders apart unpredictably. Unity Technologies recommends that you set skin width to 10 percent of your character's radius parameter.

- **Min Move Distance**: This is the lowest amount by which your character can be moved. Usually set to zero, setting this value to a larger number means that your character cannot move unless they will be moved beyond that value. This is generally only used to reduce jittering, but in most situations is left set to **0**.

- **Center**: Set as a Vector3 (x,y,z values). It allows you to position the character collider away from its local central point. Usually at zero, this is more often used for third person characters, which will have a more complex look than a simple capsule. By allowing you to move the Y coordinate, for example it enables you to account for where the character's feet hit the floor —as it is the **Character Controller collider**, that defines where the player object rests on the ground, and not the visual mesh of the character's feet.

The Character Controller collider is represented in the **Scene** view by a green capsule-shaped outline, in the same way as other colliders in Unity. In the following image, I have temporarily disabled the rendering of the visual part of the FPC **Graphics** in order to help you spot the Character Controller's outline:

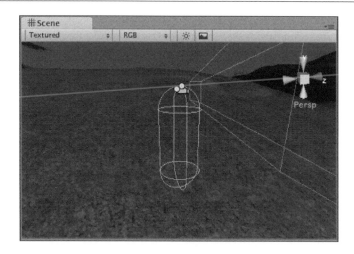

Mouse Look (Script)

Written in C#, this script is in charge of turning our character as we move the mouse, leaving the horizontal move keys to handle strafing. This script has a number of public member variables exposed for adjustment:

- **Axes**: Set to **MouseX** in this instance. This variable allows you to choose **MouseX**, **MouseY**, or **MouseXAndY**. In our FPC, we need this instance of the **Mouse Look** script (the other instance being a component of the **Main Camera** child object) to be set to the X-axis only, as this will allow mouse movement in the left and right direction in order to rotate the entire character — the **Main Camera** child object included.

  You may be wondering why we do not simply have **MouseXAndY** axes chosen on the **Mouse Look** component for the **Main Camera** object. The problem with this approach would be that while it would allow the camera to tilt and pan in both the axes, it would not keep the character facing where we are looking — it would simply rotate the camera locally. As a result, we could look around, but when we moved the character with the keys, we would run off in a random direction. By having this instance of the **Mouse Look** script on the parent object (**First Person Controller**), we are allowing it to rotate the character, which in turn pans the camera because it is a child and will match its parent's rotation.

- **Sensitivity X/Sensitivity Y**: As we are only using the X-axis of this script, this variable will only control how much the left/right movement of the mouse affects the rotation of the object. If the **Axes** variable was set to include the Y-axis, then this would control how sensitive the up or down movement of the mouse was at affecting the camera tilt. You will notice that **Sensitivity Y** has been set to **0**, as we are not using it, while **Sensitivity X** is set to **15** — the higher the value here, the faster the rotation.

- **Minimum X/Maximum X**: This allows you to restrict the amount you can pan around, as this script is in charge of turning the character. These amounts are set to **-360** and **360** respectively, allowing you to turn the player completely around on the spot.

- **Minimum Y/Maximum Y**: Again, we are not using the Y-axis, so this variable is set to **0** here, but ordinarily it would restrict the player when looking up and down, as it does in the instance of this script, which is applied to the **Main Camera** child object.

Object 2: Graphics

Because of the first person nature of this character, the player will never see their own body, as represented by the capsule. It is merely included in this prefab to help you, the developer, to easily spot the object in the **Scene** window when developing and testing the game. Often, developers will switch off the rendering of the capsule mesh by disabling the **Mesh Renderer** component in the **Inspector**. This is to ensure that the capsule stays hidden, especially in games where the player's character is viewed from another angle during cut scenes.

Select the **Graphics** child object in the **Hierarchy** panel, and take a look at the **Inspector** to view its components.

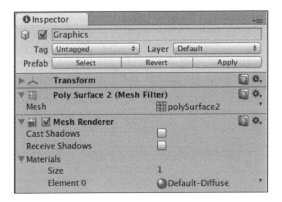

We'll take it as read that this object has a **Transform** component and that its position is (0,0,0), as it sits centrally with the parent object, **First Person Controller**. As this object's only purpose is to represent our player visually, it simply has the two key components that make it visible, a **Mesh Filter** and a **Mesh Renderer**. But what do these two components do?

Mesh filter

It is named **Poly Surface 2** in this instance. The name of the **Mesh Filter** component in any 3D mesh is usually the name of the object that it represents. Therefore, when you are introducing externally created models, you will notice that each **Mesh Filter** component is named after each part of the model.

A **Mesh Filter** is simply a component containing the mesh — the 3D shape itself. It then works with the renderer to draw a surface based on the mesh.

Mesh renderer

A **Mesh Renderer** must be present in order to draw surfaces onto the mesh of a 3D object. It is also in charge of a) how the mesh responds to lighting and b) the materials used on the surface to show color or textures.

Mesh renderers have the following parameters:

- **Cast Shadows**: Whether light cast onto this object will cause a shadow to be cast on the other surfaces (only available in Unity Pro version).

- **Receive Shadows**: Whether shadows cast by other objects are drawn onto this object (only available in Unity Pro version).

  In this example of the **Graphics** capsule, neither box is checked. Firstly, this is because we will never see the capsule, so we do not need to receive shadows. Secondly, the player does not think that their character has a body shaped like a capsule, so seeing a capsule-shaped shadow following them around would look rather odd.

- **Materials**: This area uses the **Size/Element** system seen in the **Tag Manager** earlier in this chapter. It allows you to specify one or more materials and adjust settings for them directly without having to find out the material in use, and then adjust it separately in the **Project** panel.

As our **Graphics** object requires/features no color or texture, there is no material to preview, but we'll explore material parameters further in the next few chapters.

Object 3: Main Camera

The **Main Camera** acts as your viewport. In the **First Person Controller** prefab, the **Main Camera** is positioned at the eye level (at the top of the **Graphics** capsule) and is controlled by scripts, allowing the player to move the entire parent object and the camera independently. This allows the player to look and also walk around at the same time.

Ordinarily, camera game objects are made up of three key components—**Camera**, **GUILayer**, and **Flare Layer**, in addition to the usual **Transform** component. Cameras also come with an **Audio Listener** for receiving sound, but this is usually removed as Unity requires that you only have one per scene.

In this instance, our camera also has a single script component called **Mouse Look (Script)**, which handles tilt rotation for the camera, based on the input from the mouse. To understand camera views better, let's take a look at how the core components work.

Camera

While ordinarily accompanied by the **GUILayer** and **Flare Layer** components, the **Camera** component is the main component in charge of establishing the viewpoint. In order to understand how the **Camera** component forms our viewpoint, we will examine its parameters.

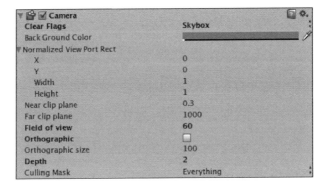

- **Clear Flags**: Ordinarily this will be set to its default, **Skybox**, so as to allow the camera to render the skybox material currently applied to the scene. But in order to allow you, the developer, to manage the use of multiple cameras to draw the game world, the **Clear Flags** parameter exists to allow you to set specific cameras, as well as to render specific parts of the game world. However, it is unlikely that you will begin utilizing techniques such as this until you have gotten to grips with much more of the basics of Unity.

- **Back Ground Color**: The background color is the color rendered behind all game objects if there is no skybox material applied to the scene. Clicking on the color block will allow you to change this color using the color picker, or you may use the ink dropper icon to the right of the color block in order to sample color from somewhere onscreen.

- **Normalized View Port Rect**: This parameter allows you to specifically state dimensions of—and position for—the camera view. Ordinarily, this is set to fit the entire screen, and this is also true in the example of the **Main Camera** attached to our player

The **X** and **Y** coordinates being set to **0** means that our camera view begins in the bottom-left of the screen. Given that the **Width** and **Height** values are set to **1**, our view from this camera will fill the screen, because these values are in Unity's screen coordinates system, which ranges from 0 to 1.

You will see this system in other 2D elements that you work with in Unity, like **graphical user interface (GUI)** elements.

The advantage of being able to set the size and position of our viewport is that we may wish to utilize more than one camera in our game. For example, in a racing game you may wish to have a camera viewport in the top corner of the screen showing the view behind the car, to allow the player to spot other drivers approaching him.

- **Near clip plane/Far clip plane**: The **clip planes** are effectively distances in which to draw the game world — the near plane being the closest distance to begin drawing, and the far plane being the furthest, or rather where drawing ends.

In order to save on memory in the graphical buffer (a part of memory used to store information on the game world's visuals), clip planes are often used to cut off the scenery that is far from the player. In older 3D games, this technique was more obvious, as computers back then had less RAM to write to, so more memory had to be saved by using closer far clip planes in order to make the game run smoothly.

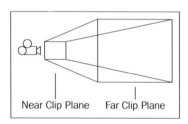

Near Clip Plane   Far Clip Plane

- **Field of view**: This parameter sets the width of the camera's viewport in degrees. This angle is set to **60** in our main camera object, as this is a sensible value in order to give the effect of a human eye view.

- **Orthographic** and **Orthographic size**: Toggling this setting would switch your camera to an **orthographic** view, as opposed to the standard 3D view, referred to as perspective view. Orthographic cameras are most often used in games, such as isometric real-time strategy games, or 2D games.

- **Depth**: The **Depth** setting can be utilized when using multiple cameras. By having a number of cameras that are switched between using scripts, the **Depth** parameter allows you to specify a priority order, that is, a camera with a higher depth value will render in front of a camera with a lower depth value. Depth can also work in conjunction with the **Normalized View Port Rect** setting in order to allow you to place camera views over the main view of the game world. In the example of the rear-view mirror of a racing game, the rear-view camera would need to have a higher depth value than the main camera in order to be rendered in front of the main forward view of the game world.

- **Culling Mask**: This parameter works with Unity's game **Layers**, as discussed previously, in order to allow you to render selectively. By placing certain elements of your game on a particular layer, you can deselect the layer they are on from the Culling Mask drop-down menu in order to exclude them from being rendered by the camera. Currently our **Main Camera** is set to render everything, as it is the only camera in the game.

GUILayer and Flare Layer

These two components have no parameters, but simply allow rendering of additional visual elements. The **GUILayer** allows the rendering of 2D elements such as menus and in-game **heads-up displays** (HUDs). The **Flare Layer** allows the camera to render lighting flares such as the one we added to our **Directional light** in Chapter 2.

Mouse Look (Script)

This is the second instance of the **Mouse Look (Script)** component we have seen so far—the other being on the parent **First Person Controller**. However, this time its **Axes** parameter is set to **MouseY**, and as a result, it is simply in charge of looking up and down by rotating the main camera object around its X-axis. This, combined with the **Mouse Look** script, which rotates the parent object, gives us the effect of a totally free look using the mouse, because by rotating the parent object our main camera is rotated left and right also.

Audio listener

The audio listener acts as our ears and allows us to hear any audio sources placed in the game. By having the audio listener on the main camera in a first person view game, mono (single channel) sounds that occur to the left of the player will be heard in the left ear, allowing you to create an environment with real-world stereo immersion.

Now that we have explored the component parts of the **First Person Controller**, let's take our first look at how the **FPSWalker** script works in order to get to grips with Unity JavaScript.

Scripting basics

Scripting is one of the most crucial elements in becoming a games developer. While Unity is fantastic at allowing you to create games with minimal knowledge of game engine source code, you will still need to understand how to write code that commands the Unity engine. Code written for use with Unity draws upon a series of ready-built **classes**, which you should think of as libraries of instructions or *behaviors*. By writing scripts, you will create your own classes by drawing upon commands in the existing Unity engine.

In this book, we will primarily focus on writing scripts in Unity's JavaScript, as it is the easiest language to get started with and is the main focus of Unity's scripting reference documentation. While this book will introduce you to the basics of scripting, it is highly recommended that you read the Unity *Scripting Reference* in parallel to it, and this is available as part of your Unity installation, and also online at:

```
http://unity3d.com/support/documentation/ScriptReference/
```

Problems encountered while scripting can often be solved with reference to this, and if that doesn't work, then you can ask for help on the Unity forums or in the **Internet Relay Chat (IRC)** channel for the software. For more information, visit:

```
http://unity3d.com/support/community
```

When writing a new script or using an existing one, the script will become active only when attached to a game object in the current scene. By attaching a script to a game object, it becomes a component of that object, and the behavior written in the script can apply to that object. However, scripts are not restricted to calling (the scripting term for *activating* or *running*) behavior on the game object they belong to, as other objects can be referenced by a name or a tag and can also be given instructions.

In order to get a better understanding of the scripts we are about to examine, let's take a look at some core scripting principles.

Commands

Commands are instructions given in a script. Although commands may be loose inside a script, you should try and ensure that they are contained within a function to give you more control over when they are called. All commands in JavaScript must be terminated (finished) with a semicolon as follows:

```
speed = 5;
```

Variables

Variables are simply containers for information. They are declared (set up) using the word **var**, followed by a word or unspaced phrase. Variables may be named anything you like, provided that:

- The name does not conflict with an existing word in the Unity engine code.
- It contains only alphanumeric characters and underscores and does not begin with a number. For example, the word *transform* already exists to represent the Transform component of a game object, so naming a variable or function with that word would cause a conflict.

Variables may contain text, numbers, and references to objects, assets, or components. Here is an example of a variable declaration:

```
var speed = 9.0;
```

Our variable begins with the word var, followed by its name, speed. It is then set (given a value) using a single equals symbol and is terminated like any other command with a semicolon.

Variable data types

When declaring variables, you should also state what kind of information they will store by defining a **data type**. Using our previous example, here is the same variable declaration including its data type:

```
var speed : float = 9.0;
```

Before the variable is set, we use a colon to specify the data type. In this example, the value that the variable is being set to is a number with a decimal place, and we state that it should have the data type float (short for 'floating point'—meaning a number with a decimal place).

By specifying the data type for any variable we declare, we are able to make our scripting more efficient, as the game engine does not need to decide upon an appropriate type for the variable it is reading. Here are a few common data types you will encounter when starting scripting with Unity:

- **string**: A combination of text and numbers stored in quotation marks "like this"
- **int**: Short for integer, meaning a whole number with no decimal place
- **float**: A floating point or a decimal placed numeric value
- **boolean**: A true or false value commonly used as a switch
- **Vector3**: A set of XYZ values

Using variables

After declaring variables, the information they contain may then be retrieved or set, simply by using the variable name. For example, if we were trying to set the speed variable, then we would simply say:

```
speed = 20;
```

As we have already established (or declared) the variable—var is only used in declaration, as is the data type.

We can also query or use the value of a variable in parts of our script. For example, if we wished to store a value that was half of the current speed variable, then we could establish a new variable, as shown in the following example:

```
var speed : float = 9.0;
var halfSpeed : float;
halfSpeed = speed/2;
```

Also, notice that where the halfSpeed variable is declared, it is not set to a value. This is because a value is given to it in the command below it by dividing the existing speed variable's value by two.

Public versus private

Variables which are declared outside of a function in a script are known as **public member variables**, because they will automatically show up as parameters of the script when it is viewed as a component in the **Inspector**. For example, when viewing the **FPSWalker** script attached as a component of the **First Person Controller** object, we see its member variables **Speed**, **Jump Speed**, and **Gravity**:

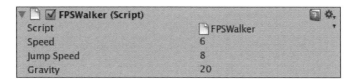

The value of each of these variables may then be adjusted in the **Inspector**.

If you are not likely to adjust the value of a variable in the **Inspector**, then you should hide it by using the prefix private. For example, if we wished to hide the variable **Jump Speed**, then we would adjust the variable declarations in the script in the following way:

```
var speed = 6.0;
private var jumpSpeed = 8.0;
var gravity = 20.0;
```

This would make our **Inspector** view of the script look as follows:

 Be aware that any value adjusted in the **Inspector** will override the original value given to a variable within the script. It will not rewrite the value stated in the script, but simply replaces it when the game runs. You can also revert to the values declared in the script by clicking on the Cog icon to the right of the component and choosing **Reset** from the drop-down menu that appears.

Functions

Functions may be described as sets of instructions that can be called at a specific point in the game's runtime. A script may contain many functions and each one may call any function within the same script. In Unity scripting, there are many in-built functions ready made to carry out your commands at predefined points in time or as a result of user input. You may also write your own functions and call them when you need to carry out specific sets of instructions.

All functions are written by specifying a function name followed by a set of brackets into which the developer may pass additional parameters and open and close with curly braces. Let's look at some examples of the existing functions that you may use:

Update()

A new JavaScript file created in Unity begins with the **Update()** function, which looks like this:

```
function Update(){
}
```

All the instructions or *commands* for a function must occur between the opening and closing braces, for example:

```
function Update(){
   speed = 5;
}
```

As long as commands are written within the curly braces, they will be called whenever this function is called by the game engine.

Games run at a certain number of **frames per second (FPS)**, and the `Update()` function is called when each frame of the game is rendered. As a result, it is mostly used for any commands that must be carried out constantly or for detecting changes in the game world that occur in real time, such as input commands—key presses or mouse clicks. When dealing with physics-related commands, the alternative function `FixedUpdate()` should be used instead, as it is a function which keeps in sync with the physics engine, whereas `Update()` itself can be variable depending on the frame rate.

OnMouseDown()

As an example of a function that is called at a specific time, **OnMouseDown()** is only called when the player's mouse clicks on a game object or on a GUI element in the game.

This is most often used for mouse controlled games or detecting clicks in menus. Here is an example of a basic `OnMouseDown()` function , which when attached to a game object, will quit the game when the object is clicked on:

```
function OnMouseDown(){
   Application.Quit();
}
```

Writing functions

In creating your own functions, you will be able to specify a set of instructions that can be called from anywhere within the scripts you are writing. If we were setting up some instructions to move an object to a specified position in the game world, then we may write a custom function to carry out the necessary instructions so that we may call this function from other functions within a script.

For example, on falling into a trap, a player character may need to be moved if they have died and are returning to the start of a level. Rather than writing the player relocation instructions onto every part of the game that causes the player to die, the necessary instructions can be contained within a single function that is called many times. It could look like this:

```
function PlayerDeath(){
   transform.position = Vector3(0,10,50);
   score-=50;
   lives--;
}
```

When calling this `PlayerDeath()` function, all three commands will be carried out—the player's position is set to X = 0, Y = 10, and Z = 50. Then a value of 50 is subtracted from a variable named `score`, and 1 is subtracted from a variable named `lives`—the two minus symbols seen here mean subtract 1, and likewise if you encounter `++` in a script, then it simply means add 1.

To call this function, we would simply write the following as part of our script that caused the player to die:

```
PlayerDeath();
```

If else statements

An **if statement** is used in scripting to check for conditions. If its conditions are met, then the `if` statement will carry out a set of nested instructions. If they are not, then it can default to a set of instructions called **else**. In the following example, the `if` statement is checking whether the `boolean` variable `grounded` is set to `true`:

```
var grounded : boolean = false;
var speed : float;
function Update(){
  if(grounded==true){
    speed = 5;
  }
}
```

If the condition in the `if` statement's brackets is met, that is, if the `grounded` variable becomes `true`, then the `speed` variable will be set to 5. Otherwise it will not be given a value.

 Note that when setting a variable, a single equals symbol '=' is used, but when checking the status of a variable, we use two '= ='. This is known as a **comparative equals**—we are comparing the information stored in a variable with the value after the two equals symbols.

If we wanted to set up a fallback condition, then we could add an `else` statement after the `if`, which is our way of saying that if these conditions are not met, then do something else:

```
var grounded : boolean = false;
var speed : float;
function Update(){
  if(grounded==true){
    speed = 5;
  }
```

```
   else{
      speed = 0;
   }
}
```

So **unless** `grounded` is `true`, `speed` will equal `0`.

To build additional potential outcomes for checking conditions, we can use an `else if` before the fallback `else`. If we are checking values, then we could write:

```
if(speed >= 6){
  //do something
}
else
   if(speed >= 3){
     //do something different
   }
   else{
      //if neither of the above are true, do this
   }
```

Be sure to remember that where I have written `//` above, I am simply writing code that would appear as a comment (non-executed code).

Multiple conditions

We can also check for more than a single condition in one `if` statement by using two ampersand symbols — **&&**.

For example, we may want to check on the condition of two variables at once and only carry out our instructions if the variable's values are as specified. We would write:

```
if(speed >= 3 && grounded == true){
  //do something
}
```

If we wished to check for one condition or another, then we can use two vertical lined characters '`||`' in order to mean **OR**. We would write this as:

```
if(speed >= 3 || grounded == true){
  //do something
}
```

Globals and dot syntax

In this section, we'll take a look at the way in which you can send information between scripts using something called a **global variable**, and how by using a technique of writing code known as **Dot Syntax**, you can address information in hierarchical manner.

Using static to define globals

When writing scripts in JavaScript, your script name is the name of your class. This means that when addressing variables or functions in other scripts, you can refer to the class by using the name of the script followed by the variable or function name using the dot syntax.

A **global** in scripting terms can be defined as a value or command accessible by any script and not simply by functions or variables within the same script. To declare a global within a Unity JavaScript file, the prefix `static` is used. For example:

```
static var speed : float = 9.0;
```

If this `speed` variable was the one seen in our **FPSWalker** script, then we would be able to access or set the value of this variable from a separate script using the script name, a dot, and then the name of the variable, followed by setting the value as follows:

```
FPSWalker.speed = 15.0;
```

We refer to this type of variable as a global variable, but we may also have global functions that may be called from other scripts. For example, the `PlayerDeath()` function mentioned previously could be a static function, which would allow you to call it from any other script in the game.

Dot syntax

In the previous example, we have used a script technique called dot syntax. This is a term that may sound more complex than it actually is, as it simply means using a dot (or full stop/period) to separate elements you are addressing in a hierarchical order.

Starting with the most general element or reference, you can use the dot syntax to narrow down to the specific parameter you wish to set.

For example, to set the vertical position of the game object, we would need to alter its Y coordinate. Therefore, we would be looking to address the position parameters of an object's Transform component. We would write:

```
transform.position.y = 50;
```

This means that any parameter can be referenced by simply finding the component it belongs to by using the dot syntax.

Comments

In many prewritten scripts, you will notice that there are some lines written with two forward slashes prefixing them. These are simply comments written by the author of the script. It is generally a good idea, especially when starting out with scripting, to write your own comments in order to remind yourself how a script works.

Further reading

As you continue to work with Unity, it is crucial that you get used to referring to the *Scripting Reference* documentation, which is installed with your copy of Unity and also available on the Unity web site at the following address:

```
http://unity3d.com/support/documentation/ScriptReference/
```

You can use the scripting reference to search for the correct use of any class in the Unity engine. Now that you have gotten to grips with the basics of scripting, let's take a look at the **FPSWalker** script, which is in charge of moving our **First Person Controller** character.

The FPSWalker script

In order to view any script in Unity, you will need to open it in the script editor. To do this, simply select the script in the **Project** panel, and then double-click on its icon to open it for editing.

On Mac, the default bundled script editor is called Unitron. On PC, the script editor is called Uniscite. These are standalone applications that simply allow you to edit various formats of text file, JavaScript and C# being two such examples.

There are other free text editors available that you may choose to use when writing scripts for Unity. You may set Unity to use a text editor of your choice. For the purposes of this book, we will refer to the default script editors Unitron and Uniscite.

Launching the script

Select the **First Person Controller** object in the **Hierarchy**, and then click on the name of the script file under the **FPSWalker (Script)** component in the **Inspector** so that it is highlighted in blue, as shown in the following screenshot:

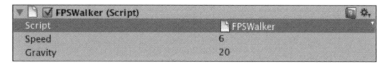

This will highlight the location of the script in the **Project** panel in yellow (see the following screenshot) to help you find it. Once you have spotted this, double-click on the file icon to launch it in the default script editor.

Mac—FPSWalker in Unitron

On Mac, **FPSWalker** opens in the default script editor **Unitron**, which appears as shown in the following screenshot:

```
1  var speed = 6.0;
2  var jumpSpeed = 8.0;
3  var gravity = 20.0;
4
5  private var moveDirection = Vector3.zero;
6  private var grounded : boolean = false;
7
8  function FixedUpdate() {
9      if (grounded) {
10         // We are grounded, so recalculate movedirection directly from axes
11         moveDirection = new Vector3(Input.GetAxis("Horizontal"), 0, Input.GetAxis("Vertical"));
12         moveDirection = transform.TransformDirection(moveDirection);
13         moveDirection *= speed;
14
15         if (Input.GetButton ("Jump")) {
16             moveDirection.y = jumpSpeed;
17         }
18     }
19
20     // Apply gravity
21     moveDirection.y -= gravity * Time.deltaTime;
22
23     // Move the controller
24     var controller : CharacterController = GetComponent(CharacterController);
25     var flags = controller.Move(moveDirection * Time.deltaTime);
26     grounded = (flags & CollisionFlags.CollidedBelow) != 0;
27 }
28
29 @script RequireComponent(CharacterController)
```

Windows PC—FPSWalker in Uniscite

On Windows PC, **FPSWalker** opens in the default script editor **UniSciTE**, which appears as shown in the following screenshot:

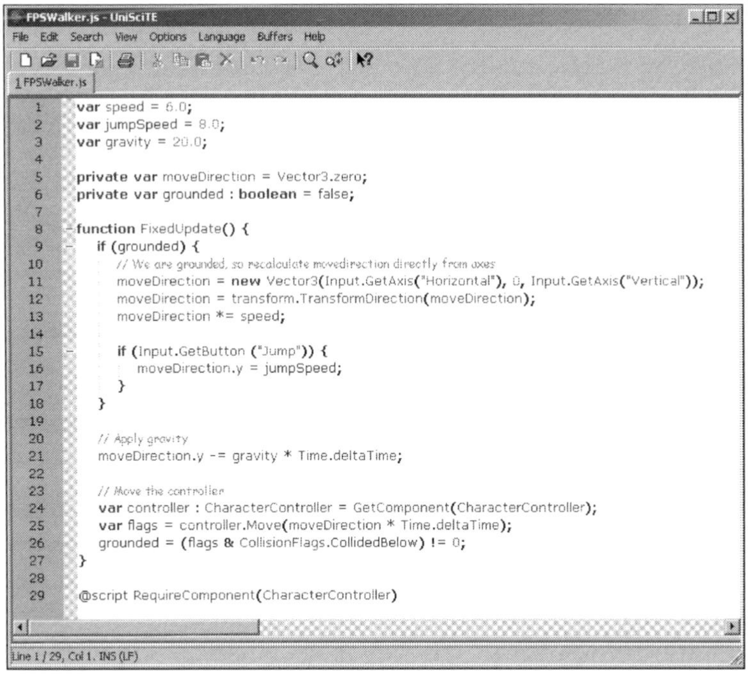

```
FPSWalker.js - UniSciTE
File  Edit  Search  View  Options  Language  Buffers  Help

1 FPSWalker.js
 1      var speed = 6.0;
 2      var jumpSpeed = 8.0;
 3      var gravity = 20.0;
 4
 5      private var moveDirection = Vector3.zero;
 6      private var grounded : boolean = false;
 7
 8      function FixedUpdate() {
 9          if (grounded) {
10              // We are grounded, so recalculate movedirection directly from axes
11              moveDirection = new Vector3(Input.GetAxis("Horizontal"), 0, Input.GetAxis("Vertical"));
12              moveDirection = transform.TransformDirection(moveDirection);
13              moveDirection *= speed;
14
15              if (Input.GetButton ("Jump")) {
16                  moveDirection.y = jumpSpeed;
17              }
18          }
19
20          // Apply gravity
21          moveDirection.y -= gravity * Time.deltaTime;
22
23          // Move the controller
24          var controller : CharacterController = GetComponent(CharacterController);
25          var flags = controller.Move(moveDirection * Time.deltaTime);
26          grounded = (flags & CollisionFlags.CollidedBelow) != 0;
27      }
28
29      @script RequireComponent(CharacterController)

Line 1 / 29, Col 1. INS (LF)
```

While this is the same script, you will see different syntax colors for different parts of the script between the two different platforms. This is down to the script editor itself and has no bearing on the functionality of the scripting.

Deconstructing the script

In this section, we will look at the parts of a potential script we have just learned in context by deconstructing their use in the **FPSWalker** script.

Variable declaration

As with most scripts, **FPSWalker** begins with a set of variable declarations from lines 1 to 6:

```
var speed = 6.0;
private var jumpSpeed = 8.0;
var gravity = 20.0;
private var moveDirection = Vector3.zero;
private var grounded : boolean = false;
```

Lines 1 to 3 are public member variables used later in the script as values to multiply by. They have decimal places in their numbers, so they ideally would feature data types set to float (as this is a simple example script from Unity Technologies, not all variables are data typed). Lines 5 and 6 are private variables, as they will only be used within the script.

The private variable moveDirection is in charge of storing the player's current forward direction as a Vector3 (set of X,Y,Z coordinates). On declaration, this variable is set to (0,0,0) in order to stop the player from facing an arbitrary direction when the game begins.

The private variable grounded is data typed to a boolean (true or false) data type. It is used later in the script to keep track of whether the player is resting on the ground, in order to allow movement and jumping, which would not be allowed if they were not on the ground (that is, if they are currently jumping).

Storing movement information

The script continues on line 8 with the opening of a FixedUpdate() function. Similar to the Update() function discussed earlier, a fixed update is called every fixed framerate frame—this means that it is more appropriate for dealing with physics-related scripting, such as rigidbody usage and gravity effects, as standard Update() will vary with game frame rate dependent upon hardware.

The FixedUpdate() function runs from lines 8 to 27, so we can assume that as all of the commands and if statements are within it, they will be checked after each frame.

In the book, you may occasionally come across a single line of code appearing on two different lines. Please note that this has been done only for the purpose of indentation and due to space constraints. When using such code make sure it's on one line in your script file.

The first if statement in the function runs from lines 9 to 18 (the developer comment has been removed in the following code snippet):

```
if (grounded) {
  moveDirection = new Vector3(Input.GetAxis("Horizontal"), 0,
    Input.GetAxis("Vertical"));
  moveDirection = transform.TransformDirection(moveDirection);
  moveDirection *= speed;

  if (Input.GetButton ("Jump")) {
    moveDirection.y = jumpSpeed;
```

```
      }
   }
```

By stating that its commands and nested `if` statements (line 15) will only run
`if (grounded)`, this is shorthand for writing:

```
   If(grounded == true){
```

When `grounded` becomes `true`, this `if` statement does three things with the
variable `moveDirection`.

Firstly, it assigns it a new Vector3 value, and places the current value of `Input.`
`GetAxis("Horizontal")` to the X coordinate and `Input.GetAxis("Vertical")`
to the Z coordinate, leaving Y set to `0`:

```
   moveDirection = new Vector3(Input.GetAxis("Horizontal"), 0,
      Input.GetAxis("Vertical"));
```

> In this example, Unity Technologies have written the code using the
> word 'new' to prefix the Vector3 they are feeding to the `moveDirection`
> variable. This is a convention of C# coding and has been written in this
> way to make their code easier to convert between JavaScript and C#.
> However, this is not necessary in JavaScript, which is why you will not
> see the use of 'new' in other instances like this within the book.

But what are the `Input.GetAxis` commands doing? They are simply representing
values between -1 and 1 according to horizontal and vertical input keys, which by
default are:

- *A/D* or Left arrow/Right arrow — horizontal axis
- *W/S* or Up arrow/Down arrow — vertical axis

When no keys are pressed, these values will be `0`, as they are axis-based inputs
to which Unity automatically gives an 'idle' state. Therefore, when holding the
Left arrow key, for example, the value of `Input.GetAxis("Horizontal")` would
be equal to -1, when holding the Right arrow, it would be equal to 1, and when
releasing either key, the value will count back towards 0.

In short, the line:

```
   moveDirection = new Vector3(Input.GetAxis("Horizontal"), 0,
      Input.GetAxis("Vertical"));
```

is giving the variable `moveDirection` a Vector3 value with the X and Z values based
upon key presses, while leaving the Y value set to `0`.

Next, our `moveDirection` variable is modified again on line 12:

```
moveDirection = transform.TransformDirection(moveDirection);
```

Here, we set `moveDirection` to a value based upon the Transform component's `TransformDirection`. The **Transform Direction** command converts local XYZ values to world values. So in this line, we are taking the previously set XYZ coordinates of `moveDirection` and converting them to a set of world coordinates. This is why we see `moveDirection` in the brackets after `TransformDirection` because it is using the value set on the previous line and effectively just changing its format.

Finally, `moveDirection` is multiplied by the `speed` variable on line 13:

```
moveDirection *= speed;
```

Because `speed` is a member variable, multiplying the XYZ values of `moveDirection` by it will mean that when we increase the value of `speed` in the **Inspector**, we can increase our character's movement speed without editing the script. This is because it is the resultant value of `moveDirection` that is used later in the script to move the character.

Before our `if (grounded)` statement terminates, there is another nested `if` statement from lines 15 to 17:

```
if (Input.GetButton ("Jump")) {
   moveDirection.y = jumpSpeed;
}
```

This `if` statement is triggered by a key press with the name `Jump`. By default, the jump button is assigned to the *Space bar*. As soon as this key is pressed, the Y-axis value of the `moveDirection` variable is set to the value of variable `jumpSpeed`. Therefore, unless `jumpSpeed` has been modified in the **Inspector**, `moveDirection.y` will be set to a value of `8.0`.

When we move the character later in the script, this sudden addition from `0` to `8.0` in the Y-axis will give the effect of jumping. But how will our character return to the ground? This character object does not have a Rigidbody component attached, so it will not be controlled by gravity in the physics engine.

This is why we need line 21, on which we subtract from the value `moveDirection.y`:

```
moveDirection.y -= gravity * Time.deltaTime;
```

You'll notice that we are not simply subtracting the value of gravity here, as the result of doing that would not give the effect of a jump, but instead take us straight up and down again between two frames. We are subtracting the sum of the `gravity` variable multiplied by a command called `Time.deltaTime`.

By multiplying any value within an `Update()` or `FixedUpdate()` function by `Time.deltaTime`, you are overriding the frame-based nature of the function and converting the effect of your command into seconds. So by writing:

```
moveDirection.y -= gravity * Time.deltaTime;
```

we are actually subtracting the value of gravity every second, rather than every frame.

Moving the character

As the comment on line 23 points out, lines 24 to 26 are in charge of the character's movement.

Firstly, on line 24, a new variable named `controller` is established and given the data type `CharacterController`. It is then set to represent the `Character Controller` component, by using the `GetComponent()` command:

```
var controller : CharacterController =
  GetComponent(CharacterController);
```

By using `GetComponent()`, you can access any component that is attached to the object that your script is attached to, simply by using its name within the brackets.

So now, whenever we use the variable reference `controller`, we can access any of the parameters of that component and use the `Move` function in order to move the object.

On line 25, this is exactly what we do. As we do so, we place this movement into a variable called `flags` as shown:

```
var flags = controller.Move(moveDirection * Time.deltaTime);
```

The `CharacterController.Move` function expects to be passed a Vector3 value—in order to move a character controller in directions X, Y, and Z—so we utilize the data that we stored earlier in our `moveDirection` variable and multiply by `Time.deltaTime` so that we move in meters per second, rather than meters per frame.

Checking grounded

Our `moveDirection` variable is only given a value if the boolean variable `grounded` is set to `true`. So how do we decide if we are grounded or not?

Character Controller colliders, like any other colliders, can detect collisions with other objects. However, unlike the standard colliders, the character controller collider has four specific collision shortcuts set up in a set of responders called `CollisionFlags`. These are as follows:

- None
- Sides
- Above
- Below

They are in charge of checking for collisions, with the specific part of the collider they describe — with the exception of None, which simply means no collision is occurring.

These flags are used to set our `grounded` variable on line 26:

```
grounded = (flags & CollisionFlags.CollidedBelow) != 0;
```

This may look complex due to the multiple equals symbols, but is simply a shorthand method of checking a condition and setting a value in a single line.

Firstly, the `grounded` variable is addressed, and then set using an equals symbol. Then, in the first set of brackets, we use a **bit mask** technique to determine whether collisions in the variable `flags` (our controller's movement) match the internally defined `CollidedBelow` value:

```
(flags & CollisionFlags.CollidedBelow)
```

The use of a single ampersand symbol here specifies a comparison between two values in binary form, something which you need not understand at this stage because Unity's class system offers shorthand for most calculations of this type.

If our controller is indeed colliding below, and therefore must be on the ground, then this comparison will be equal to 1.

This comparison is followed by `!=0`. An exclamation mark before an equals symbol means "does not equal". Therefore, here we are setting `grounded` to not equal `0`, if we are colliding below, and in these terms, setting `grounded` to `1` is the same as setting it to `true`.

@Script commands

The `FixedUpdate()` function terminates on line 27, leaving only a single command in the rest of the script, that is, an `@script` command as shown:

```
@script RequireComponent(CharacterController)
```

`@script` commands are used to perform actions that you would ordinarily need to perform manually in the Unity Editor.

In this example, a `RequireComponent()` function is executed, which forces Unity to add the component specified in brackets, should the object the script is being added to not currently have one.

Because this script uses the `CharacterController` component to drive our character, it makes sense to use an `@script` command to ensure that the component is present and, therefore, can be addressed. It is also worth noting that `@script` commands are the only examples of commands that must not terminate with a semicolon.

Summary

In this chapter, we've taken a look at the first interactive element in our game so far — the **First Person Controller**. We have also taken a broad look at scripting for Unity games, an important first step that we will be building on throughout this book.

In the next chapter, you will begin to write your own scripts and look further into collision detection. To do this, we'll be returning to the outpost model asset we imported in Chapter 2, introducing it to our game scene, and making our player character interact with it using a combination of animation and scripting.

4
Interactions

In this chapter, we'll be looking at further interactions and dive into two of the most crucial elements of game development, namely, **Collision Detection** and **Ray Casting**.

To detect physical interactions between game objects, the most common method is to use a Collider component—an invisible net that surrounds an object's shape and is in charge of detecting collisions with other objects. The act of detecting and retrieving information from these collisions is known as collision detection.

Not only can we detect when two colliders interact, but we can also pre-empt a collision and perform many other useful tasks by utilizing a technique called **Ray Casting**, which draws a Ray—put simply, an invisible (non-rendered) vector line between two points in 3D space—which can also be used to detect an intersection with a game object's collider. Ray casting can also be used to retrieve lots of other useful information such as the length of the ray (therefore—distance), and the point of impact of the end of the line.

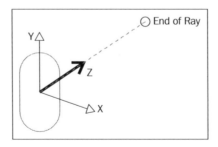

In the given example, a ray facing the forward direction from our character is demonstrated. In addition to the direction, a ray can also be given a specific length, or allowed to cast until it finds an object.

Over the course of the chapter, we will work with the outpost model that we imported in Chapter 2. Because this asset has been animated for us, the animation of the outpost's door opening and closing is ready to be triggered—once the model is placed into our scene. This can be done with either collision detection or ray casting, and we will explore what you will need to do to implement either approach.

Let's begin by looking at collision detection and when it may be appropriate to use ray casting instead of, or in complement to, collision detection.

Exploring collisions

When objects collide in any game engine, information about the **collision event** becomes available. By recording a variety of information upon the moment of impact, the game engine can respond in a realistic manner. For example, in a game involving physics, if an object falls to the ground from a height, then the engine needs to know which part of the object hit the ground first. With that information, it can correctly and realistically control the object's reaction to the impact.

Of course, Unity handles these kinds of collisions and stores the information on your behalf, and you only have to retrieve it in order to do something with it.

In the example of opening a door, we would need to detect collisions between the player character's collider and a collider on or near the door. It would make little sense to detect collisions elsewhere, as we would likely need to trigger the animation of the door when the player is near enough to walk through it, or to expect it to open for them.

As a result, we would check for collisions between the player character's collider and the door's collider. However, we would need to extend the depth of the door's collider so that the player character's collider did not need to be pressed up against the door in order to trigger a collision, as shown in the following illustration. However, the problem with extending the depth of the collider is that the game interaction with it becomes unrealistic.

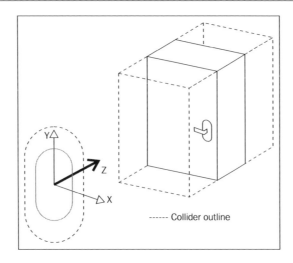

------ Collider outline

In the example of our door, the extended collider protruding from the visual surface of the door would mean that we would bump into an invisible surface which would cause our character to stop in their tracks, and although we would use this collision to trigger the opening of the door through animation, the initial bump into the extended collider would seem unnatural to the player and thus detract from their immersion in the game. So while collision detection will work perfectly well between the player character collider and the door collider, there are drawbacks that call for us as creative game developers to look for a more intuitive approach, and this is where ray casting comes in.

Ray casting

While we can detect collisions between the player character's collider and a collider that fits the door object, a more appropriate method may be to check for when the player character is facing the door we are expecting to open and is within a certain distance of this door. This can be done by casting a ray forward from the player's forward direction and restricting its length. This means that when approaching the door, the player needn't walk right up to it—or bump into an extended collider—in order for it to be detected. It also ensures that the player cannot walk up to the door facing away from it and still open it—with ray casting they must be facing the door in order to use it, which makes sense.

In common usage, ray casting is done where collision detection is simply too imprecise to respond correctly. For example, reactions that need to occur with a frame-by-frame level of detail may occur too quickly for a collision to take place. In this instance, we need to preemptively detect whether a collision is likely to occur rather than the collision itself. Let's look at a practical example of this problem.

The frame miss

In the example of a gun in a 3D shooter game, ray casting is used to predict the impact of a gunshot when a gun is fired. Because of the speed of an actual bullet, simulating the flight path of a bullet heading toward a target is very difficult to visually represent in a way that would satisfy and make sense to the player. This is down to the frame-based nature of the way in which games are rendered.

If you consider that when a real gun is fired, it takes a tiny amount of time to reach its target—and as far as an observer is concerned it could be said to happen instantly—we can assume that even when rendering over 25 frames of our game per second, the bullet would need to have reached its target within only a few frames.

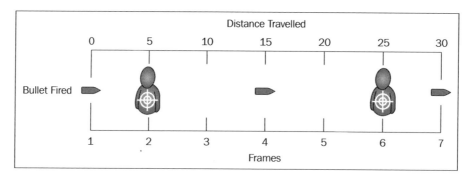

In the example above, a bullet is fired from a gun. In order to make the bullet realistic, it will have to move at a speed of 500 feet per second. If the frame rate is 25 frames per second, then the bullet moves at 20 feet per frame. The problem with this is a person is about 2 feet in diameter, which means that the bullet will very likely miss the enemies shown at 5 and 25 feet away that would be hit. This is where prediction comes into play.

Predictive collision detection

Instead of checking for a collision with an actual bullet object, we find out whether a fired bullet will hit its target. By casting a ray forward from the gun object (thus using its forward direction) on the same frame that the player presses the fire button, we can immediately check which objects intersect the ray.

We can do this because rays are drawn immediately. Think of them like a laser pointer—when you switch on the laser, we do not see the light moving forward because it travels at the speed of light—to us it simply appears.

Rays work in the same way, so that whenever the player in a ray-based shooting game presses fire, they draw a ray in the direction that they are aiming. With this ray, they can retrieve information on the collider that is hit. Moreover, by identifying the collider, the game object itself can be addressed and scripted to behave accordingly. Even detailed information, such as the point of impact, can be returned and used to affect the resultant reaction, for example, causing the enemy to recoil in a particular direction.

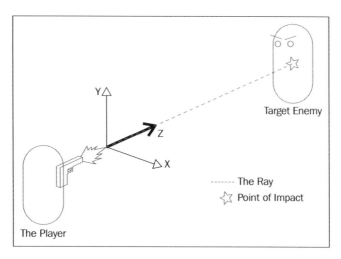

In our shooting game example, we would likely invoke scripting to kill or physically repel the enemy whose collider the ray hits, and as a result of the immediacy of rays, we can do this on the frame after the ray collides with, or *intersects* the enemy collider. This gives the effect of a real gunshot because the reaction is registered immediately.

It is also worth noting that shooting games often use the otherwise invisible rays to render brief visible lines to help with aim and give the player visual feedback, but do not confuse these lines with ray casts because the rays are simply used as a path for line rendering.

Adding the outpost

Before we begin to use both collision detection and ray casting to open the door of our outpost, we'll need to introduce it to the scene. In Chapter 2, we set up the animation states for the model, and it will be those states that we'll be addressing when we write a script later in the chapter.

To begin, drag the outpost model from the **Project** panel to the **Scene view** and drop it anywhere—bear in mind you cannot position it when you drag-and-drop; this is done once you have dropped the model (that is, let go off the mouse).

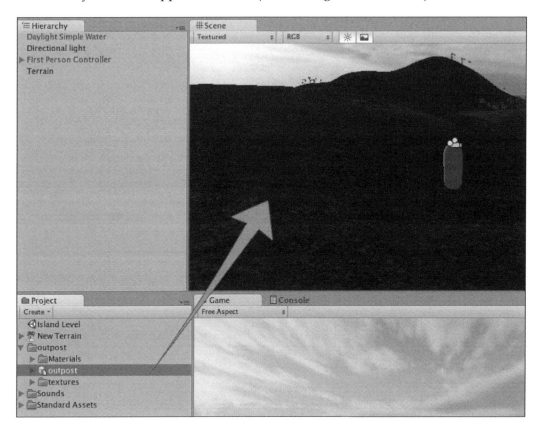

Once the outpost is in the **Scene**, you'll notice its name has also appeared in the **Hierarchy** panel and that it has automatically become selected. Now you're ready to position and scale it!

Positioning

As your terrain design from Chapter 2 may be different to mine, select the **Transform** tool and position your **outpost** in a free area of land by dragging the axis handles in the scene.

Be careful when using the axis handles for positioning. Dragging the white square where the handles converge will adjust all three axes at once—not something you'll want to use when in perspective mode, so ensure that you drag handles individually by keeping your cursor outside of the white square.

If you'd like to constrain an object to the surface of the terrain in perspective mode, then you can hold the *Command* key (Mac) or *Ctrl* key (PC) and drag within the white square.

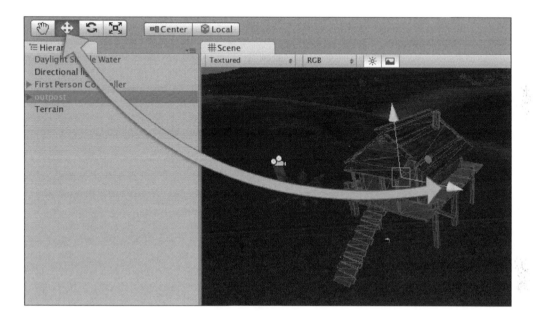

I have positioned my outpost at (500, 30.8, 505) but you may need to reposition your object manually. Remember that once you have positioned using the axis handles in the **Scene** window, you can enter specific values in the **Position** values of the **Transform** component in the **Inspector**.

Scaling

As we are working with two applications—the modeling application our **outpost** asset was created in and Unity itself—often the scale of the imported asset will not match the meter units in Unity and will need scaling up or down.

While we can set up **Scale** values in the **Inspector**, it is best wherever possible, to set up your scale by using the **Scale Factor** setting on the original asset. Select the **outpost** model inside the **Outpost** folder in the **Project** panel. Now in the **Inspector**, you will see a component called **FBXImporter**. This component has import settings available that will affect any instances of the model you place into the Scene. Here you should set the **Scale Factor** value from **1** to **2**. This makes the outpost model large enough for our **Character Controller** to fit through the doorframe and making it a realistically sized room once we get inside.

Colliders and tagging the door

In order to open the door, we need to identify it as an individual object when it is collided with by the player—this can be done because the object has a collider component and via this we can check the object for a specific tag. Expand the **outpost** parent object by clicking on the dark gray arrow to the left of its name in the **Hierarchy** panel.

You should now see the list of all child objects beneath it. Select the object named **door** and then with your mouse cursor over the **Scene** window, press *F* on the keyboard to focus your view on it.

You should now see the door in the **Scene** window, and as a result of selecting the object, you should also see its components listed in the **Inspector** panel. You should notice that one of the components is a **Mesh Collider**. This is a detailed collider assigned to all meshes found on the various children of a model when you select **Generate Colliders**, as we did for the **outpost** asset in Chapter 2.

The mesh collider is assigned to each child element, as Unity does not know how much detail will be present in any given model you could choose to import. As a result, it defaults to assigning mesh colliders for each part, as they will naturally fit to the shape of the mesh they encounter. Because our door is simply a cube shape, we should replace this mesh collider with a simpler and more efficient box collider.

From the top menu, go to **Component | Physics | Box Collider**.

You will then receive two prompts. Firstly, you will be told that adding a new component will cause this object to lose its connection with the parent object in the **Project** panel. This dialog window, titled **Losing Prefab**, simply means that your copy in the **Scene** will no longer match the original asset, and as a result, any changes made to the asset in the **Project** panel in Unity will not be reflected in the copy in the **Scene**. Simply click on the **Add** button to confirm that this is what you want to do.

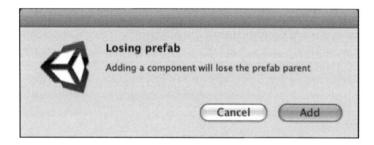

This will happen whenever you begin to customize your imported models in Unity, and it is nothing to worry about. This is because, generally, you will need to add components to a model, which is why Unity gives you the opportunity to create your own prefabs.

Secondly, as the object already has a collider assigned to it, you will be prompted whether you wish to **Add**, **Replace**, or **Cancel** this collider to your object. Generally, you'll use a single collider per object, as this works better for the physics engine in Unity. This is why Unity asks if you'd like to **Add** or **Replace** rather than assuming the addition of colliders.

As we have no further need for the mesh collider, choose **Replace**.

You will now see a green outline around the door representing the **Box Collider** component you have added.

A box collider is an example of a **Primitive Collider**, so called as it is one of several scalable primitive shape colliders in Unity—including Box, Sphere, Capsule, and Wheel—that have predetermined collider shapes, and in Unity, all primitive colliders are shown with this green outline. You may have noticed this when viewing the character controller collider, which is technically a capsule collider shape and as such also displays in green.

Finally, we need to tag the door object, as we will need to address this object in our scripting later. With the door child object still selected, click on the **tag** drop-down at the top of the **Inspector** panel, and choose **Add Tag**. In the **Tag Manager** that replaces your current **Inspector** view, add the tag **outpostDoor**, as shown in the following screenshot:

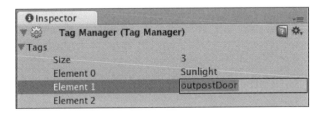

Because adding tags is a two step process, you will need to reselect the **door** child object in the **Hierarchy** panel, and choose your newly added **outpostDoor** tag from the **Tag** drop-down menu to finish adding the tag.

Disabling automatic animation

By default, Unity assumes that all animated objects introduced to the scene will need to be played automatically. Although this is why we create an idle animation—in which our asset is doing nothing; allowing Unity to play automatically will often cause animated objects to appear a frame into one of their intended animations. To correct this issue, we simply deselect the **Play Automatically** checkbox in the **Inspector** for the parent object of our model. Ordinarily, we would not need to do this if our asset was simply a looped animation constantly playing in the game world. For example, a billowing flag or rotating lighthouse lamp, but we need our outpost not to animate until the player reaches the door, so we avoid automatically playing any animation.

To do this, reselect the parent object called **outpost** in the **Hierarchy** panel, and in the **Animation** component in the **Inspector** panel, deselect **Play Automatically**.

The **Inspector** panel view of the outpost object should now look like the following screenshot:

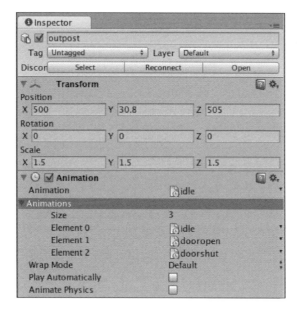

Note that I have expanded the **Animations** parameter here in the **Animation** component to view the animation states currently applied to this object.

The outpost object is now ready to be interacted with by our player character, so we will need to begin scripting to detect collisions with our newly tagged door using either collision detection or ray casting as outlined above.

Opening the outpost

In this section, we will look at the two differing approaches for triggering the animation giving you an overview of the two techniques that will both become useful in many other game development situations. In the first approach, we'll use collision detection—a crucial concept to get to grips with as you begin to work on games in Unity. In the second approach, we'll implement a simple ray cast forward from the player.

Approach 1—Collision detection

To begin writing the script that will trigger the door-opening animation and thereby grant access to the outpost, we need to consider which object to write a script for.

In game development, it is often more efficient to write a single script for an object that will interact with many other objects, rather than writing many individual scripts that check for a single object. With this in mind, when writing scripts for a game such as this, we will write a script to be applied to the player character in order to check for collisions with many objects in our environment, rather than a script made for each object the player may interact with, which checks for the player.

Creating new assets

Before we introduce any new kind of asset into our project, it is good practice to create a folder in which we will keep assets of that type. In the **Project** panel, click on the **Create** button, and choose **Folder** from the drop-down menu that appears.

Rename this folder **Scripts** by selecting it and pressing *Return* (Mac) or by pressing *F2* (PC).

Next, create a new JavaScript file within this folder simply by leaving the **Scripts** folder selected and clicking on the **Project** panel's **Create** button again, this time choosing **JavaScript.**

By selecting the folder, you want a newly created asset to be in before you create them, you will not have to create and then relocate your asset, as the new asset will be made within the selected folder.

Rename the newly created script from the default—`NewBehaviourScript`—to `PlayerCollisions`. JavaScript files have the file extension of `.js` but the Unity **Project** panel hides file extensions, so there is no need to attempt to add it when renaming your assets.

You can also spot the file type of a script by looking at its icon in the **Project** panel. JavaScript files have a 'JS' written on them, C# files simply have 'C#' and Boo files have an image of a Pacman ghost, a nice little informative pun from the guys at Unity Technologies!

Scripting for character collision detection

To start editing the script, double-click on its icon in the **Project** panel to launch it in the script editor for your platform—Unitron on Mac, or Uniscite on PC.

Working with OnControllerColliderHit

By default, all new JavaScripts include the `Update()` function, and this is why you'll find it present when you open the script for the first time. Let's kick off by declaring variables we can utilise throughout the script.

Our script begins with the definition of four variables, public member variables and two private variables. Their purposes are as follows:

- `doorIsOpen`: a private `true`/`false` (boolean) type variable acting as a switch for the script to check if the door is currently open.

- `doorTimer`: a private floating-point (decimal-placed) number variable, which is used as a timer so that once our door is open, the script can count a defined amount of time before self-closing the door.

- `currentDoor`: a private `GameObject` storing variable used to store the specific currently opened door. Should you wish to add more than one outpost to the game at a later date, then this will ensure that opening one of the doors does not open them all, which it does by remembering the most recent door hit.

- doorOpenTime: a floating-point (potentially decimal) numeric public member variable, which will be used to allow us to set the amount of time we wish the door to stay open in the **Inspector**.
- doorOpenSound/doorShutSound: Two public member variables of data type AudioClip, for allowing sound clip drag-and-drop assignment in the **Inspector** panel.

Define the variables above by writing the following at the top of the **PlayerCollisions** script you are editing:

```
private var doorIsOpen : boolean = false;
private var doorTimer : float = 0.0;
private var currentDoor : GameObject;

var doorOpenTime : float = 3.0;
var doorOpenSound : AudioClip;
var doorShutSound : AudioClip;
```

Next, we'll leave the Update() function briefly while we establish the collision detection function itself. Move down two lines from:

```
function Update(){
}
```

And write in the following function:

```
function OnControllerColliderHit(hit : ControllerColliderHit){
}
```

This establishes a new function called OnControllerColliderHit. This collision detection function is specifically for use with player characters such as ours, which use the **CharacterController** component. Its only parameter hit is a variable that stores information on any collision that occurs. By addressing the hit variable, we can query information on the collision, including—for starters—the specific game object our player has collided with.

We will do this by adding an if statement to our function. So within the function's braces, add the following if statement:

```
function OnControllerColliderHit(hit: ControllerColliderHit){
    if(hit.gameObject.tag == "outpostDoor" && doorIsOpen == false){

    }
}
```

In this `if` statement, we are checking two conditions, firstly that the object we hit is tagged with the tag `outpostDoor` and secondly that the variable `doorOpen` is currently set to `false`. Remember here that two equals symbols (`==`) are used as a comparative, and the two ampersand symbols (`&&`) simply say 'and also'. The end result means that if we hit the door's collider that we have tagged and if we have not already opened the door, then it may carry out a set of instructions.

We have utilized the dot syntax to address the object we are checking for collisions with by narrowing down from `hit` (our variable storing information on collisions) to `gameObject` (the object hit) to the `tag` on that object.

If this `if` statement is valid, then we need to carry out a set of instructions to open the door. This will involve playing a sound, playing one of the animation clips on the model, and setting our boolean variable `doorOpen` to `true`. As we are to call multiple instructions—and may need to call these instructions as a result of a different condition later when we implement the ray casting approach—we will place them into our own custom function called `OpenDoor`.

We will write this function shortly, but first, we'll call the function in the `if` statement we have, by adding:

```
OpenDoor();
```

So your full collision function should now look like this:

```
function OnControllerColliderHit(hit: ControllerColliderHit){
    if(hit.gameObject.tag == "outpostDoor" && doorIsOpen == false){
        OpenDoor();
    }
}
```

Writing custom functions

Storing sets of instructions you may wish to call at any time should be done by writing your own functions. Instead of having to write out a set of instructions or "commands" many times within a script, writing your own functions containing the instructions means that you can simply call that function at any time to run that set of instructions again. This also makes tracking mistakes in code—known as **Debugging**—a lot simpler, as there are fewer places to check for errors.

In our collision detection function, we have written a call to a function named `OpenDoor`. The brackets after `OpenDoor` are used to store parameters we may wish to send to the function—using a function's brackets, you may set additional behavior to pass to the instructions inside the function. We'll take a look at this in more depth later in this chapter under the heading **Function Efficiency**. Our brackets are empty here, as we do not wish to pass any behavior to the function yet.

Declaring the function

To write the function we need to call, we simply begin by writing:

```
function OpenDoor(){
}
```

In between the braces of the function, much in the same way as the instructions of an `if` statement, we place any instructions to be carried out when this function is called.

Playing audio

Our first instruction is to play the audio clip assigned to the variable called `doorOpenSound`. To do this, add the following line to your function by placing it within the curly braces after { "and before" }:

```
audio.PlayOneShot(doorOpenSound);
```

To be certain, it should look like this:

```
function OpenDoor(){
    audio.PlayOneShot(doorOpenSound);
}
```

Here we are addressing the **Audio Source** component attached to the game object this script is applied to (our player character object, `First Person Controller`), and as such, we'll need to ensure later that we have this component attached; otherwise, this command will cause an error.

Addressing the audio source using the term `audio` gives us access to four functions, `Play()`, `Stop()`, `Pause()`, and `PlayOneShot()`. We are using `PlayOneShot` because it is the best way to play a single instance of a sound, as opposed to playing a sound and then switching clips, which would be more appropriate for continuous music than sound effects. In the brackets of the `PlayOneShot` command, we pass the variable `doorOpenSound`, which will cause whatever sound file is assigned to that variable in the **Inspector** to play. We will download and assign this and the clip for closing the door after writing the script.

Checking door status

One condition of our `if` statement within our collision detection function was that our boolean variable `doorIsOpen` must be set to `false`. As a result, the second command inside our `OpenDoor()` function is to set this variable to `true`.

This is because the player character may collide with the door several times when bumping into it, and without this boolean, they could potentially trigger the OpenDoor() function many times, causing sound and animation to recur and restart with each collision. By adding in a variable that when false allows the OpenDoor() function to run and then disallows it by setting the doorIsOpen variable to true immediately, any further collisions will not re-trigger the OpenDoor() function.

Add the line:

```
doorOpen = true;
```

to your OpenDoor() function now by placing it between the curly braces after the previous command you just added.

Playing animation

In Chapter 2, we imported the outpost asset package and looked at various settings on the asset before introducing it to the game in this chapter. One of the tasks performed in the import process was the setting up of animation clips using the **Inspector**. By selecting the asset in the **Project** panel, we specified in the **Inspector** that it would feature three clips:

- idle (a 'do nothing' state)
- dooropen
- doorshut

In our openDoor() function, we'll call upon a named clip using a **String** of text to refer to it. However, first we'll need to state which object in our scene contains the animation we wish to play. Because the script we are writing is to be attached to the player, we must refer to another object before referring to the animation component. We do this by stating the line:

```
var myOutpost : GameObject = GameObject.Find("outpost");
```

Here we are declaring a new variable called myOutpost by setting its type to be a GameObject and then selecting a game object with the name outpost by using GameObject.Find. The Find command selects an object in the current scene by its name in the **Hierarchy** and can be used as an alternative to using tags.

Now that we have a variable representing our outpost game object, we can use this variable with dot syntax to call animation attached to it by stating:

```
myOutpost.animation.Play("dooropen");
```

This simply finds the animation component attached to the `outpost` object and plays the animation called **dooropen**. The `play()` command can be passed any string of text characters, but this will only work if the animation clips have been set up on the object in question.

Your finished `OpenDoor()` custom function should now look like this:

```
function OpenDoor(){
    audio.PlayOneShot(doorOpenSound);
    doorIsOpen = true;
    var myOutpost : GameObject = GameObject.Find("outpost");
    myOutpost.animation.Play("dooropen");
}
```

Reversing the procedure

Now that we have created a set of instructions that will open the door, how will we close it once it is open? To aid playability, we will not force the player to actively close the door but instead establish some code that will cause it to shut after a defined time period.

This is where our `doorTimer` variable comes into play. We will begin counting as soon as the door becomes open by adding a value of time to this variable, and then check when this variable has reached a particular value by using an `if` statement.

Because we will be dealing with time, we need to utilize a function that will constantly update such as the `Update()` function we had awaiting us when we created the script earlier.

Create some empty lines inside the `Update()` function by moving its closing curly brace } a few lines down.

Firstly, we should check if the door has been opened, as there is no point in incrementing our timer variable if the door is not currently open. Write in the following `if` statement to increment the timer variable with time if the `doorIsOpen` variable is set to `true`:

```
if(doorIsOpen){
    doorTimer += Time.deltaTime;
}
```

Here we check if the door is open—this is a variable that by default is set to `false`, and will only become `true` as a result of a collision between the player object and the door. If the `doorIsOpen` variable is `true`, then we add the value of `Time.deltaTime` to the `doorTimer` variable. Bear in mind that simply writing the variable name as we have done in our `if` statement's condition is the same as writing `doorIsOpen == true`.

Time.deltaTime is a Time class that will run independent of the game's frame rate. This is important because your game may be run on varying hardware when deployed, and it would be odd if time slowed down on slower computers and was faster when better computers ran it. As a result, when adding time, we can use Time.deltaTime to calculate the time taken to complete the last frame and with this information, we can automatically correct real-time counting.

Next, we need to check whether our timer variable, doorTimer, has reached a certain value, which means that a certain amount of time has passed. We will do this by nesting an if statement inside the one we just added—this will mean that the if statement we are about to add will only be checked if the doorIsOpen if condition is valid.

Add the following code below the time incrementing line inside the existing if statement:

```
if (doorTimer > doorOpenTime) {
    shutDoor();
    doorTimer = 0.0;
}
```

This addition to our code will be constantly checked as soon as the doorIsOpen variable becomes true and waits until the value of doorTimer exceeds the value of the doorOpenTime variable, which, because we are using Time.deltaTime as an incremental value, will mean three real-time seconds have passed. This is of course unless you change the value of this variable from its default of 3 in the **Inspector**.

Once the doorTimer has exceeded a value of 3, a function called shutDoor() is called, and the doorTimer variable is reset to zero so that it can be used again the next time the door is triggered. If this is not included, then the doorTimer will get stuck above a value of 3, and as soon as the door was opened it would close as a result.

Your completed Update() function should now look like this:

```
function Update() {
    if (doorIsOpen) {
        doorTimer += Time.deltaTime;

        if (doorTimer > 3) {
            shutDoor();
            doorTimer = 0.0;
        }
    }
}
```

Now, add the following function called `shutDoor()` to the bottom of your script. Because it performs largely the same function as `openDoor()`, we will not discuss it in depth. Simply observe that a different animation is called on the outpost and that our `doorIsOpen` variable gets reset to `false` so that the entire procedure may start over:

```
function shutDoor(){
audio.PlayOneShot(doorShutSound);
doorIsOpen = false;

var myOutpost : GameObject = GameObject.Find("outpost");
myOutpost.animation.Play("doorshut");
}
```

Function efficiency

Now that we have a script in charge of opening and closing our door, let's look at how we can expand our knowledge of bespoke functions to make our scripting more efficient.

Currently we have two functions we refer to as custom or bespoke—`openDoor()` and `shutDoor()`. These functions perform the same three tasks—they play a sound, set a boolean variable, and play an animation. So why not create a single function and add parameters to allow it to play differing sounds and have it choose either `true` or `false` for the boolean and play differing animations? Making these three tasks into parameters of the function will allow us to do just that. Parameters are settings specified in the brackets of the function. They must be separated by commas and should be given a specified type when declared in the function.

At the bottom of your script, add the following function:

```
function Door(aClip : AudioClip, openCheck : boolean, animName :
String, thisDoor : GameObject){
    audio.PlayOneShot(aClip);
    doorIsOpen = openCheck;

    thisDoor.transform.parent.animation.Play(animName);
}
```

You'll notice that this function looks similar to our existing `open` and `shut` functions, but has four parameters in its declaration—`aClip`, `openCheck`, `animName`, and `thisDoor`. These are effectively variables that get assigned when the function is called, and the value assigned to them is used inside the function. For example, when we wish to pass values for opening the door to this function, we would call the function and set each parameter by writing:

```
Door(doorOpenSound, true, "dooropen", currentDoor);
```

This feeds the variable `doorOpenSound` to the `aClip` parameter, a value of `true` to the `openCheck` parameter, string of text `"dooropen"` to the `animName` parameter, and sends the variable `currentDoor` to the `thisDoor` parameter.

Now we can replace the call to the `openDoor()` function inside the collision detection function. However, we are yet to set the `currentDoor` variable, so we will need to do this as well. First, remove the following line that calls the `OpenDoor()` function inside the `OnControllerColliderHit()` function:

```
OpenDoor();
```

Replace it with the following two lines:

```
currentDoor = hit.gameObject;
Door(doorOpenSound, true, "dooropen", currentDoor);
```

Here we are setting the `currentDoor` variable to whichever object has been most recently collided with. This allows us to then pass this information to our function, ensuring that we only open—that is trigger animation on—the specific outpost we're colliding with, rather than any outpost with a tagged door.

In the last line of this function, we play the correct animation by using `thisDoor.transform.parent.animation`—by using the dot syntax here, we are tracing steps back to the `animation` component we need to address. The `thisDoor` variable has been fed the object most recently hit—stored in the `currentDoor` variable—and we then address the door's parent object—the outpost itself, as it is this that has the animation component attached to it, not the door. For example, we could not say:

```
thisDoor.animation.Play(animName);
```

Unity would tell us that there is no animation component. So, instead, we address the door child object's `transform parent`—the object it belongs to in the **Hierarchy**—and then simply select the `animation` component from there.

Finally, because we are using this new method of opening and closing the doors, we'll need to amend the door closing code within the `Update()` function. Within the `if` statement that checks for the `doorTimer` variable exceeding the value of the `doorOpenTime` variable, replace the call to the `shutDoor()` function with this line:

```
Door(doorShutSound, false, "doorshut", currentDoor);
```

You may now delete the original two functions—`openDoor()` and `shutDoor()` as our customizable `Door()` function now supersedes both of them. By creating functions in this way, we are not repeating ourselves in scripting, and this makes our script more efficient and saves time writing two functions.

Finishing the script

To complete the script, we will make sure that the object it gets added to has an `AudioSource` component—this is needed to play back sound clips as we do in our `Door` function.

Add the following line to the very bottom of the script, ensuring that the line is NOT terminated with a semi-colon as you'd expect. This is because this command is Unity-specific, and not part of the JavaScript calls expected.

```
@script RequireComponent (AudioSource)
```

Attaching the script

Save your script in the script editor to ensure that the Unity editor receives any updates you have made—this should be done with any changes you make to your scripts; otherwise Unity cannot re-compile the script.

Next, switch back to Unity. Check the bottom bar of the Unity interface, as this is where any errors made in the script will be shown. If there are any errors, then double-click on the error and ensure that your script matches that written above. As you continue to work with scripting in Unity, you'll get used to using the error reporting to help you correct any mistakes you may make. The best place to begin double-checking that you have not made any mistakes in your code is to ensure that you have an even number of opening and closing curly braces—this means that all functions and `if` statements are correctly closed.

If you have no errors, then simply select the object you wish to apply the script to in the **Hierarchy**—the **First Person Controller** object.

There are two methods of attaching a script to any object in Unity. Firstly, you may drag-and-drop the script itself from the **Project** panel onto the object in the **Hierarchy** or **Scene views**, or simply select the object you wish to apply the script to (as you just did), and from the top menu, go to **Component | Scripts | Player Collisions**. The **Scripts** sub-menu of the **Component** menu simply lists any scripts it finds in the current **Project**; so as soon as your script is created and saved, it will be available to choose from that menu.

The **Inspector** panel for the **First Person Controller** should now show **Player Collisions Script** as a component along with an **Audio Source** component that automatically was added as a result of using the `RequireComponent` command at the end of our script.

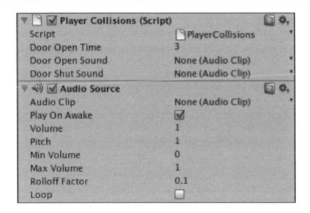

You should note that our public member variables, `doorOpenTime`, `doorOpenSound`, and `doorShutSound` appear in the **Inspector** so that you may adjust the value of `doorOpenTime` and drag-and-drop sound files from the **Project** panel to assign to the two sound variables. This is true of any member variables you may encounter while writing scripts—remember you can hide public member variables from appearing in this manner simply by using the prefix `private`, as we have done with the other three variables used in the script. Bear in mind that when using private variables, they should be assigned a type or value in the script to avoid errors, otherwise they will be `"null"`—have no value.

The `Door Open` and `Door Close` sound clips are available in the code bundle provided on packtpub.com (`www.packtpub.com/files/code/8181_Code.zip`). Extract the files and locate the package named `doorSounds.unitypackage`. To import this package, return to Unity and go to **Assets | Import Package**, navigate to the file you have downloaded and select it. The **Import Assets** dialog window will appear listing the two files in the package. Simply click on the **Import** button on this window to confirm the import. You should now have **doorSlideOpen** and **doorSlideShut** audio clips in your **Project** panel's list of assets, as shown in the following screenshot. To keep things neat, drag them both into the existing **Sounds** folder, where we already have our hillside ambient audio clip.

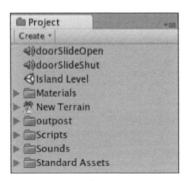

Now that the assets are in your project folder, drag-and-drop the appropriate clip to the public member variables in the **Inspector** for the **Player Collisions (Script)** component. Once this is done, the script component should look like this:

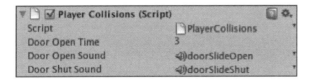

Now try playing the game and opening the door. Click the **Play** button at the top of the interface to start testing, and walk up to the door of the outpost and bump into it.

The collision between the player and the door will be detected, causing the door to open, and after **3** seconds the door will close automatically. Press the **Play** button again to finish testing.

To allow the door to open without being pressed against it, we will extend the collider of the door, as discussed at the beginning of the chapter. Expand the child objects beneath the **outpost** game object in the **Hierarchy** panel by clicking on the gray arrow next to the object, and then select the child object named **door**. Now with your mouse cursor over the **Scene** view, press *F* to focus the view on that object:

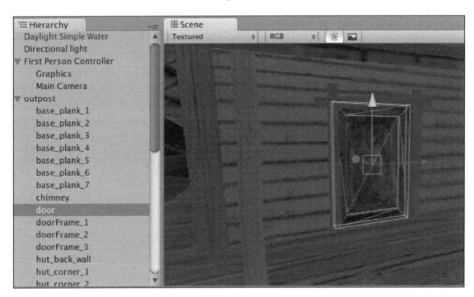

In the **Inspector** for this object, expand the **Size** parameter of the **Box Collider** component, so that you can adjust the **Z** value (depth) of the collider itself. Change the existing value to a value of **1.5**, so that the collider becomes extended, as shown in the following screenshot:

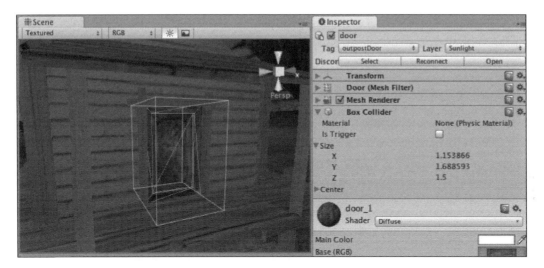

Now try playing the test again, and you will notice that the door opens sooner upon approaching it, as the boundary of the collider extends further from the visible door.

However, you should also note the physical bumping into the collider that occurs. This can be countered by utilizing the Trigger mode of the collider, but we will be looking into triggers further in the next chapter. So for now, we will implement the second approach discussed earlier—ray casting. By casting a ray forward from the player, we will negate the need for our player character's collider to actually touch the door's collider.

Approach 2—Ray casting

In this section, we will implement an alternate approach to opening the door with collision detection. Although collision detection or trigger detection would be a valid approach, by introducing the concept of ray casting, we can ensure that our player only opens the door of the outpost when they are facing it, because the ray will always face the direction the First Person Controller is facing, and as such not intersect the door if, for example, the player backs up to it.

Disabling collision detection—using comments

To avoid the need to write an additional script, we will simply comment out—that is, temporarily deactivate part of the code that contains our collision detection function. To do this, we will add characters to turn our working collision code into a comment.

In programming, comments can be left as a reminder but are never executed. So to deactivate a piece of code, you can turn it into a comment—we refer to this as **commenting out**.

Switch back to your script editor (Unitron/Uniscite) and before the line:

```
function OnControllerColliderHit(hit: ControllerColliderHit){
```

place the following characters:

```
/*
```

Putting a forward slash and asterisk into your script begins a mass comment (as opposed to two forward slashes that simply comment out a single line). After the collision detection function, place the reverse of this, that is, an asterisk followed by a forward slash. Your entire function should have changed the syntax color in the script editor and be written like this:

```
/*
function OnControllerColliderHit(hit: ControllerColliderHit){
    if(hit.gameObject.tag == "outpostDoor" && doorIsOpen == false){
        currentDoor = hit.gameObject;
        Door(doorOpenSound, true, "dooropen", currentDoor);
    }
}
*/
```

Resetting the door collider

As we do not want the effect of bumping into the invisible collider on the door, return to the **Box Collider** component of the door by selecting the **door child** object in the **Inspector** and then setting the **Size** value of the Z axis to **0.1**. This will match the door's depth visually.

Adding the ray

Switch back to the script editor and move your cursor a couple of lines down from the opening of the Update() function. We place ray casts in the Update() function, as we need to technically cast our ray forward every frame. Add in the following code:

```
var hit : RaycastHit;

    if(Physics.Raycast (transform.position,
                    transform.forward, hit, 5)) {

    if(hit.collider.gameObject.tag=="outpostDoor"
                    && doorIsOpen == false){
       currentDoor = hit.collider.gameObject;
       Door(doorOpenSound, true, "dooropen", currentDoor);
    }

}
```

At the outset, a ray is created by establishing a private variable called hit, which is of type RaycastHit. Note that it does not need a private prefix to not be seen in the **Inspector**—it is simply private by default because it is declared inside a function. This will be used to store information on the ray when it intersects colliders. Whenever we refer to the ray, we use this variable.

Then we use two if statements. The parent if is in charge of casting the ray and uses the variable we created. Because we place the casting of the ray into an if statement, we are able to only call the nested if statement if the ray hits an object, making the script more efficient.

Our first if contains Physics.Raycast, the actual command that casts the ray. This command has four parameters within its own brackets:

- The position from which to create the ray (transform.position—the position of the object this script applies to, that is **First Person Controller**)
- The direction of the ray (transform.forward—the forward direction of the object this script applies to)
- The RaycastHit data structure we set up called hit—the ray stored as a variable
- The length of the ray (5—a distance in the game units, meters)

Then we have a nested `if` statement that first checks the `hit` variable for collision with colliders in the game world, specifically whether we have hit a collider belonging to a game object tagged `outpostDoor`, so:

```
hit.collider.gameObject.tag
```

Secondly, this `if` statement ensures — as our collision detection function did — that the `doorIsOpen` boolean variable is `false`. Again, this is to ensure that the door will not re-trigger many times once it has started to open.

Once both `if` statements' conditions are met, we simply set the `currentDoor` variable to the object stored in `hit` and then call the `Door()` function in the same way that we did in our collision detection function:

```
currentDoor = hit.collider.gameObject;
Door(doorOpenSound, true, "dooropen");
```

Playtest the game once more and you will notice that when approaching the door, it not only opens before you bump into it, but also only opens when you are facing it, because the ray that detects the door is cast in the same direction that the player character faces.

Summary

In this chapter, we have explored two key methods for detecting interactions between objects in 3D games. Both ray casting and collision detection have many individual uses, and they are key skills that you should expect to reuse in your future use of Unity.

In the next chapter, we'll look into another method of collision detection while using colliders of objects set to trigger mode. This mode allows collision detection but removes the physical presence of an object, allowing — for example — the collection of objects without the player bumping into them. Try to think of triggers as collisions with no impact. While we could have taken this approach with the outpost door, it is important to learn the core concept of collision detection first, which is why we are learning in this particular order.

We will create a collection game in which the player must find four batteries in order to recharge the lock on the outpost door, and not allow entry to the outpost unless these batteries have been collected.

5
Prefabs, Collection, and HUD

In this chapter, we'll continue our work from Chapter 4. Working with a similar approach to the previous chapter, we will be expanding our knowledge of collision detection by using a third method of collision, that is, by using colliders as **Triggers**.

Triggers are often referred to as actual components. However, in simple terms, they are the primitive colliders you are already familiar with, but with the trigger mode set in the **Inspector** using the **Is Trigger** checkbox, as shown in the following screenshot:

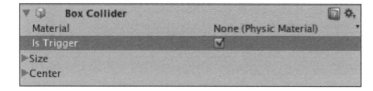

As we have already set up an outpost with an opening door, we will now restrict player access by making them find objects in order to open the door. By creating onscreen instructions when the player approaches the door, we will inform him that the door requires a power source to be opened. We will then add a 2D display of an empty battery on the screen. This will prompt the player to look for more objects, that is, batteries, which are scattered nearby, so as to charge up enough power to open the door.

By creating this simple puzzle, you will learn the following:

- Working with 2D objects using GUI Textures
- How to control onscreen text with GUI Text elements
- How to utilize prefabs to create multiples of a game object, which are stored as an asset

Creating the battery prefab

In this section, we will import a downloaded model of a battery and turn it into a Unity prefab—a data template that we can use to make multiple copies of the model with predetermined settings applied. If you've worked with Adobe Flash before, then you might compare this idea to the *MovieClip* concept, wherein you can create many identical copies, or modify individual copies post creation.

Download, import, and place

To begin creating the puzzle, you'll need the battery asset package which is available in the code bundle provided on packtpub.com (`www.packtpub.com/files/code/8181_Code.zip`). Locate the package called `batteries.unitypackage` from the extracted files. Once you have done this, switch back to Unity and go to **Assets | Import Package**. Browse to the location you downloaded the package to, and select it as the file to import. You will be presented with a list of the assets inside this package in the **Import Assets** dialog window, then click on **Import** to import these assets. In this package, you are provided with:

- A 3D model of a battery
- Five image files of a battery filling with charge
- An audio clip to be played, upon collection of the battery by the player

Simply click **Import** to confirm here. You should then have the following files in your project, as seen in the **Project** panel in the following screenshot:

Drag-and-drop the battery model from the **Other Models** folder in the **Project** panel onto the **Scene** view. Then hover your cursor over the **Scene** view and press *F* to focus the view on it. Your battery will be placed at an arbitrary position—we will reposition it once we have finished making our prefab.

Tagging the battery

As we need to detect a collision with the **battery** object, we should give it a tag to help us identify the object in scripting that we will write shortly. Click on the **Tag** drop-down menu, and at the bottom of the menu select **Add Tag**.

The **Inspector** panel then switches to display the **Tag Manager**. In the next available **Element** slot, add a tag called **battery**, as shown in the next screenshot:

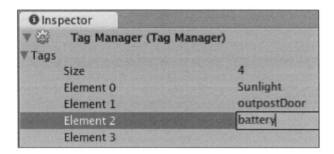

Press *Enter* to confirm the tag, then reselect the **battery** object in the **Hierarchy** panel, and choose the new **battery** tag from the **Tag** drop-down menu in the **Inspector** for that object.

Scale, collider, and rotation

Now, we will prepare the **battery** as a prefab by applying components and settings that we'd like to keep in each new copy of the **battery**.

Enlarging the battery

We are creating something that the player is required to collect, so we should ensure that the object is of a reasonable size for the player to spot in the game. As we have already looked at scaling objects in the **FBXImporter** for the asset, we'll take a look at simple resizing with the **Transform** component in the **Inspector**. With the **battery** object still selected in the **Hierarchy**, change all the **Scale** values in the **Transform** component of the **Inspector** to **6**.

Adding a trigger collider

Next, we should add a primitive collider to the **battery** to enable the player to interact with it. Go to **Component | Physics | Capsule Collider**. We have selected this type of collider as it is the closest shape to our **battery**. As we do not want the player to bump into this object while collecting it, we will set its collider to trigger mode. So, on the newly added **Capsule Collider** component, select the box to the right of the **Is Trigger** setting.

Creating a rotation effect

Now we will write a script to make the **battery** object rotate, so as to add a visual effect and make it easier for the player to notice it. On the **Project** panel, select the Scripts folder to ensure that the script we are about to create gets created within that folder. Go to the **Create** button on the **Project** panel, and choose **JavaScript**. Press *F2* and type to rename the newly created file from **NewBehaviourScript** to **RotateObject**. Double-click its icon to launch it in the script editor.

At the top of your new script outside the Update() function, create a floating-point public member variable called rotationAmount, and set its value to 5.0 by adding the following line:

```
var rotationAmount : float = 5.0;
```

We will use this variable to define how quickly the **battery** object rotates. Because it is a public member variable (outside of any function and not declared as private), we will also be able to adjust this value in the **Inspector** once the script is attached to the **battery**.

Within the Update() function, add the following command to rotate our **battery** around its Y-axis with a value equal to the rotationAmount variable:

```
function Update () {
   transform.Rotate(Vector3(0,rotationAmount,0));
}
```

The Rotate() command expects a Vector3 (X, Y, Z) value, and we provide values of 0 for X and Z by feeding the variable's value into the Y-axis. As we have written this command within the Update() function, it will be executed in every frame, and so the battery will be rotated by 5 degrees each frame. In the script editor, go to **File | Save** and then switch back to Unity.

To attach this script to our **battery** object, ensure that it is selected in the **Hierarchy** panel. Then, go to **Component | Scripts | RotateObject** or simply drag-and-drop the script from the **Project** panel onto the object in the **Hierarchy** panel.

Press the **Play** button at the top of the interface, and watch the **battery** in the **Scene** view to make sure that the rotation works. If it does not work, then return to your script and check that you have not made any mistakes—double-check whether you have applied the script to the correct object! Remember to press **Play** again to end your testing before continuing.

Saving as a prefab

Now that the **battery** object is complete, we'll need to clone the object three times, giving us a total of four batteries. The best way to do this is with Unity's prefab system. Creating a prefab simply means making a data template that stores the settings of an object created in the scene. This can then be cloned while editing, or instantiated (created on the fly in the game) at runtime.

Create a new folder within the **Project** panel for storing this and any future prefabs. To do this, first ensure that you do not have an existing folder selected by clicking in some gray space beneath the objects in your **Project** panel. Click on the **Create** button and choose **Folder**, then rename the resultant new folder to **Prefabs** by pressing *Return* (Mac) or *F2* (PC) and retyping.

Select the newly made **Prefabs** folder. From the **Create** button, choose **Prefab**. This creates a new empty prefab within the **Prefabs** folder.

 You can spot an empty prefab, as it will have a gray cube icon, as opposed to a finished prefab, which has a light blue cube icon.

Rename the new empty prefab to **battery**. Now drag the **battery** object we have been working on from the **Hierarchy** panel, and drop it onto the empty **battery** prefab object in the **Project** panel.

This makes your battery into a prefab and also makes the copy in the current scene related to that prefab, which means that any changes made to the prefab in the **Project** panel will be reflected in the copy in the scene. Objects in the scene related to assets in the project are shown in the **Hierarchy** panel with blue text, as opposed to the black text of scene-only objects.

Scattering batteries

Now that we have our battery object stored as a prefab, when we duplicate the copy in the scene, we are creating further instances of the prefab. Ensure that you still have the **battery** selected in the **Hierarchy** and then duplicate the **battery** object three times so that you have four in total, this can be done either by going to **Edit** | **Duplicate** or using the keyboard shortcut *Command + D* (on Mac) or *Ctrl + D* (on PC).

When objects in the scene are duplicated, the duplicates are created at the same position—don't let this confuse you. Unity simply does this to standardize where new objects in the scene end up, and this is because when an object is duplicated, every setting is identical—including the position. Moreover, it is easier to remember that they are in the same position as the original and simply need moving from that position.

Now, select each of the four batteries in the **Hierarchy** panel, and use the **Transform tool** to reposition them around the outpost. Remember, you can use the view gizmo in the top-right of the **Scene** view to switch from perspective view to top, bottom, and side views. Remember to place the batteries at a height at which the player can pick them up, so do not set them too high to reach.

Once you have placed the four batteries around the outpost, you should have something like this:

Displaying the battery GUI

Now that we have our battery collectables in place, we'll need to show the player a visual representation of what they have collected. The textures imported with the batteries package have been designed to clearly show that the player will need to collect four batteries to fully charge the door. By swapping an empty battery image onscreen for one with 1 unit of charge, then for an image with 2 units of charge, and so on, we can create the illusion of a dynamic interface element.

Creating the GUI Texture object

Part of the assets imported with the batteries package was the `textures` folder. This folder contains five image files—one of an empty battery cell and the others of the four stages of battery charge. Created in Adobe Photoshop, these images have a transparent background, and are saved in a **PNG (Portable Network Graphics)** format. The PNG format was selected because it is compressed but still supports high quality **alpha channels**. Alpha channels are what many pieces of software refer to as the channel of the image (besides the usual red, green, and blue channels) that creates transparency.

We will begin to create the GUI showing the progress of the battery, by adding the empty battery graphic to the scene using Unity's **GUI Texture** component. In the **Project** panel, expand the **textures** folder, and select the file named **battery_nocharge**.

In a way different to our normal method of dragging and dropping assets into the **Scene** view, we need to specifically create a new object with a GUI Texture component and specify the `battery_nocharge` graphic as the texture for that component to use.

While this is technically a three-step procedure, it can be done in a single step by selecting the texture to be used in the **Project** panel, and then going to **GameObject | Create Other | GUI Texture** from the top menu. Do this now.

A new object will be created with a **GUITexture** component attached. In the **Inspector**, the **Pixel Inset** fields will already be defined (see the following screenshot) based on the chosen texture's dimensions, which Unity reads from the file:

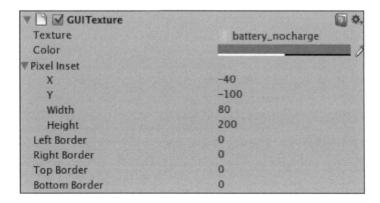

Pixel Inset fields define the dimensions and display area of an object. Typically the **Width** and **Height** parameters should be specified to match the original dimensions of your texture file, and the **X** and **Y** values should be set to half of the dimensions. Again, this is set up for you when you create the object, having selected the texture first.

> By selecting the graphic you wish to use first, Unity knows that when it creates a new object with the **GUITexture** component, it should select that file as the texture and fill in the dimensions of the texture also.
>
> Also, when you select a graphic and create a **GUI Texture** object using the top menu, the object created is named after your texture asset for the sake of convenience — remember this, as it will help you find the object in the **Hierarchy** panel, post creation.

Choose the object you have created in the **Hierarchy** panel by selecting **battery_nocharge**, and rename it to **Battery GUI** by pressing *Return* (Mac) or *F2* (PC) and retyping.

Positioning the GUI Texture

When dealing with 2D elements, you will need to work in screen coordinates. Because they are 2D, these only operate in the X and Y axes — with the Z-axis used for layer priority between multiple GUI Texture elements.

Screen coordinates go incrementally in decimals from 0 to 1, and in order to position the **Battery GUI** where we want to see it (in the lower-left of the screen), we need to type values into the **X** and **Y** boxes of the **Battery GUI** object's **Transform** component.

Fill in a value of **0.05** in **X** and **0.2** in **Y**.

You should now see the graphic displayed on the **Game** view, as shown in the following screenshot:

You can also show 2D details in the **Scene** view by clicking on the **Game Overlay** button, as shown in the following screenshot:

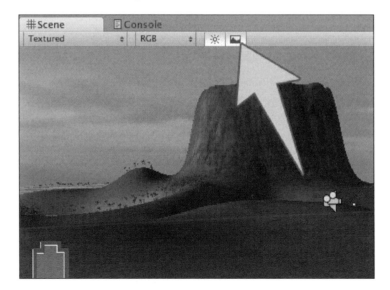

Scripting for GUI change

Now that we have several batteries to collect, and as it is the first stage of our battery GUI onscreen, we need to write a script to address the GUI Texture component and swap its texture based upon how many batteries have been collected.

Select the **Scripts** folder inside the **Project** panel, and then click on the **Create** button and choose **JavaScript**. Rename the **NewBehaviourScript** you have created to **BatteryCollect**, and then double-click its icon to open it in the script editor.

Because we are writing a script to control the **Battery GUI** object's GUI Texture component, it is best to write a script to be attached to that object, so that related scripts are attached to their relevant objects.

By writing the following script, the texture that is used onscreen will be based upon how many batteries have been collected—this information will be stored in an integer (whole number) variable. After we're finished writing this script, we'll append to our `PlayerCollisions` script, adding trigger collision detection for the batteries. Each time a collision is detected with a battery, we will increment the integer in our `BatteryCollect` script, which will swap the texture of the GUI Texture component on **Battery GUI**.

Our script begins by establishing a `static` variable—a global, accessible from other scripts—to store the amount of charge collected. We make this variable an integer, as there is no chance of it not being a whole number. Add the following line to the top of the script now:

```
static var charge : int = 0;
```

Then we need five variables to store the textures that represent the five different states of our **Battery GUI**—empty, plus four stages of charge. So, we'll add five unassigned variables of type `Texture2D`:

```
var charge1tex : Texture2D;
var charge2tex : Texture2D;
var charge3tex : Texture2D;
var charge4tex : Texture2D;
var charge0tex : Texture2D;
```

As these are public member variables, we will simply assign image files to them from the **Project** panel, using drag-and-drop to the variable slots which will be created in the **Inspector** (component) view of this script.

To set up defaults for the GUI Texture component, add the following `Start()` function to the script, beneath the variables you just declared:

```
function Start(){
  guiTexture.enabled = false;
  charge = 0;
}
```

The `Start()` function will execute once when the current level (or scene, in Unity terms) has started. By placing in the line:

```
guiTexture.enabled = false;
```

We are ensuring that the component is not enabled, so that the battery will not be visible when the game begins. We have also set the charge variable to `0` when the game begins, to ensure that the script assumes that no batteries are collected on scene start.

Next, move the closing right curly brace of the `Update()` function down by a few lines, and place the following `if` statement inside it:

```
if(charge == 1){
  guiTexture.texture = charge1tex;
  guiTexture.enabled = true;
}
```

Here we are checking the `charge` variable for a value of `1`, and then executing two commands:

- `guiTexture.texture = charge1tex;`: This line sets the texture slot of the GUI Texture component (of the object this script is attached to) to use the image file assigned to the `charge1tex` variable.

- `guiTexture.enabled = true;`: This line enables the component itself. We have set the **Battery GUI** to not be visible (that is, not enabled) when the game starts, so as not to confuse the user, and to avoid cluttering the screen—we only want them to see the empty battery GUI once they have tried to open the door.

  This line of the script is in charge of enabling the GUI when the player has collected one battery because it is governed by the `if` statement. Later, we will add scripting to the door ray collision in our `PlayerCollisions` script in order to switch on the empty battery GUI if the user happens to try entering the door before picking up his first battery.

Next we will add three more `if` statements to the `Update()` function, checking for other states of the `charge` variable. As there will never be an occasion where charge equals both `1` and another value, we will use `else if` statements, as these are checked when any of the other `if` statements are already in play.

If we were to use `if` for each of the following statements, they would all be checked simultaneously, making the script inefficient. Add the following code after the closing curly brace of your existing `if` statement:

```
else if(charge == 2){
   guiTexture.texture = charge2tex;
}
else if(charge == 3){
   guiTexture.texture = charge3tex;
}
else if(charge >= 4){
   guiTexture.texture = charge4tex;
}
```

In these `else if` statements, we simply set the texture displayed by the GUI Texture component to use differing textures by using the public member variables established at the top of the script (we will assign the image files to these variables in the **Inspector** later). We don't need to enable the component in any of these `else if` statements as it would have already been enabled when the player picked up his first battery.

Finally, to address when our `charge` variable is at `0`, we can simply add an `else` statement to the end of our `if` and `else if` statements, which effectively says "if none of the above is true, then do the following." Therefore, as our existing `if` and `else if` statements are looking for a charge value of `1` to `4`, the following `else` statement will take care of display when the game starts (when the charge variable will equal `0`). This essentially backs up the `Start()` function:

```
else{
   guiTexture.texture = charge0tex;
}
```

Now that the script is complete, go to **File | Save** in the script editor and switch back to Unity.

Select the **Battery GUI** object in the **Hierarchy** panel and go to **Component | Scripts | BatteryCollect** from the top menus. This assigns our script to the **Battery GUI** object, and you should see it in the **Inspector** with the five public member variables awaiting assignment, as shown in the following screenshot:

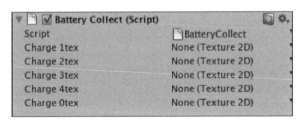

Drag-and-drop the five texture files from the **Project** panel's **textures** folder you imported earlier to the appropriate member variables, as shown in the following screenshot:

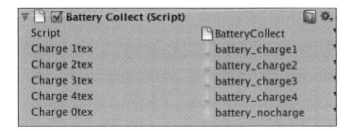

Now that our onscreen GUI for battery collection is ready, we simply need to add it to the `PlayerCollisions` script attached to the **First Person Controller**, in order to detect our player character's interaction with the battery objects' trigger colliders.

Battery collection with triggers

To trigger the differing states of our **Battery GUI**, we will use a function called `OnTriggerEnter()` to detect interaction with objects that have trigger mode colliders, that is, our collectable batteries.

Before we add this function to our `PlayerCollisions` script, we will add a public member variable at the top to hold an audio clip to be played when the player picks up a battery as a form of audio-based feedback to back up the GUI element.

Open the **PlayerCollisions** script by double-clicking on its icon in the **Scripts** folder of the **Project** panel. This will launch the script in the script editor, or simply switch back to it for you, if you already have the file opened. Add a public member variable for the audio clip to the top of the script by adding the line:

```
var batteryCollect : AudioClip;
```

Remember that this is not assigned in the script, but simply left with a data type (**AudioClip**) so that it may be assigned in the **Inspector** later.

Next, place your cursor above the final line of the script:

```
@script RequireComponent(AudioSource)
```

And add in the following function:

```
function OnTriggerEnter(collisionInfo : Collider){
}
```

This is a function specifically for detecting collisions with trigger mode colliders. Any collision with such a collider is placed into the parameter called `collisionInfo`, which is of type `Collider`, meaning that the information queried from it must be done in reference to the object attached to the collider that has been hit.

Inside the `OnTriggerEnter()` function (that is, before its right-facing [closing] curly brace), add the following `if` statement to query any triggers that are collided with:

```
if(collisionInfo.gameObject.tag == "battery"){
  BatteryCollect.charge++;
  audio.PlayOneShot(batteryCollect);
  Destroy(collisionInfo.gameObject);
}
```

With this `if` statement, we query the function's `collisionInfo` parameter, checking whether the collider in the current collision is attached to a game object tagged with the word `battery`—as our battery collectables are. If this is the case, then we do three things:

- Address the `BatteryCollect` script's `charge` static (global) variable using dot syntax, and add one to its value using the ++ method. By adding to the value of `charge` with each collision with a battery, we are making the `BatteryCollect` script swap the textures that represent the charge, completing the link between our collisions and the onscreen GUI.

- Play a one-shot (single instance) of the audio clip assigned to the `batteryCollect` variable in the **Inspector**.

- Remove the object collided with from the current scene using the `Destroy()` command. Using the dot syntax again, we have specified that the object to be destroyed is the one currently collided with. As this is governed by an `if` statement, calling it only if the collided-with object is tagged `battery`, then there is no chance of destroying the wrong object. The `Destroy()` command simply takes a game object as its main parameter in this instance, but it can also be used with a second parameter after a comma, that is, a float value to represent a delay in time before it removes an object.

Now save the script by going to **File | Save** in the script editor, and switch back to Unity. Select the **First Person Controller** object in the **Hierarchy**, and locate the **Player Collisions (Script)** component in the **Inspector**. You should now see that there is a new public member variable called **Battery Collect**, which is awaiting assignment of an **Audio Clip** asset, as shown in the following screenshot:

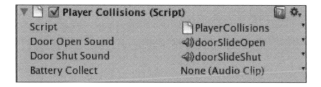

Drag-and-drop the audio clip asset called **battery_collect** from the **Sounds** folder in the **Project** panel, or click on the gray down arrow to the right of **None (Audio Clip)**, and select **battery_collect** from the drop-down list that appears.

Press the **Play** button and test the game, you should now be able to walk the player character into each of the batteries, and they should disappear, causing the battery GUI to appear onscreen and then increment with each battery collected. You should also hear the sound effect being played with each battery you collect, so make sure your computer's audio is turned up! Press **Play** again to stop testing, once you have ensured that you can collect all the batteries.

Restricting outpost access

The main point of this exercise is to demonstrate how you can control certain situations within your game development. In this example, we wish to allow the player access to the outpost, only if they have charged the sliding door by collecting four batteries.

This puzzle presents us as developers with two main issues to be addressed:

- How does the player know they need to collect the batteries to enter the door?
- How can we code our game to open the door only if all of the batteries have been collected?

To address the first issue, we'll aim to maintain the element of mystery about our game. We will only present the player with a hint to collect batteries should they be inquisitive enough to attempt to enter the outpost. To do this, we will need to add onscreen instructions when the door is approached for the first time. We will add further instructions if the door is approached again, if the player has collected some but not all of the batteries required.

In order to check whether the player can open the door—and therefore, whether to display instructions—we can use the `BatteryCollect` script we have already written. Because this script has the amount of batteries collected and stored in a static variable called `charge`, we can query the value of `charge` to see if it equals 4—meaning all batteries have been collected.

Restricting access

Before we give the player instructions, we will restrict the door opening part of our `PlayerCollisions` script to activate only when the player has collected all of the four batteries. In the previous chapter, we wrote a custom function in the `PlayerCollisions` script called `Door()`, to which we could feed parameters in order to use it for opening or closing doors the player encountered. It looked like this:

```
function Door(aClip : AudioClip, openCheck : boolean, animName :
   String, thisDoor : GameObject){
   audio.PlayOneShot(aClip);
   doorIsOpen = openCheck;
   thisDoor.transform.parent.animation.Play(animName);
}
```

This function plays sound, it ensures that the door cannot be re-opened, and then plays the animation of it opening. We called this function within the ray cast code we created in the `Update()` function (the vector line which faces the same direction as the player checking for the door). To remind you, it looked like this:

```
var hit : RaycastHit;
   if (Physics.Raycast (transform.position, transform.forward,
      hit, 5)) {
      if(hit.collider.gameObject.tag=="outpostDoor" && doorIsOpen ==
         false){
         currentDoor = hit.collider.gameObject;
         Door(doorOpenSound, true, "dooropen", currentDoor);
      }
   }
```

Open the `PlayerCollisions` script by double-clicking on it in the **Project** panel, and then locate the last code snippet inside the `Update()` function near the top of the script, which calls the `Door()` function to open:

```
if(hit.collider.gameObject.tag=="outpostDoor" && doorIsOpen ==
   false){
   Door(doorOpenSound, true, "dooropen", currentDoor);
}
```

To restrict access before all of the four batteries are collected, simply add a third condition to this `if` statement by using another pair of ampersands—&&, as shown in the following code snippet:

```
if(hit.collider.gameObject.tag=="outpostDoor" && doorIsOpen ==
   false && BatteryCollect.charge >= 4){
   Door(doorOpenSound, true, "dooropen", currentDoor);
}
```

By adding the following condition:

```
BatteryCollect.charge >= 4
```

We are checking the `BatteryCollect` script's `charge` static variable for a value of `4`. The door will not open until we attempt to enter the door having collected all of the batteries we have laid out.

Utilizing GetComponent()

When we gain access, we will need to remove the **Battery GUI** from the screen. To do this, we will need to access the GUI Texture component on that object. Given that the triggering of the door is in the `PlayerCollisions` script we are currently working on, we will need to address a component which is not on the same object as this script (**First Person Controller**), but instead is on the **Battery GUI** object. While in the `BatteryCollect` script, we could simply say:

```
guiTexture.enabled = false;
```

This is because it was attached to the same object as the **GUITexture** component— this cannot be done in a script that is not on an object with a **GUITexture** component.

This is where the `GetComponent()` command comes in. By referencing the object that has the particular component you need to address and followed by the `GetComponent()` command, you can easily adjust components on external objects.

Beneath the line that calls the `Door()` function in the `if` statement you just altered, add the following line of code:

```
GameObject.Find("Battery
   GUI").GetComponent(GUITexture).enabled=false;
```

Here, we are using `GameObject.Find`, specifying the name of the object in the **Hierarchy**, and then—using the dot syntax—we address the `GUITexture` as a parameter of `GetComponent()`. Finally, we disable the component by setting it to `false` in the usual manner—`enabled = false;`.

We do not want to destroy the object, as we still need the script to exist within the game, so that we may reference the amount of batteries already collected. This is why we simply disable the visual component.

Go to **File** | **Save** in the script editor, and then switch back to Unity.

Press the **Play** button now to test the game, and ensure that you cannot enter the outpost door without having collected all of the four batteries. If this is not the case, then double-check your code to ensure that it matches what we have outlined so far. Remember to press **Play** again to stop testing.

Hints for the player

What if the player, less intrigued by batteries than the outpost door itself, goes up to the door and tries to enter? We should ideally do two things:

- Tell the player in text form that the door needs charging — while we could easily say "Collect some batteries!", it is much better in gameplay terms to provide hints, such as "The door seems to be lacking power..".

- Switch on the Battery GUI so that they can tell they need to charge up the battery.

The latter of those two hints is much easier to implement, so we'll address that first.

Battery GUI hint

Switch back to the script editor where you still have the **PlayerCollisions** script open. If you have closed it for any reason, then remember that you can simply re-open it from the **Project** panel.

After the closing curly brace of the `if` statement we have been working on, add an `else if` statement that checks for the same conditions as the original one — except this time, we will check if the `charge` variable of `BatteryCollect` is less than 4:

```
else if(hit.collider.gameObject.tag=="outpostDoor" &&
  doorIsOpen == false && BatteryCollect.charge < 4){
}
```

In this `else if` statement, we will use the same line that we previously added to the first `if` statement, which disabled the `Battery GUI`'s `GUITexture` component, but this time we will enable it. Place the following line into the `else if` statement:

```
GameObject.Find("Battery GUI").
  GetComponent(GUITexture).enabled=true;
```

Now, go to **File** | **Save** in the script editor and switch back to Unity. Press the **Play** button and test that when you approach the door without any four batteries, the Battery GUI appears as a visual hint. Press **Play** again to stop testing.

GUI Text hint

Whenever you need to write text on the screen in 2D, the most straightforward way to do this is by using a **GUIText** component. By creating a new GUI Text object from the top menus, you will get a new object with both Transform and GUI Text components. Create one of these now by going to **GameObject** | **Create Other** | **GUI Text**. You should now have a new object in the **Hierarchy** called **GUI Text** and some 2D text on the screen that says **Gui Text**, as shown in the following screenshot:

Rename this object in the **Hierarchy** by selecting it and pressing *Return* (Mac) or *F2* (PC). Name it **TextHint GUI**.

Select the **GUI Text** object in the **Hierarchy** panel in order to see the component itself in the **Inspector**. As we want to inform the player, we'll leave the current position in the **Transform** component as **0.5** in **X** and **Y** — GUI Text positioning works in screen coordinates also, so **0.5** in both axes places this in the middle of the screen, demanding the player's attention.

In addition to the positioning of the entire element, **GUI Text** also features an **Alignment** parameter that works in a similar manner to justification settings in word processing software. Click the Up/Down arrows to the right of the **Alignment** parameter and choose **middle center** — this means that text will spread out from the center of the screen rather than starting in the center and then filling out to the right.

While you can easily type in what you wish this **GUI Text** element to say in the **Text** parameter in the **Inspector** (see the following screenshot)—we are instead going to control what it says dynamically, through scripting.

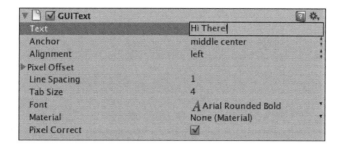

Create a new JavaScript file by selecting the **Scripts** folder in the **Project** panel. From the drop-down menu of the **Create** button, select **JavaScript**.

Rename the **NewBehaviourScript** this creates to **TextHints**, and then double-click its icon to launch it in the script editor.

Begin the script by declaring three variables:

```
static var textOn : boolean = false;
static var message : String;
private var timer : float = 0.0;
```

Our first static variable—textOn—is a boolean, as it needs to simply act as a switch. We will cover more on this shortly.

Then, we establish a string type static variable called message, which we will use to pass any information to the Text parameter of the component. These two variables are static, as we will need to address them from a separate script, PlayerCollisions.

Our third variable—timer—is private, as it need not be addressed by other scripts nor seen in the **Inspector**. We will use this timer to count from the moment the message appears onscreen, in order to make it disappear after a defined amount of time.

Next, add the following Start() function, in order to set certain states when the scene begins:

```
function Start(){
  timer = 0.0;
  textOn = false;
  guiText.text = "";
}
```

Here, we simply ensure that the `timer` is set to `0`, that the `textOn` variable is `false` (we need not see any instruction when the game begins), and that no text is currently in the `text` parameter of the `guiText` component. We do this by simply using two quotation marks with no text inside. This is known as an **empty string**.

Next, append the following code to the `Update()` function that already exists in the script:

```
function Update () {
  if(textOn){
    guiText.enabled = true;
    guiText.text = message;
    timer += Time.deltaTime;
  }
  if(timer >=5){
    textOn = false;
    guiText.enabled = false;
    timer = 0.0;
  }
}
```

This simple two-step procedure does the following:

- Checks for the `textOn` variable to become `true`. When it is, it:
  - Switches on the **GUIText** component
  - Sets the `text` parameter equal to the string variable called `message`
  - Begins to increment the `timer` variable using the `Time.deltaTime` command

- Checks for the `timer` variable to have reached a value of `5` seconds. If it has, then it:
  - Sets the `textOn` boolean to `false` (meaning the first `if` statement will no longer be valid)
  - Disables the **GUIText** component
  - Resets the `timer` variable to `0.0`

Go to **File** | **Save** in the script editor, and switch back to Unity. Select the **TextHint GUI** object in the **Hierarchy** and go to **Component** | **Scripts** | **TextHints** to add the script you have just written to the object.

We now have a script that controls our **TextHint GUI**, and all we need to do is trigger it into action by calling the static variables it contains. Given that the moment we wish to trigger instructions is related to the collisions with the door, we'll address these static variables from the `PlayerCollisions` script—open this in the script editor now.

Find the `else if` statement we most recently added to this script's `Update()` function that accompanies the ray casting detection of the door, and add the following two lines:

```
TextHints.message = "The door seems to need more power..";
TextHints.textOn = true;
```

Here we are sending some text to the `message` static variable of the `TextHints` script and setting the same script's `textOn` boolean variable to `true`. Here is the complete `else if` statement:

```
else if(hit.collider.gameObject.tag=="outpostDoor" &&
  doorIsOpen == false && BatteryCollect.charge < 4){
  GameObject.Find("Battery GUI").GetComponent(GUITexture).
    enabled=true;
  TextHints.message = "The door seems to need more power..";
  TextHints.textOn = true;
}
```

As we have switched on the component by setting `textOn` to `true`, our `TextHints` script will do the rest! Go to **File | Save** in the script editor, then switch back to Unity and press **Play** to test the game. Walk up to the door without the four required batteries, and you will be shown five seconds of the text-based hint on the screen. Press **Play** again to stop testing the game.

Go to **File | Save** in Unity to update your progress.

Finally, let's improve the look of our onscreen text hint by adding our own font.

Using fonts

When utilizing fonts in any Unity project, they must be imported as an asset in the same way as any other piece of media you include. This can be done by simply adding any **TTF** (**TrueType font**) or **OTF** (**OpenType font**) file to your **Assets** folder in Finder (Mac) or Windows Explorer (PC) or in Unity itself by going to **Assets | Import New Asset**.

For this example, I'll be using a commercially free-to-use font from www.dafont. com, which is a web site of free-to-use fonts that is very useful when starting out in any kind of typographic design. Be aware that some font web sites provide fonts with a restriction, stating that you should use them in projects that could make the font extractable—this is not a problem with Unity as all fonts are converted to textures in the exported build of the game.

Visit this site now and download a font whose look you like, and which is easy to read. Remember, you'll be using this font to give instructions, so anything overly complex will be counterintuitive to the player. If you would like to use the same font that I am using, then search for a font called **Sugo**. Download the font, unzip it, and then use the methods just outlined to add the Sugo.ttf file as an asset.

Once this is in your project, find the font inside the **Project** panel and select it. Then, to make it easier to read, we'll increase the font size for whenever this font is used. In the **Inspector** for the **Sugo** font under **True Type Font Importer** (refer to the following screenshot), set the **Font Size** to **24** and then press the **Apply** button. If you have chosen a font of your own, be aware that sizing may differ, but you may return and alter the **Font Size** setting at any time.

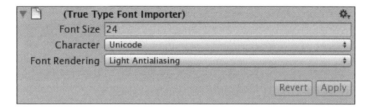

Next, choose this as the font to use for the **TextHint GUI** by selecting it in the **Hierarchy** panel and then choosing your font from the drop-down menu to the right of the **Font** parameter of the **GUIText** component in the **Inspector**. Alternatively, remember you can also drag-and-drop to assign in Unity, by dragging the font asset from the **Project** panel and dropping it onto this parameter in the **Inspector**.

Now press the **Play** button, and test your game. This time, when you approach the door with less than four batteries, your message will appear on the screen. When you are no longer colliding with the door, it will disappear after the five seconds we specified earlier. Press **Play** again to stop testing the game and go to **File** | **Save** to update your progress.

Summary

In this chapter, we have successfully created and solved a game scenario. By assessing what your player will expect to see in the game you present to them—outside of your prior knowledge of its workings—you can best devise the approach you must take as a developer.

Try to consider each new element in your game from the player's perspective—play existing games, think about real-world scenarios, and most of all, assume no prior knowledge. The most intuitive gameplay is always found in games that strike a balance between the difficulties in achieving the tasks set and properly equipping the player for the task in terms of information and familiarity with the intended approach. Appropriate feedback for the player is crucial here, be it visual or audio based—always consider what feedback the player has at all times when designing any game.

Now that we have explored a basic game scenario and looked at how we can build and control GUI elements, in the next chapter we'll move on to a more advanced game scenario, in which we will look at two more crucial concepts—**Instantiation** and **Rigid Body** physics.

Instantiation and Rigid Bodies

6

In this chapter, we'll be exploring two crucial concepts in 3D game design. In the first half, we'll look at the concept of **Instantiation**—the process of creating objects during runtime. We will then explore a practical example of instantiation, as we learn about the use of **Rigid Body** physics.

When you first begin to build game scenes, you'll realize that not all of the objects required within any given scene would be present at the start of the the game. This is true of a wide variety of game genres like puzzle games, such as *Tetris*. Puzzle pieces of random shapes are created or *instantiated* at the top of the screen at set intervals because all of them cannot be stored at the top of the screen infinitely.

Now take our island exploration game as another example. In this chapter, we'll be taking a look at rigid body physics by creating a method for our player character to play a simple coconut shy game, but the coconuts that will be thrown will not be present in the game scene when it begins. This is where instantiation comes in again. By specifying an asset (most likely a prefab of an object), a position, and a rotation, objects can be created while the game is being played—this will allow us to create a new coconut whenever the player presses the fire button.

In order to tie this new part of our game into the game as it stands, we'll be removing one of the batteries that is required to enter the outpost from the game. We will give the player a chance to win the final battery they require by playing the coconut shy game. You will be provided with a model of the coconut shy platform. You will need to create the coconut prefab and control the animation of the targets within the game through scripting—detecting collisions between the coconuts and the targets.

As the targets we provide you with have a 'knocked down' and 'reset' animation, we will also write scripting to ensure that the targets reset after being knocked down for a defined number of seconds. This means that the player may win this minigame only if all of the three targets are down at the same time. This adds an extra layer of skill for the player.

In this chapter, you will learn the following:

- Preparation of prefabs for instantiation
- The instantiation command put into practice
- Checking for player input
- Adding physics to an object with rigid bodies
- Providing feedback for the player

Introducing instantiation

In this section, we will learn how to spawn and duplicate objects while the game is running. This is a concept that is used in many games to create projectiles, collectable objects, and even characters, such as enemies.

In concept

Instantiation is simply a method of creating (also referred to as **spawning**) objects from a template (a prefab in Unity terms) during runtime. It can also be used to duplicate existing game objects already in the scene.

The approach when using instantiation will usually take this form:

- Create the object that you wish to instantiate in your scene, and add components as necessary
- Create a new prefab in your project, and drop the object you have been working on into that prefab
- Delete the original object from the scene so that it is only stored as a prefab asset
- Write a script that involves the `Instantiate()` command, attach it to an active game object, and set the prefab you created as the object that the `Instantiate()` command creates

In code

At its core, the `Instantiate()` command has three parameters and is written as follows:

```
Instantiate(object to create, position to create it,
   rotation to give it);
```

By understanding how to assign these three parameters, you will be in a good stead to tackle any use of the `Instantiate()` command that you may encounter.

Passing in an object

In order to pass in an object, you may simply feed a public member variable name to the first parameter of `Instantiate()`. By creating a public member variable of type `GameObject` at the top of a script, you will be able to drag-and-drop a prefab onto it in the Unity **Inspector** and then utilize this variable as the object parameter, as follows:

```
var myPrefab : GameObject;
Instantiate(myPrefab, position to create it, rotation to give it);
```

We can also ensure that only certain types of prefab can be dropped into this `myPrefab` variable by being more specific in its data typing, for example, we could say:

```
var myPrefab : Rigidbody;
Instantiate(myPrefab, position to create it, rotation to give it);
```

This ensures that only prefab objects with a Rigidbody component may be used.

Position and rotation

Position and rotation of objects to be created must be specified as Vector3 values (X,Y,Z). These can be passed directly as follows:

```
Instantiate(myPrefab, Vector3(0, 12, 30), Vector3(0, 0, 90));
```

They can also be inherited from another object by taking values that represent its position.

When assigning the position of an object to be instantiated, you must consider where your object will be created and whether it should be created in local space or world space.

For example, when creating our coconut prefabs, we'll be creating them at a point in the world defined by an empty game object, which will be a child of our player character object. As a result, we can say that it will be created in local space—not in the same place every time, but relative to where our player character is standing and facing.

This decision helps us to decide where to write our code, that is, to which object to attach a script. By attaching a script to the empty object that represents the position where the coconuts must be created, we can simply use dot syntax and reference `transform.position` as the position for the `Instantiate()` command. By doing this, the object created inherits the position of the empty object's **Transform** component because this is what the script is attached to. This can be done for rotation too—giving the newly spawned object a rotation that matches the empty parent object.

This would give us an `Instantiate()` command that looked like this:

```
var myPrefab : GameObject;
Instantiate(myPrefab, transform.position, transform.rotation);
```

We will put this into practice later in the chapter, but first let's take a look at rigid body physics and its importance in games.

Introducing rigid bodies

Physics engines give games a means of simulating realism in physical terms, and they are a feature in almost all game engines either natively or as a plugin. Unity utilizes the **Nvidia PhysX** physics engine, a precise modern physics engine that is used in many commercial games in the industry. Having a physics engine means that not only physical reactions, such as weight and gravity are possible, but realistic responses to friction, torque, and mass-based impact, are also possible.

Forces

The influence of the physics engine on objects is known as **force**, and forces can be applied in a variety of ways through components or scripting. In order to apply physics forces, an object must be what is known as a rigid body object.

The Rigidbody component

In order to invoke the physics engine in Unity, you must give an object a rigidbody component. This simply tells the engine to apply the physics engine to a particular object—you need not apply it to an entire scene. It simply works in the background.

Having added a **Rigidbody** component, you would see settings for it in the **Inspector** in the same way as any other object, as shown in the following screenshot:

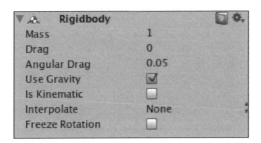

Rigidbody components have the following parameters to be adjusted or controlled through scripting:

- **Mass**: The weight of the object in kilograms. Bear in mind that setting mass on a variety of different rigid bodies will make them behave realistically. For example, a heavy object hitting a lighter object will cause the light object to be repelled further.

- **Drag**: Drag, as in real terms, is simply the amount of air resistance affecting an object as it moves. The higher the value, the quicker will the object slow when simply affected by air.

- **Angular Drag**: Similar to the previous parameter, but angular drag simply affects the rotational velocity, defining how much air affects the object, slowing it to a rotational halt.

- **Use Gravity**: Does exactly as it states. It is a setting that determines whether the rigid body object will be affected by gravity or not. With this option disabled, the object will still be affected by forces and impacts from the physics engine and will react accordingly, but as if in zero gravity.

- **Is Kinematic**: This option allows you to have a rigid body object that is not affected by the physics engine. For example, if you wished to have an object repel a rigid body with gravity on, such as the trigger in a pinball machine hitting the ball—but without the impact causing the trigger to be affected—then you might use this setting.

- **Interpolate**: This setting can be used if your rigid body objects are jittering. Interpolation and extrapolation can be chosen in order to smooth the transform movement, based on the previous frame or predicted next frame respectively.

- **Freeze Rotation**: This can be used to lock objects so that they do not rotate as a result of forces applied by the physics engine. This is particularly useful for objects that need to use gravity but stay upright, such as game characters.

Making the minigame

To put into practice what we have just looked at, we'll create a coconut shy game that ties into our access to the outpost. By playing the game, the player will be rewarded with the final battery they require to charge the outpost door.

As we have already set up the battery charge element of the game, we simply need to remove one of the batteries from the existing scene, leaving the player with one less.

Select one of the objects called **battery** in the **Hierarchy** panel, and then remove it with *Command + Backspace* (Mac) or *Delete* (PC).

Creating the coconut prefab

Now that we have learnt about instantiation, we'll begin our minigame by creating the object to be thrown, that is, the coconut.

Go to **Game Object | Create Other | Sphere**.

This creates a new sphere primitive object in the scene. While it will not be created directly in front of the editor viewport, you can easily zoom to it by hovering your cursor over the **Scene** view and pressing *F* (focus) on the keyboard. Rename this object from **Sphere** to **Coconut**, by selecting the object in the **Hierarchy** and pressing *Return* (Mac) or *F2* (PC) and retyping.

Next, we'll make this object a more appropriate size and shape for a coconut by scaling down and subtly extending its size in the Z-axis. In the **Transform** component of the **Inspector** for the **Coconut** object, change the **Scale** value for **X** and **Z** to **0.5** and **Y** to **0.6**.

The textures to be used on the coconut are available in the code bundle provided on packtpub.com (`www.packtpub.com/files/code/8181_Code.zip`). Locate the package called `CoconutGame.unitypackage`. Import this package by going to **Assets | Import Package**. Navigate to the file you have extracted, select it, and confirm the **Import**.

You should now have a folder in your **Project** panel called `Coconut Game` containing the following:

- A coconut image texture
- A crosshair texture
- Four audio clips
- Two 3D models — one called **platform**, and the other called **target**
- A `Materials` folder for the 3D models

Creating the textured coconut

To apply the coconut texture, we'll need to make a new material to apply it to. On the **Project** panel, click on the **Create** button, and from the drop-down menu that appears, select **Material**. Rename the new material you have made to **Coconut Skin** by pressing *Return* (Mac) or *F2* (PC), and retyping.

To apply the texture to this material, simply drag-and-drop the **coconut** texture from the **Project** panel over to the empty square to the right of the **Base (RGB)** setting for the material in the **Inspector**. When this is done, you should see a preview of the material in the window in the lower half of the **Inspector**, as shown in the following screenshot:

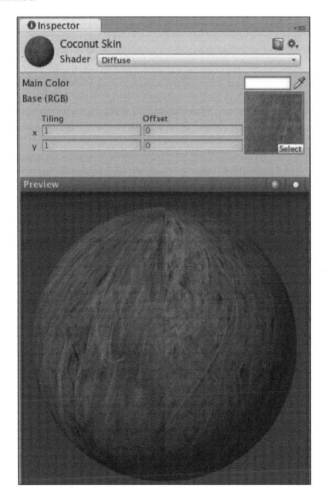

Remember that this preview simply demonstrates the material's appearance on a sphere—this is the default for Unity material previews and has nothing to do with the fact that we will be using this on a spherical object.

Next, we need to apply the **Coconut Skin** material to the **Coconut** game object that we have placed into our scene. In order to do this, we simply drag-and-drop the material from the **Project** window to either the object's name in the **Hierarchy** or to the object itself in the **Scene** view.

Adding physics

Now because our **Coconut** game object needs to behave realistically, we'll need to add a Rigidbody component in order to invoke the physics engine for this object. Select the object in the **Hierarchy** and go to **Component | Physics | Rigidbody**.

This adds the Rigidbody component that will apply gravity. As a result, when the player throws the object forward it will fall over time as we would expect it to in real life. The default settings of the Rigidbody component can be left unadjusted, so you will not need to change them at this stage.

We can test that the coconut falls and rolls now by pressing the **Play** button and watching the object in the **Scene** or **Game** views. When you are satisfied, press the **Play** button again to stop testing.

Saving as a prefab

Now that our coconut game object is complete, we'll need to store it as a prefab in our project, in order to ensure that we can instantiate it using code as many times as we like, rather than simply having a single object.

On the **Project** panel, select the **Prefabs** folder, and then click on the **Create** button and select **Prefab**. Rename the new prefab **Coconut Prefab**. Drag-and-drop the **Coconut** game object from the **Hierarchy** onto the new prefab in the **Project** panel to save it, and then delete the original copy from the scene by selecting it in the **Hierarchy** and pressing *Command + Backspace* (Mac) or *Delete* (PC).

Creating the Launcher object

As we are going to allow our player to throw the coconut prefabs we have just created, we will need two things—a script to handle the instantiation and an empty game object to act as a reference point for the position to create the objects in the world.

In real life when we throw a ball (overarm style), it comes into view to the side of our head, as our arm comes forward to release the ball. Therefore, we should position an object just outside of our player's field of view and make sure it will follow wherever they look. As the player view is handled by the **Main Camera** child object of **First Person Controller**, making an empty object a child of this will allow it to move with the camera, as its position will always stay relative to its parent.

Begin by creating a new empty game object in your scene by going to **GameObject | Create Empty**. Select this new object in the **Hierarchy** (by default, it will be called GameObject) and rename it **Launcher**. Next, expand the **First Person Controller** object by clicking on the gray arrow to the left of its name in the **Hierarchy**. Now drag-and-drop the **Launcher** object onto the **Main Camera** so that it becomes a child of it—you will know that you have done this correctly if a gray arrow appears next to the **Main Camera**, indicating that it can be expanded to show its child objects. The **Launcher** object is indented beneath it, as shown in the following screenshot:

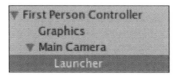

Making this object a child of the **Main Camera** will mean that it moves and rotates with its parent, but it still needs repositioning. Begin by resetting the position of the **Launcher** object in the **Transform** component in the **Inspector**. This can be done either by replacing all values with **0**, or to save time, you can use the Cog button to reset by selecting **Reset Position** from the pop-out menu, as shown in the following screenshot:

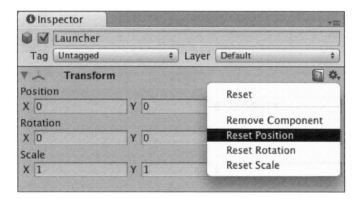

 The Cog button acts as a quick way of performing operations on components, and you'll see one next to each component in the **Inspector**. They are also useful as they allow you to remove components you no longer need or which have been added by mistake.

Setting the **Launcher** child object to a position of **0** means it is exactly in the center(same position) as its parent. Of course, this is not what we want, but it is a good starting point to go from. We must not leave the launcher in this position for two reasons:

- When coconuts are thrown, they would appear to be coming out from the player's head, and this would look odd.

- When you are instantiating objects, you must ensure that they are not created at a position where their collider will intersect with another collider, because this forces the physics engine to push the colliders apart and could interrupt the force applied when throwing the coconut.

To avoid this, we simply need to move the **Launcher** object forward and to the right of its current position. In the **Transform** component, set the **X** and **Z** positions to a value of **1**. Your **Launcher** object should now be positioned at the point where you would expect to release an object thrown by the player character's right arm, as shown in the following screenshot:

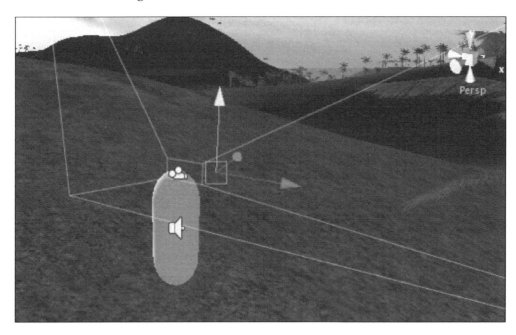

Finally, in order to make the thrown coconut head towards the center of our view, we need to rotate the launcher slightly around the Y-axis. Under **Rotation** in the **Transform** component, place in a value of **352** to rotate it by 8 degrees.

Next, we'll need to script the instantiation of the coconut and its propulsion when the player presses the fire button.

Scripting coconut throws

As we need to launch coconuts when the player presses fire, we'll need to check whether they are pressing a key—tied to an input in Unity—each frame. Keys and mouse axes/buttons are tied to default named inputs in the Unity **Input Manager**, but these can be changed at your leisure by going to **Edit** | **Project Settings** | **Input**. Do this now, then expand the **Axes** by clicking the gray arrow to the left of it, and then finally expand the axis entry called **Fire1**.

The three crucial fields to observe here are the **Name** parameter, the **Positive** parameter, and the **Alt Positive** parameter. We will be addressing this axis by its name, and the **Positive** and **Alt Positive** are the actual keys themselves to listen for. New axes can be created by simply increasing the **Size** value at the top of the **Input Manager**—resulting in a new input being added, which you can then customize.

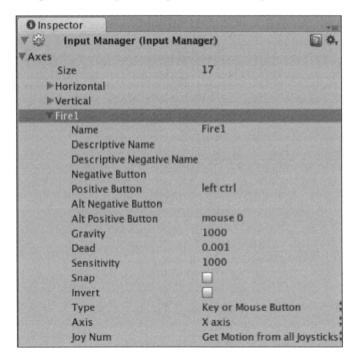

For the player to launch coconuts at the targets—which we'll place into our scene later—they must have a script that implements two key steps:

- Instantiation of the **Coconut** object to be thrown upon fire button press
- Assigning a velocity to the Rigidbody component to propel the coconut forward, as soon as it has been created

In order to achieve this, first create a new JavaScript file:

- Select the **Scripts** folder in the **Project** panel
- Click on the **Create** button drop-down menu and choose **JavaScript**
- Rename the **NewBehaviourScript** to **CoconutThrow** by pressing *Return* (Mac) or *F2* (PC)
- Launch this in the script editor by double-clicking its icon

Checking for player input

Given that we need to listen for player key presses each frame, we need to write our code for the launcher inside the Update() function. Move the closing right curly brace } of this function down by a few lines, and then add the following if statement to listen for the Fire1 keypress:

```
if(Input.GetButtonUp("Fire1")){
}
```

This checks the Input class and waits for the buttons tied to the **Fire1** input (Left *Ctrl* key and left mouse button) to be released. Into this if statement, we'll need to place actions we'd like the script to perform when the player releases either button.

Firstly, we should play a sound that acts as an audio-based feedback for throwing. If we were creating a shooting game, then this would likely be the sound of the gun being fired. However, in this instance, we simply have a subtle whooshing sound to represent the launch of the coconut.

Playing feedback sound

We'll need a variable to represent the sound clip we need to play, so place the following public member variable at the very top of the script before we continue:

```
var throwSound : AudioClip;
```

This creates what is known as a public member variable, which means we will be able to assign the actual audio clip to this variable using the **Inspector** once we're finished writing this script.

Now, let's set up the playing of this audio clip inside our if statement. After the opening curly brace, add the following line:

```
audio.PlayOneShot(throwSound);
```

This will play the sound as the player releases the **Fire1** button.

Instantiating the coconut

Next, we need to create the actual coconut itself, also within the current `if` statement. Given that we have created the coconut and saved it as a prefab, we should establish another public member variable so that we can assign our prefab to a variable in the **Inspector** later. At the top of the script, below your existing `throwSound` variable line, place the following:

```
var coconutObject : Rigidbody;
```

This places in a public member variable with a data type of `Rigidbody`. Although our coconut is stored as a prefab asset, when we instantiate it, we'll be creating a game object with a Rigidbody attached in our scene, and therefore the data type. This ensures that we cannot drag a non-rigidbody object to this variable in the **Inspector**. By strictly data typing to Rigidbody, this also means that if we wish to address the Rigidbody component of this object, then we wouldn't need to use the `GetComponent()` command to select the Rigidbody component first—we can simply write code that speaks directly to the Rigidbody.

Now, in the `if` statement in `Update()`, place the following line below the existing audio line:

```
var newCoconut : Rigidbody = Instantiate(coconutObject,
   transform.position, transform.rotation);
```

Here, we establish a private variable called `newCoconut`—it is private because it is within the `Update()` function, and so does not need to be implicitly written with the `private` prefix. Into this variable, we are passing the creation (Instantiation) of a new `GameObject`—and therefore the data type.

Remember that the three parameters of `Instantiate()` are object, position, and rotation. You'll see that we have used the public member variable to create an instance of our prefab and then inherited the position and rotation from the object this script is attached to—the **Launcher** object.

Naming instances

Whenever you create objects during runtime with `Instantiate()`, Unity takes the name of the prefab and follows it with the text "(clone)" when naming new instances. As this is rather a clunky name to reference in code—which we will need to do for our targets later—we can simply name the instances that are created by adding the following line beneath the line we just added:

```
newCoconut.name = "coconut";
```

Here, we have simply used the variable name we created, which refers to the new instance of the prefab, and used dot syntax to address the name parameter.

Assigning velocity

While this variable will create an instance of our coconut, our script is not yet complete, as we need to assign a velocity to the newly created coconut too. Otherwise, it will simply be created and fall to the ground. To allow us to adjust the speed of the thrown coconut, we can create another public member variable at the top of our script to handle this. In order to give us precision, we'll make this variable a float data type, allowing us to type in a value with a decimal place:

```
var throwForce : float;
```

Now, beneath the `Instantiate()` line in your `if` statement, add the following line:

```
newCoconut.rigidbody.velocity = transform.
    TransformDirection(Vector3(0,0, throwForce));
```

Here, we are referencing the newly instantiated coconut by its variable name, then using dot syntax to address the Rigidbody component, and then setting the velocity for the rigid body.

We have set the velocity using `transform.TransformDirection`, as this command creates a direction from local to world space. We must do this because our **Launcher** will be constantly moving and never facing a consistent direction.

The Z-axis of the world *does* face a consistent direction. When assigning velocity, we can take a specific local axis simply by assigning it a value inside a Vector3. This is why we have values of `0` in the `x` and `y` parameters of the Vector3.

Ensuring component presence

If we wish to safeguard against errors resulting from an attempt to address a component that is not attached, then we can check if the component exists, and add it if it is not present. For example, with our rigidbody, we could check the new instance `newCoconut` for a Rigidbody component by saying:

```
if(!newCoconut.rigidbody) {
  newCoconut.AddComponent(Rigidbody);
}
```

Here we are saying that if there is no rigidbody attached to this variable instance, then add a component of that type. We say 'no rigidbody' by simply placing an exclamation mark in front of the statement inside the `if` condition—a common practice in scripting. As we have already prepared our prefab with a rigidbody, we do not need to do it in this case.

Safeguarding collisions

While we have set up our **Launcher** in a position that is away from the player character's collider (the Controller Collider)—we should still include this last piece of code in order to safeguard against instantiating new coconuts that accidentally intersect our player's collider.

This can be done using the `IgnoreCollision()` command of the `Physics` class. This command typically takes three arguments:

```
IgnoreCollision(Collider A, Collider B, whether to ignore or not);
```

As a result, we simply need to feed it the two colliders, which we do not want the physics engine to react to, and set the third parameter to `true`.

Add the following line beneath the last line you added:

```
Physics.IgnoreCollision(transform.root.collider,
    newCoconut.collider, true);
```

Here we are finding the player character's collider by using `transform.root`—this simply finds the ultimate parent object of any objects that the **Launcher** is attached to. While the **Launcher** is a child of the **Main Camera** object, the camera itself does not have a collider. So, we really want to find the object it is attached to—**First Person Controller**, which we find by using `transform.root`.

Then we simply pass in the variable name `newCoconut`, which represents our newly instantiated coconut. For both the parameters, we use the dot syntax to refer to the `collider` component.

 Here we needed to find the ultimate parent of these objects, but if you are only referring to the parent of an object, you may address it using `transform.parent`.

Including the Audio Source component

Finally, as your throwing action involves playing audio, we can use the `@script` command to make Unity include an Audio Source component when this script is added to an object.

Below the closing of the `Update()` function, which is at the very bottom of the script, add the following line:

```
@script RequireComponent(AudioSource)
```

Save your script now by going to **File | Save** and return to Unity.

Script and variable assignment

Ensure that the **Launcher** object is still selected in the **Hierarchy** panel, and then go to **Component | Scripts | Coconut Throw** from the top menus. Unity will add the script you have just written as a component, as well as the Audio Source component you were required to add.

You should notice that the public member variables of the `CoconutThrow` script need to be assigned values/assets as we did not do this manually in the script.

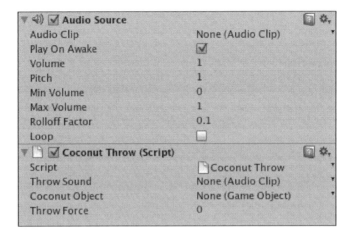

The two public member variables that require assets to be assigned to them are **Throw Sound** and **Coconut Object**—you can easily spot this as they indicate the data type that has been set for them in the script. The third public member variable, although data typed in the script, simply provides you with a default value in the appropriate format—a numeric value of **0**.

Click on the drop-down arrow to the right of **None (Audio Clip)** and select the **throw** audio clip from the list of available sound clip assets. Click on the arrow to the right of **None (Rigidbody)** and select **Coconut Prefab** as the object to assign from the list that appears. This ties the coconut prefab asset directly to this variable, meaning that the script will create instances of that object. Finally, assign the **Throw Force** variable a value of **25**. Bear in mind that altering values in the **Inspector** does not adjust what is written in the script but simply overrules any script-assigned values. Remember that these publicly exposed member variables can be changed, without having to recompile or edit the source code. Get used to adjusting these values in the **Inspector**, as the convenience of using public member variables in this way is a real time saver.

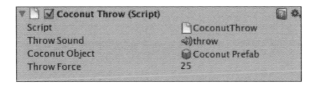

Now, it's time to test the throwing script by play testing the game. Press the **Play** button now and either click the left mouse button, or press the left *Ctrl* key on the keyboard to throw a coconut! Press the **Play** button again to stop testing, once you are satisfied that this works correctly. If anything does not work correctly, then return to your script and double-check that it matches the full script, which is as follows:

```
var throwSound : AudioClip;
var coconutObject : Rigidbody;
var throwForce : float;
function Update () {
  if(Input.GetButtonUp("Fire1")){
    audio.PlayOneShot(throwSound);
    var newCoconut : Rigidbody = Instantiate(coconutObject,
      transform.position, transform.rotation);
    newCoconut.name = "coconut";
    newCoconut.rigidbody.velocity = transform.TransformDirection
      (Vector3(0,0, throwForce));
    Physics.IgnoreCollision(transform.root.collider,
      newCoconut.collider, true);
  }
}
@script RequireComponent(AudioSource)
```

Instantiate restriction and object tidying

Instantiating objects in the manner in which we have done is an ideal use of Unity's prefab system, making it easy to construct any object in the scene and create many clones of it during runtime.

However, creating many clones of an object with a rigid body can prove costly, as each one invokes the physics engine, and as it negotiates its way around the 3D world—interacting with other objects—it will be using CPU cycles (processing power). Now imagine if you were to allow your player to create an infinite amount of physics-controlled objects, and you can appreciate that your game may slow down after a while. As your game uses too many CPU cycles and memory, the frame rate becomes lower, creating a jerky look to your previously smooth-motioned game. This will of course be a poor experience for the player, and in a commercial sense, would kill your game.

Rather than hoping that the player does not throw many coconuts, we will instead do two things to avoid too many objects clogging up the game's frame rate:

- Allow the player to throw coconuts only while in a defined spot in the game world
- Write a script to remove coconuts from the world after a defined time since their instantiation

If we were working on an instantiation of a larger scale, for example, a gun, then we would also add a time-based delay to ensure a 'reload' period. This is not necessary in this instance, as we avoid too many coconuts being thrown at once by using the GetButtonUp() command—the player must release the key before a coconut is thrown.

Activating coconut throw

We will address the first point by simply having a switching boolean variable that must be true for the player to throw coconuts, and we will only set this variable to true when the player character is standing on a part of the platform model—which will be our coconut target arena.

Having the player randomly throwing coconuts around the level away from this minigame would not really make sense, so it's a good thing to restrict this action in general regardless of our performance considerations.

Re-open the **CoconutThrow** script if you have closed it, by double-clicking its icon in the **Project** panel. Otherwise, simply switch back to the script editor and continue working on it. Previously, we have looked at activating and deactivating scripts through the enabled parameter of a component. Similarly, in this instance, we could very well use a GetComponent() command, select this script, and disable it when we do not want the player to throw coconuts. However, as with all scripting issues, there are many solutions to any one problem, and in this instance, we'll take a look at using static variables to communicate across scripts. Add the following line at the very top of the **CoconutThrow** script:

```
static var canThrow : boolean = false;
```

This static prefix before our variable is Unity JavaScript's way of creating a global—a value that can be accessed by other scripts. As a result of this, we'll be adding another condition to our existing if statement that allows us to throw, so find that line within the Update() function. It should look like this:

```
if(Input.GetButtonUp("Fire1")){
```

To add a second condition, simply add two ampersand symbols before the right closing bracket of the `if` statement along with the name of the static variable, as follows:

```
if(Input.GetButtonUp("Fire1") && canThrow){
```

Bear in mind here that simply writing the name of the variable is a shorter way of stating:

```
if(Input.GetButtonUp("Fire1") && canThrow==true){
```

As we have set the `canThrow` variable in the script to `false` when it was declared, and because it is static (therefore not a public member variable), we will need to use another piece of scripting to set this variable to `true`. Given that our player must be standing in a certain place, our best course of action for this is to use collision detection to check if the player is colliding with a particular object, and if so, set this static variable to `true`, allowing them to throw.

Open the **PlayerCollisions** script now and locate the commented-out `OnControllerColliderHit()` function. It should look like this:

```
/*
function OnControllerColliderHit(hit: ControllerColliderHit){
  if(hit.gameObject.tag == "outpostDoor" && doorIsOpen == false){
    Door(doorOpenSound, true, "dooropen");
  }
}
*/
```

Remove the `/*` and `*/` characters in order to uncomment it, making it an active code again. However, remove the `if` statement, as we no longer need this function to handle door opening and closing. You should now only have the function itself remaining, like this:

```
function OnControllerColliderHit(hit: ControllerColliderHit){
}
```

In the **platform** model you have downloaded, there is a part of the model called **mat** on which the player should be standing in order to throw coconuts, so we will ensure that they are colliding with this object. Inside this function, add the following `if else` statement:

```
if(hit.collider == GameObject.Find("mat").collider){
  CoconutThrow.canThrow=true;
}else{
  CoconutThrow.canThrow=false;
}
```

Here we are checking whether the current collider being hit is equal to (double equals is a comparative) the collider of the game object in the scene with the name mat. If this condition is met, then we simply address the static variable canThrow inside the script named CoconutThrow using the dot syntax, and set this variable to true. This allows the Instantiate() commands of the CoconutThrow script to work. Otherwise, we make sure that this variable it set to false, meaning that the player will not be able to throw coconuts when he is not standing on the platform's throwing mat.

In the script editor, go to **File | Save** and return to Unity.

Removing coconuts

As explained earlier, too many physics-controlled objects in your scene can seriously affect the performance. Therefore, in cases such as this, where your objects are simply throwaway objects (objects that need not be kept), we can write a script to automatically remove them after a defined amount of time.

Select the **Scripts** folder inside the **Project** panel, click on the **Create** button, and select **JavaScript** to make a new script. Rename this script **CoconutTidy** by pressing *Return* (Mac) or *F2* (PC) and retyping. Then double-click the icon of the script to launch it in the script editor.

Remove the default Update() function from this script as we do not need it. To remove any object from a scene, we can simply use the **Destroy()** command. Implement its second parameter in order to establish a waiting period. Add the following function and command to your script now:

```
function Start(){
   Destroy(gameObject, 5);
}
```

By using the Start() command, we will call Destroy() as soon as this object appears in the world, that is, as soon as it is instantiated by the player pressing the fire button. By referring to gameObject, we are simply saying 'the object this script is attached to'. After the comma, we simply state a time in seconds to wait until activating this command.

As a result of this script—as soon as a coconut is thrown, it will stay in the world for five seconds, and then be removed. Go to **File | Save** in the script editor and return to Unity.

Previously, when we had written scripts, we had attached them to objects in the scene we had been working on. However, in this instance, we have already finished working on our coconut prefab, and we no longer have a copy in the scene.

There are two ways of applying the script we have just written to the prefab. To do this the easy way, you can:

- Select the **Coconut** prefab you made earlier in the **Project** panel, and go to **Component | Scripts | CoconutTidy**

Or to take a more long-winded route, you can modify the prefab in the **Scene** in the following way:

- Drag the **Coconut** prefab to the **Scene** window or the **Hierarchy** panel
- Go to **Component | Scripts | CoconutTidy**, click **Add** to confirm when told that '**Adding a component will lose the prefab parent**'
- Echo this update to the original prefab by going to **GameObject | Apply Changes to prefab**
- Delete the instance in the scene using the shortcut *Command + Backspace* (Mac) or *Delete* (PC).

In this instance, I recommend the former, that is, the single step route, so let's do that now. But in some instances it can be useful to take a prefab back into the scene, and modify it before you apply changes to the prefab. For example, if you are working on something visual, such as a particle system, then you would need to see what effect your adjustments or newly added components will have. Therefore, taking a prefab of such an object into the scene to edit would be essential.

Go to **File | Save Project** in Unity now to update your progress so far.

Adding the coconut shy platform

Now we are ready to implement our minigame from the assets you downloaded earlier. By placing the platform and three targets into the scene, we'll check for collisions between the coconuts and the targets, and write a script to check if all of the three targets are knocked down at once—the goal of the minigame.

In the **Project** panel, there is a **Coconut Game** folder that was imported when you downloaded the assets to complete this chapter. Select the 3D model in this folder named **platform** to see its properties in the **Inspector**.

Import settings

Before we place the platform and targets into the scene, we will ensure that they are correctly scaled and can be walked on by the player by generating colliders for each part of the models.

The platform

In the **FBXImporter** component in the **Inspector**, set the **Scale Factor** to **1.25**, then select the box for **Generate Colliders** to ensure that Unity assigns a mesh collider to each part of the model, meaning the player character will be able to walk on the platform.

To confirm this change, click the **Apply** button at the bottom of the **Inspector** now.

Now drag the model from the **Project** panel to the **Scene** window, and use the **Transform tool** to position it somewhere near the outpost in order to ensure that the player understands that the two features are related. Make sure that you lower the platform model into the ground so that the player character will be able to walk up the steps at the front of the model. Here is the positioning that I have chosen:

Targets and coconut collisions

Now find the **target** model inside the **Coconut Game** folder in the **Project** panel, and select it in order to see the various import setting components in the **Inspector**.

In the **FBXImporter** component in the **Inspector**, select the box for **Generate Colliders** to ensure that any part of the model that a coconut hits should cause it to repel—remember that with no colliders, 3D objects will pass through one another. Also, set the **Scale Factor** to a value of **1** here.

In the **Animations** component, we'll need to specify frames and give names for each animation state we would like this model to have, in the same way as we did for the outpost door animations. By adding these animation states, we can call upon them in our scripts if a collision between a coconut and the correct part of the target occurs.

Add three animation states, as shown in the following screenshot, by clicking on the plus (+) icon to the right of the animations table, then filling in a **Name** and the **Start** and **End** frames:

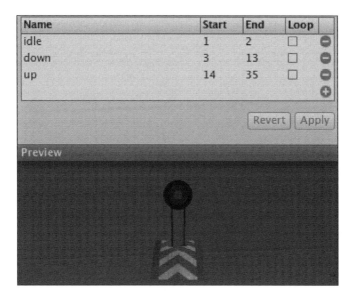

When you have completed the **Animations** table, remember to press the **Apply** button at the bottom to confirm this and the other import changes you have made to the asset.

Placement

To place the targets easily on the platform, we will add them as children of the **platform** object already in our scene. To do this, simply drag the target model from the **Coconut Game** folder in the **Project** panel, and drop it onto the **platform** parent object in the **Hierarchy** panel.

You will be prompted with a dialog window informing you that adding this child object will **Lose the prefab connection**. Simply click the **Continue** button here. This is simply informing you that changes made to components attached to the original model in the **Project** panel—for example, script parameters—will no longer apply to this copy in the scene because you are severing the connection between this instance and the original asset or prefab.

Adding the target as a child of the platform will cause the platform to expand and reveal its existing child objects along with the target you have just added.

As the target will be positioned in the center of the platform by default, move it to the correct position by changing values in the **Transform** component in the **Inspector** — placing it at (**0, 1.7, 1.7**).

Coconut detection script

As we need to detect collisions between the target part of the target model — as opposed to the stem or base, for example — we'll need to write a script with collision detection to be applied to that part of the model. Select the **Scripts** folder in the **Project** panel, then click on the **Create** button, and select **JavaScript** from the drop-down menu. Rename this from **NewBehaviourScript** to **CoconutCollision**, and then double-click the icon to open it in the script editor.

Establishing variables

Firstly, we need to establish five variables, and they are as follows:

- A `GameObject` public member variable storing the target object itself

- A `beenHit` boolean to check if the target is currently down

- A private floating-point `timer` variable to wait for a defined amount of time before the target is reset

- A `hitSound` audio public member variable

- A `resetSound` audio public member variable

To do this, add the following code to the start of the script:

```
var targetRoot : GameObject;
private var beenHit : boolean = false;
private var timer : float = 0.0;
var hitSound : AudioClip;
var resetSound : AudioClip;
```

Note here that `beenHit` and `timer` are private variables, as they do not need to be assigned in the **Inspector** — their values are set and used only within the script. Setting the `private` prefix will hide them from view in the **Inspector**, meaning that they are not public member variables.

Collision detection

Next, move the existing Update() function down by a few lines and write in the following collision detection function:

```
function OnCollisionEnter(theObject : Collision) {
  if(beenHit==false && theObject.gameObject.name=="coconut"){
    audio.PlayOneShot(hitSound);
    targetRoot.animation.Play("down");
    beenHit=true;
  }
}
```

Different from the OnControllerColliderHit() and OnTriggerEnter() functions we've used previously, OnCollisionEnter() handles ordinary collisions between objects with primitive colliders, that is, not character controller colliders and not colliders in trigger mode.

In this function, the parameter theObject is an instance of the Collision class, which stores information on velocities, rigidbodies, colliders, transform, GameObjects, and contact points involved in a collision. Therefore, here we simply check the class with an if statement, checking whether that parameter has stored a gameObject with the name coconut. To ensure that the target cannot be hit many times, we have an additional condition in the if statement, which checks that beenHit is set to false. This will be the case when the game starts, and when this collision occurs, beenHit gets set to true so that we cannot accidentally trigger it twice.

This function also plays an audio file assigned to the variable hitSound, and plays the animation state named down on whatever object we drag-and-drop to the targetRoot variable. After writing the script, we will assign the target model parent object to this variable in the **Inspector**.

Resetting the target

Now in the Update() function, we'll need to use the beenHit variable to start the timer counting up to 3 seconds. This means that from the frame that it is hit by the coconut, the timer will count to 3 before triggering a reset. For this, we will need two if statements, one to handle checking for beenHit to be true and incrementing the timer and the other to check if the timer has reached 3 seconds. Move the closing right curly brace of the Update() function down by a few lines, and add the following code:

```
if(beenHit){
  timer += Time.deltaTime;
}
```

```
if(timer > 3){
  audio.PlayOneShot(resetSound);
  targetRoot.animation.Play("up");
  beenHit=false;
  timer=0.0;
}
```

Our first `if` statement waits for `beenHit` to be `true`, and then adds to the `timer` variable using the `Time.deltaTime` counter. This is non-frame rate specific, and therefore counts in real time.

The second `if` statement waits for the `timer` variable to exceed 3 seconds, then plays the sound assigned to `resetSound` variable, plays the animation state of the model assigned to `targetRoot`, and resets `beenHit` and `timer` to their original states so that the target can be hit again.

Including audio source

As we are playing sounds, we'll need to add the usual `RequireComponent` command to the bottom of our script in order to ensure that an audio source gets added to the object this script gets attached to. Place the following line at the very bottom of the script after the closing curly brace of the `Update()` function:

```
@script RequireComponent(AudioSource)
```

Go to **File** | **Save** in the script editor, and switch back to Unity now.

Script assignment

In the **Hierarchy** panel, expand the **target** model that you have added to the platform, in order to see its constituent parts, and then expand the **target_pivot** child group to reveal the target itself and its supports. They should look like this:

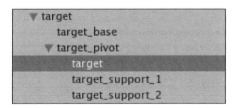

In the last screenshot, I have selected the target itself. You need to do the same now as we must ensure that the script we just wrote is assigned to this object, as opposed to the parent target model. We need to check for collisions with this child part as we don't want collisions to be triggered if the player throws a coconut at the base or supports, for example.

With this object selected, go to **Component | Scripts | CoconutCollision**. The script we just wrote will be added, along with an **Audio Source** component. Now drag the **target** parent from the **Hierarchy** panel to the **Target Root** public member variable and the **targetHit** and **targetReset** audio files from the **Project** panel to the relevant public member variables in the **Inspector**, as illustrated in the following screenshot:

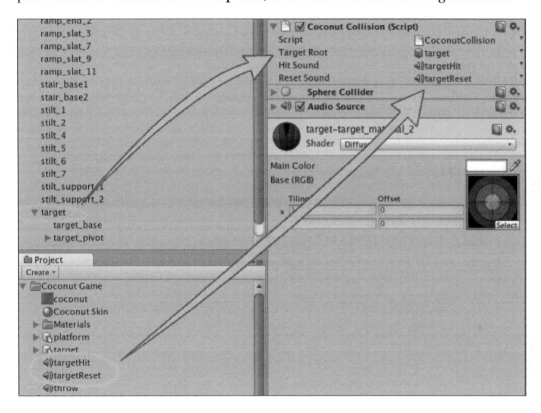

Now go to **File | Save Scene** in Unity to update your progress. Press the **Play** button to test the game and walk over to the platform, making sure you stand on the mat—you should now be able to throw coconuts and knock down the target. Press **Play** again to stop testing.

To complete our minigame setup, we'll make three more targets using the prefab system.

Making more targets

To make more targets, we'll duplicate our existing target, having turned it into a prefab. Make a new prefab by selecting the **Prefabs** folder in the **Project** panel and going to the **Create** button and selecting **Prefab**. Rename this from **new prefab** to **Target Prefab**. Now, drag-and-drop the target parent object in the **Hierarchy** onto this new prefab to save it.

The text of the parent **target** in the **Hierarchy** should turn blue, indicating that it is connected to a prefab in the project.

Now select the parent **target** in the **Hierarchy** panel, and press *Command + D* (Mac) or *Ctrl + D* (PC) to duplicate this object.

With the duplicate selected, set its **X** position in the **Transform** component in the **Inspector** to **1.8**. Repeat this duplicating step again now to make a third target, but this time, setting the **X** position to **-1.8**.

Winning the game

To complete the function of our minigame—to give the player the final battery they need to charge the outpost door—we'll need to write a script that checks if all of the three targets are knocked down at once.

Select the **Scripts** folder in the **Project** panel, and use the **Create** button to make a new **JavaScript** file. Rename this script **CoconutWin**, and then double-click its icon to launch it in the script editor.

Variable setup

At the top of the script, add the following four variables:

```
static var targets : int = 0;
private var haveWon : boolean = false;
var win : AudioClip;
var battery : GameObject;
```

Here we begin with a static variable called `targets`, which is effectively a counter to store how many targets are currently knocked down—this will be assigned by a change that we will make to our `CoconutCollision` script later. We then have a private variable called `haveWon` that will stop this minigame from being replayed, by simply being set to `true` after the first win.

We then have two public member variables—one to store a winning audio clip, and the other to store the battery prefab, so that this script can instantiate it when the player has won.

Checking for a win

Now add the following code to the `Update()` function:

```
if(targets==3 && haveWon == false){
  targets=0;
  audio.PlayOneShot(win);
  Instantiate(battery, Vector3(transform.position.x,
    transform.position.y+2, transform.position.z),
    transform.rotation);
  haveWon = true;
}
```

This `if` statement has two conditions. It ensures that the `targets` count has reached `3`, meaning that they must all be knocked down, and also that the `haveWon` variable is `false`, meaning that this is the first time the player has attempted playing this minigame.

When these conditions are met, the following commands are carried out:

- The script resets the `targets` variable to `0` (this is simply another measure to ensure that the `if` statement does not retrigger)
- The `win` audio clip is played as player feedback
- An instance of the object that we will assign to the `battery` variable is instantiated, taking its position with a manual Vector3 that uses the constituent `x` and `z` values of the platform (as that is what this script will be applied to), while adding `2` to the value of `y`
- We set the `haveWon` variable to `true`, which means that the game cannot be won again, and stops the player from generating more batteries

Finally, as we are playing sound, add the following line to the very bottom of the script:

```
@script RequireComponent(AudioSource)
```

Now go to **File | Save** in the script editor, and switch back to Unity.

Script assignment

Select the platform parent object in the **Hierarchy** panel and go to **Component | Scripts | Coconut Win**.

To complete this, assign the **battery** prefab from the **Prefabs** folder in the **Project** panel to the **battery** member variable, and the **Win** sound effect from the **Coconut Game** folder to the **Win** member variable. When done, the script component should look like this:

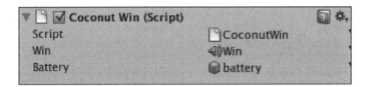

Incrementing and decrementing targets

Finally, to make the game work, we must return to our **CoconutCollision** script, and add one to the static variable `targets` in `CoconutWin` when we knock down a target, and subtract one when the target resets.

This is simple to do, as our script is already set up to handle those two events. Double-click on the icon of the **CoconutCollision** script in the **Scripts** folder to launch it in the script editor.

Adding

In the collision detection function—`OnCollisionEnter()`—the `if` statement features a line setting `beenHit` to `true`. Find the line:

```
beenHit=true;
```

and after it, add the following line:

```
CoconutWin.targets++;
```

Subtracting

In the `Update()` function, the second `if` statement handles resetting the target, meaning we should subtract from the `targets` count. Find the line:

```
beenHit=false;
```

and then add the following line after it:

```
CoconutWin.targets--;
```

In both these cases, we are using dot syntax to address the script (effectively a class), followed by the name of the variable, namely, `targets`.

Go to **File** | **Save** in the script editor, and return to Unity.

Press the **Play** button now and test the game. Throwing coconuts and knocking down all of the three targets at once should cause the platform to instantiate a battery for you to collect. When it does, you simply press the *Space* bar to jump over the barrier and collect the battery. Press **Play** again to stop testing the game, and go to **File** | **Save Scene** in Unity to update your progress.

Finishing touches

To make this minigame feel a little more polished, we'll add a crosshair to the heads-up display when the player is standing on the throwing mat, and use our existing **TextHint GUI** object to give the player instructions on what to do to win the coconut shy game.

Adding the crosshair

To add the crosshair to the screen, do the following:

- Open the **Coconut Game** folder in the **Project** panel.
- Select the **Crosshair** texture file.
- Go to **GameObject** | **Create Other** | **GUI Texture**. This will take dimensions of the texture file and assign them for you while creating a new GUI Texture object named after the **Crosshair** texture.

This will automatically get selected in the **Hierarchy** panel, so you can see its **GUITexture** component in the **Inspector**. The crosshair graphic should have become visible in the **Game** view and in the **Scene** view if you have the **Game Overlay** button toggled. As this is centered by default, it works perfectly with our small 64 x 64 texture file. When we created the texture file for this example, it was important that we used light and dark edges so that the cross is easy to see regardless of whether the player is looking at something light or dark.

 Bear in mind that when not selecting the texture file and simply creating the GUI Texture, you will be presented with a Unity logo. You then have to swap this for your texture in the **Inspector**, as well as fill in the dimensions manually. For this reason, it is always best to select the texture you wish to form your GUI Texture object first.

Toggling the crosshair GUI Texture

Open the **PlayerCollisions** script from the `Scripts` folder of the **Project** panel. In the `OnControllerColliderHit()` function, you'll notice that we already have scripting that checks if we are on the throwing mat. As we want the crosshair to be visible only when we are on this mat, we will add more code to these `if` statements.

Before the `if` statement that reads:

```
if(hit.collider == GameObject.Find("mat").collider){
    CoconutThrow.canThrow=true;
}
```

Add the following two lines:

```
var crosshairObj : GameObject = GameObject.Find("Crosshair");
var crosshair : GUITexture = crosshairObj.
    GetComponent(GUITexture);
```

Here we are establishing two variables, one which finds the crosshair object using `GameObject.Find` and the object's name and another which uses `GetComponent()` to represent the previous variable's `GUITexture` component. By doing this, we can simply enable and disable the crosshair using the `if` and `else` statements.

Now in the `if` statement shown previously, we add the following line:

```
crosshair.enabled = true;
```

And in the accompanying `else` statement, we add the line:

```
crosshair.enabled=false;
```

Informing the player

To help the player understand what they need to do, we'll use our **TextHints GUI** object from Chapter 5 to show a message on screen when the player stands on the throwing mat.

In the `if` statement of `OnControllerColliderHit()` in **PlayerCollisions**, add the following lines:

```
TextHints.textOn=true;
    TextHints.message = "Knock down all 3 at once to win a
        battery!";
    GameObject.Find("TextHint GUI").transform.position.y = 0.2;
```

Here we are switching on the **TextHint GUI** by setting its static variable `textOn` to `true`, then sending a string of text to its `message` static variable. The timer within the `TextHints` script will take care of switching off this message once the player leaves the mat.

Here we have also used `GameObject.Find` to address the `TextHint GUI` object itself and set its `y` position to `0.2`. This is because, by default, our TextHint GUI messages appear in the center of the screen, which would mean they would be in the same place as our crosshair. As we do not want this, we use the latter of the three lines in the previous code snippet to set the position lower on the screen.

Now, in the `else` statement of `OnControllerColliderHit()`, add the following:

```
GameObject.Find("TextHint GUI").transform.position.y = 0.5;
```

This simply resets the `TextHint GUI` object back to its original position when the player is done with the coconut game and leaves the mat.

Your completed `OnControllerColliderHit()` function should look like this:

```
function OnControllerColliderHit(hit: ControllerColliderHit){
  var crosshairObj : GameObject = GameObject.Find("Crosshair");
  var crosshair : GUITexture =
    crosshairObj.GetComponent(GUITexture);
  if(hit.collider == GameObject.Find("mat").collider){
    CoconutThrow.canThrow=true;
    crosshair.enabled = true;
    TextHints.textOn=true;
    TextHints.message = "Knock down all 3 to win a battery!";
    GameObject.Find("TextHint GUI").transform.position.y = 0.2;
  }
  else{
    CoconutThrow.canThrow=false;
    crosshair.enabled = false;
    GameObject.Find("TextHint GUI").transform.position.y = 0.5;
  }
}
```

Go to **File | Save** in the script editor to update your progress and return to Unity.

Press the **Play** button and test the game. Now when standing on the throwing mat, you should see a crosshair and a message telling you what to do. Leave the mat and the crosshair should disappear from the screen, followed by the message after a few seconds. Press **Play** again to stop testing the game, and go to **File | Save Project** to update your progress so far.

Summary

In this chapter, we have covered various topics that you will find crucial when creating any game scenario. We have looked at implementing rigid body objects that use the physics engine. This is something you'll likely expand upon in many other game scenarios while working with Unity. We also explored the concept of instantiation, something that is very important to get to grips with, as it means you can create or clone any prefab asset or game object during runtime—a very useful tool in your game-designing arsenal.

We also gave the player further feedback by reusing our TextHint GUI object made in Chapter 5 and worked across scripts in order to send the information to this object.

These are concepts you will continue to use in the rest of this book and in your future Unity projects. In the next chapter, we'll take a break from coding and take a look at more of Unity's aesthetic effects. We'll explore the use of particle systems to create a fire outside the outpost cabin—giving the player a visual reward for winning the minigame and opening the door.

7
Particle Systems

In this chapter, we will take a look at some of the rendering effects available to you as a Unity developer. To create more dynamic 3D worlds, rendering effects outside of simple materials and texturing are used to simulate, and often accentuate, the features of the real world. Many 3D games have adopted visual conventions of camera-captured imagery, introducing such effects as lens flares and light trails as part of a simulated viewpoint which in real terms would never witness such effects.

We have already taken advantage of the lens flare rendering effect in Chapter 2, where we utilized a Sun lens flare on the light component of our main directional light. In this chapter, we will look at more versatile effects that can be achieved by using particle systems within your 3D world. Games use particle effects to achieve a vast range of effects from fog and smoke to sparks, lasers, and simple patterns. In this chapter, we'll look at how we can use two particle systems to achieve the effect of a simulated fire.

In this chapter, you will learn:

- What makes up a particle system—its components and settings
- How to build particle systems to simulate fire and smoke
- Further work with on-screen player instructions and feedback
- Using variables to activate particle systems during runtime

What is a particle system?

A particle system is referred to in Unity as a system—rather than a component—as it requires a number of components working together in order to function properly. Before we begin to work with the systems themselves, we need to understand the component parts and their role in the system.

Particle emitter

Within any particle system, the emitter component is in charge of instantiating individual particles. In Unity, there is an **Ellipsoid Particle Emitter** and a **Mesh Particle Emitter** available.

The ellipsoid is most commonly used for effects such as smoke, dust, and other such environmental elements that can be created in a defined space. It is referred to as the ellipsoid because it creates particles within a sphere that can be stretched to accommodate the system.

The mesh emitter creates particles which are tied directly to a 3D mesh and can either be animated along vertices of a mesh or simply emitted upon the points of the mesh. This is more commonly used when there is a need for direct control over particle position — giving the developer the ability to follow vertices of a mesh means that they can design precise particle systems in whatever 3D shape they desire.

In component terms, both emitters have the following settings in common:

- Size: the visible size of an individual particle
- Energy: the amount of time a particle exists in the world before auto-destructing
- Emission: the number of particles emitted at a time
- Velocities: the speed at which particles travel

We will look at some of the more detailed settings specific to either kind of emitter as we go further in the chapter. For the task of creating a fire, we'll be using the ellipsoid emitter — this will allow a more random effect as it is not tied to a mesh.

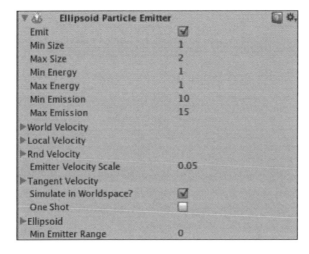

Particle Animator

The **Particle Animator** is in charge of how individual particles behave over time. In order to appear dynamic, particles have a lifespan, after which they will auto-destruct. As in our example of creating a fire, particles should ideally be animated so that each individual particle's appearance changes during its lifespan in the world. As flames burst and fade in real fire—we can use the animator component to apply color and visibility variance, as well as apply forces to the particles themselves.

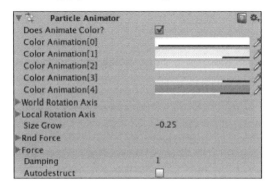

Particle Renderer

Particle renderers define the visual appearance of individual particles. Particles are effectively square sprites (2D graphics), and in most instances are rendered in the same manner as the grass we added to our terrain in Chapter 2—by using the billboarding technique to give the appearance of always facing the camera. Particle renderers in Unity can display particles in other ways, but billboarding is appropriate for most uses.

The Particle Renderer component also handles the materials applied to the particle system. As particles are rendered simply as sprites, applying particle shaders to materials in the renderer component means you can create the illusion of non-square sprites by using alpha channel (transparency) surrounded textures. Here is an example that we'll be using shortly on our fire material—the dark area here is the transparent part:

As a result of using transparency for particles, they no longer have a square appearance—as rendered 2D sprites would ordinarily. By combining the render of only the visible part of this texture with higher emission values of the emitter, the effect of density can be achieved.

Particle renderers can also animate particles using UV animation, by using a grid of images to effectively swap textures during a particle's lifespan, but this is slightly more advanced than the scope of this book, so it is recommended that you refer to the Unity manual for more information on this.

In summary

A particle system works because it has a series of components that work together, namely, the emitter creating the particles, the animator defining their behavior/ variation over time, and the renderer defining their aesthetic using materials and display parameters.

Now, we'll take a look at creating the next part of our tutorial game, which will culminate in lighting a fire made of two particle systems, one for flames and the other creating a smoke plume.

Making the task

Our existing game consists of a task for the player to complete in order to enter the outpost—they must collect four batteries to power the door, one of which has to be won by winning the coconut shy game we added in the previous chapter.

Currently, having entered the outpost, the player is met with a sense of disappointment—as there is nothing to be found inside. In this chapter, we will change that by adding a box of matches to be picked up by the player when they enter the outpost. We will then create our fire outside, which can only be lit if the player is carrying the box of matches. In this way, we can show the player a set of logs waiting to be lit, leading them to attempt to find matches by completing the tasks laid out (that is, opening the door).

To create this game, we will need to implement the following in Unity:

- Locate an asset package, and add a log fire model to our scene near the outpost.
- Create the particle systems for fire and smoke for when the fire is lit. Then set them to not emit until triggered by a script.
- Set up collision detection between the player character and the log fire object in order to light the fire by switching on the emitter component.

- Add the matches model to the outpost and set up collision detection to function as collection of the object, and make this restrict whether the fire can be lit.

- Use our `TextHint` GUI object to show the player a hint if they approach the fire with no matches.

Asset download

To get the assets necessary to complete this exercise, locate the file named `firePack.unitypackage` from our extracted code bundle. In Unity, go to **Assets | Import Package**, and navigate to the location you have downloaded the package to, and choose it.

This will import several files required to create the fire exercise:

- A 3D model of the campfire logs
- A Flame texture for our fire particle system material
- A Smoke texture for our smoke particle system material
- A Sound clip of the fire crackling
- Material folders for the 3D models

The files will be imported into a folder in the **Project** panel called **Fire feature**.

Adding the log pile

In the **Fire feature** folder in the project panel, you'll find a model called **campfire**. Select it, and change the **Scale factor** to **0.5** in the **FBX Importer** component of the **Inspector**. This will ensure that the model is imported into our scene at a reasonable size compared to the other objects already present. Press the **Apply** button at the bottom of the components in the **Inspector** to confirm this change.

Now drag this model over to the **Scene**, and use the **Transform tool** to position it near the outpost and coconut shy that are already present. Here is the positioning that I have used:

Now, because we do not want our player to walk through this model, it needs to have a collider. Ordinarily, with complex models such as this, we'd use the FBX Importer to generate mesh colliders for each individual mesh in the model. However, given that we only need to ensure that the player bumps into this object, we can simply use a capsule collider instead. This will work just as well for the purpose and save on processing power because the processor will not have to build a collider for every part.

Select the **campfire** object in the **Hierarchy** and go to **Component | Physics | Capsule Collider**. You will be prompted to confirm that you wish to disconnect this instance from the original with a dialog window saying **Losing Prefab Parent**—simply click on **Continue** as usual.

This will give you a small spherical looking collider at the base of the fire model. We need to increase the size of this to cover the boundary of the fire—in the newly added **Capsule Collider** component in the **Inspector**, set the **Radius** to **2**, **Height** to **5**, and in the values for **Center**, set **Y** to a value of **1.5**. Your collider should now look something like what is shown in the following screenshot, and upon play testing, should cause the player to bump into the object.

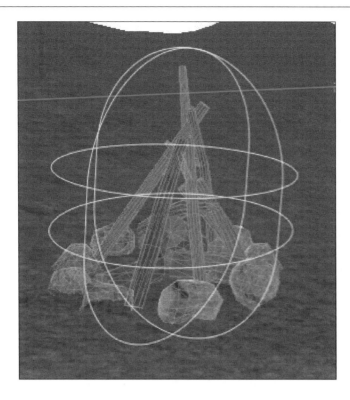

Creating the fire particle systems

In this section, we'll create two different particle systems, one for the fire and the other for smoke emanating from it. By using two separate systems, we will have more control over the animation of the particles over time, as we will not need to animate from fire to smoke in a single system.

Making fire

To begin building our fire particle systems, we can add a game object with all three essential particle components. Go to **GameObject | Create Other | Particle System**. This creates a new game object in the **Scene/Hierarchy** named **Particle System**. Press *Return* (Mac) or *F2* (PC) and type to rename this to **FireSystem**, ensuring that there is no space in the name—this is crucial for our scripting later.

Bear in mind that at this stage, we needn't position the fire until we have finished making it. Therefore, it can be designed at the arbitrary point in the 3D world that the Unity editor has placed it at.

By default, your particle system has the default particle appearance of white softened dots, in a cluster not too dissimilar from fireflies in a cluster. This simply demonstrates the most generic settings for each component—the particle emitter is emitting and has a modest number of particles, the animator is simply making particles fade in and out, and the renderer has no material set up yet.

Let's go through each component now and set them up individually. You'll be able to see a preview of the particle system in the **Scene** view, so watch as you adjust each setting in the **Inspector**.

Ellipsoid Particle Emitter Settings

Begin by setting the **Min Size** value to **0.5** and **Max Size** value to **2**. Our flames are considerably larger than the firefly-like dots seen in the default settings. As with all Min and Max settings, the emitter will spawn particles of a size between these two values.

Now set **Min Energy** to **1** and **Max Energy** to **1.5**—this is the lifespan of the particles, and as a result, particles will last between 1 and 1.5 seconds before autodestructing.

Set the **Min Emission** value to **15** and **Max Emission** value to **20**. This is the value defining how many particles are in the scene at any given time. The higher these values go, the more particles will be on screen, giving more density to the fire. However, particles can be expensive to render for the CPU. So, generally speaking, it is best to keep emission values like these to the lowest possible setting that you can aesthetically afford.

Set the **Y** value of **World Velocity** to **0.1**. This will cause the particles to rise during their lifespan, as flames would due to natural heat.

We do this with **World Velocity** with objects that must always go up in the game world. If this was done on an object that was movable with **Local Velocity** and that object rotated during the game, then its local Y axis would no longer face the World Y.

For example, a flaming barrel with physics may fall over, but its fire should still rise in World terms. While our campfire is not movable, it is a good practice to understand the difference between Local and World here.

Then set the **Y** value of **Rnd Velocity** (Random) to **0.2**—this will cause occasional random flames to leap a little higher than others.

Tangent Velocity should be set to **0.2** in the **X** and **Z** axes, leaving the **Y** axis on **0**. **Tangent Velocity** defines the starting speed of individual particles. So by setting a small value in **X** and **Z**, we are giving the flames of the fire a boost out horizontally.

Emitter Velocity Scale can be set to **0**, as this is only relevant to moving particle systems as it controls how quickly the particles themselves move if the system's parent object is moved. As our fire will remain static, it can be left at **0**.

Simulate in Worldspace can be left deselected, as we would like our particles to be created relative to the position of the system, as opposed to a world space position.

One Shot can be left deselected, as we need our particles to flow continuously. **One Shot** would be more useful in something such as a puff of smoke from a cannon for example.

Ellipsoid values can be set to **0.1** for all axes — this is a small value, but our particle system is only on a small scale — the ellipsoid value for the smoke plume particle system, for example, will need to be much taller.

Particle Animator settings

Next we need to set up the Particle Animator component, which will define behavior of our particles over the course of their lifespan. Here we will need to make the particles fade in and out, and animate through colors (shades of red/orange), as well as apply forces to them which will cause the flames to leap and billow at the sides more realistically.

Begin by ensuring that **Does Animate Color** is selected, which will cause the five **Color Animation** boxes to come into play. Now go through each box by clicking on the color space — and in the color picker that appears, set colors that fade from white in **Color Animation [0]** through to dark orange in **Color Animation [4]**.

As you do this, also set the A (alpha) value at the bottom of the color picker to a value so that **Color Animation [0]** and **Color Animation [4]** have an alpha of **0**, and the states in between fade up and back. Alpha is illustrated in the **Inspector** by the white/black line beneath each color block. See the following screenshot for a visual representation of what you need to do here:

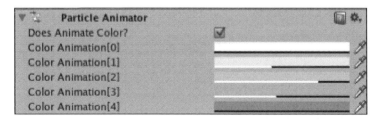

Your particle system in the **Scene** view should now be billowing more naturally and animating through the colors and alpha values that you have specified.

The effect of the **Color Animation** system may look more or less effective depending upon whether materials applied to your particle system use particular **Shaders**—some show color more so than others; for example, shaders with transparency may appear to show colors less effectively.

After leaving the **Rotation Axis** settings at their default of **0** in all axes, set **Size Grow** to a value of **-0.3**. We set this to a minus value in order to cause particles to shrink during their lifespan, giving a more dynamic look to the fire.

Next we'll add forces to give a more realistic motion to the fire. Forces are different to the velocities added in the **Emitter** settings, as they are applied when the particles are instantiated—causing a boost of speed following by deceleration. Expand the **Rnd Force** parameter by clicking on the gray arrow to the left of it and place a value of **1** into the **X** and **Z** axes. Then expand the **Force** parameter in the same way, and set the **Y** axis value to **1**.

Set the value for **Damping** to **0.8**. Damping defines the amount that particles slow down during their lifespan. With a default value of 1 meaning no damping occurs, values between 0 and 1 cause slow down, 0 being the most intensive slowing. We are setting a mild value of 0.8 so that our particles do not slow too unnaturally.

The final setting, **Autodestruct,** can be left deselected. All particles themselves naturally autodestruct at the end of their lifespan, but the autodestruct setting here relates to the parent game object itself—if selected, and all particles in the system have auto-destructed, then the game object will be destroyed. This only comes into play when using the **One Shot** setting in the emitter component—in the example of a cannon blast, the developer would likely instantiate an instance of a one-shot particle system with autodestruct selected. This means that as soon as it had been created, once all the particles had died, the game object would be destroyed, thus saving system resources such as CPU, GPU, and RAM.

Particle Renderer settings

In our fire particle system, we simply need to apply a particle-shaded material containing the fire graphic you downloaded and imported. But before we do that, we'll ensure that the **Particle Renderer** is set up correctly for our purpose.

As the particles or flames of a fire should technically emit light, we'll deselect both **Cast** and **Receive** shadows to ensure that no shadow is cast on or by the fire—bear in mind that this is only valid for users of Unity Pro version, as Indie does not feature dynamic shadows at the time of writing.

Currently there are no materials applied to this particle system, so there are no entries in the **Materials** area—we will rectify this shortly. Next, ensure that **Camera Velocity Scale** is set to **0**—this would only be used if we were not billboard rendering our particles. If we planned to stretch particles, then we would use this setting to define how much of an effect camera movement had on particle stretching.

Stretch Particles should be set to **Billboard** as discussed earlier—ensuring that no matter where the player views the fire from, particles are drawn facing them. As **Length** and **Velocity** scale are only used in stretched particles, we can happily leave these two settings at **0**—altering these values will not affect billboarded particles.

The final setting to consider—bearing in mind that we are not using UV Animation—is **Max Particle Size**. This setting controls how large a particle can be in relation to the height of the screen. For example if set to **1**, particles can be of a size up to the height of the screen, at **0.5** they can be up to half the height of the screen, and so on. As our fire particles will never need to be of a size as large as the screen height—we can leave this setting on its default of **0.25**.

Adding a material

Now that our particle system is set up, all that is left to do is to create a material for it using our fire texture. Select the **Fire feature** folder in the **Project** panel, and click on the **Create** button at the top of the panel, and choose **Material**. This will make a new asset called **New Material** in the folder—simply rename this **Flame**, and then select it to see its properties in the **Inspector**.

From the **Shader** drop–down menu, choose **Particles | Additive (soft)**. This will give us an alpha-based particle with a soft render of the texture we apply. Now, drag the texture called **Fire 1** from the **Fire Feature** folder in the **Project** panel, and drop it onto the empty square to the right of **Particle Texture** where it currently says **None (Texture2D)**.

To apply this material, simply drag the material from the **Fire feature** folder in the **Project** panel and drop it onto the **FireSystem** object in the **Hierarchy** panel.

Positioning the FireSystem

In order to position the fire particle system more easily, we'll need to make it a child of the **campfire** object already in our scene. In the **Hierarchy** panel, drag the **FireSystem** object, and drop it onto the parent object called **campfire** to make it a child object. Then reset its position by clicking on the **Cog** icon to the right of the **Transform** component of **FireSystem**, and choose **Reset**:

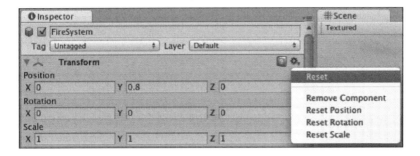

Now that you have reset the position, your particle system will be directly in the center of its parent object; as you'll notice, this is too low down. If you cannot see this, then select the object in the **Hierarchy** and hover your mouse cursor over the **Scene** view and press *F* to focus your view on it. Still in the **Transform** component, set the **Y** axis position to **0.8** to raise it slightly.

Time to Test!

Press the **Play** button to test the game now and admire your handiwork! Remember to press **Play** again to stop testing before you continue.

Making smoke

As the saying goes, "There's no smoke without fire", and vice versa. With this in mind, we'll need a smoke plume emerging from above our campfire, if it is to look realistic at all.

Begin by adding a new particle system to the Scene; go to **GameObject | Create Other | Particle System**. Rename the **Particle System** that you have just made in the Hierarchy to **SmokeSystem** (again, note that I am not using a space in this object name).

Ellipsoid Particle Emitter settings

As we have already discussed the implications of settings in the previous step, now you can simply use the following list and observe the changes as you make them. Any settings not listed should be left at their default setting:

- **Min Size: 0.8**
- **Max Size: 2.5**
- **Min Energy: 8**
- **Max Energy: 10**
- **Min Emission: 10**
- **Max Emission: 15**
- **World Velocity Y: 1.5**
- **Rnd Velocity Y: 0.2**
- **Emitter Velocity Scale: 0.1**

Particle Animator settings

Set up your particle animator to animate through shades of gray, as shown in the image below:

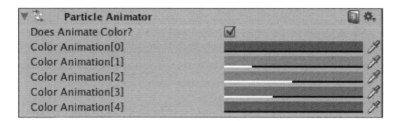

Again, here you should notice that particles should be animated between two zero-alphas so that they start and end invisibly. This will avoid a visual "pop" as the particles are removed—if they are visible when they are removed, the removal is a lot more noticeable, and less natural.

Now alter the following settings:

- **Size Grow**: 0.2
- **Rnd Force**: (1.2, 0.8, 1.2)
- **Force**: (0.1, 0 0.1)
- **Autodestruct**: Not selected

Particle Renderer settings

We will create a material to apply to the smoke shortly, but first, ensure that the following settings are applied to the particle renderer component:

- **Cast/Receive Shadows**: both deselected
- **Stretch Particles: Billboard**
- **Camera Velocity Scale, Length Scale, Velocity Scale: 0**
- **Max Particle Size: 0.25**

Now, follow the step titled **Adding a Material** under **Making fire** above. However, this time, name your material **Smoke** and assign the texture file called **smoke 1**, and drop the material you make onto the **SmokeSystem** game object.

Positioning

Repeat the step for positioning of the fire for the smoke system by dragging and dropping the **SmokeSystem** object onto the **campfire** parent in the **Hierarchy**. Then using the **Cog** icon, choose **Reset**, and set the **Y** position value to **0.9**. Press the **Play** button now and your campfire should light, and the smoke plume should rise, looking something like the following screenshot. As always, remember to press **Play** again to stop testing.

Adding audio to the fire

Now that our fire looks aesthetically pleasing, we'll need to add atmospheric sound of the fire crackling. In the package you downloaded, you are provided with a sound file called `fire_atmosphere`, which is a mono audio clip, which can be looped. Being mono, when we apply this file to an audio source, walking away from the fire will mean the audio will fade away with distance, which should make sense to the player.

Select the **campfire** object in the **Hierarchy**, and go to **Component | Audio | Audio Source**. This adds an audio source component to the object, so now simply drag the **fire_atmosphere** audio clip from the **Fire feature** folder in the **Project** panel, and drop it onto the **Audio Clip** parameter of the **Audio Source** in the **Inspector**. To finish, simply select the box next to the **Loop** parameter.

Press the **Play** button and approach the fire while listening for the sound of the fire crackling; then walk away, and listen to the fading effect.

Lighting the fire

Now that our fire is complete, let's switch off the particle systems and audio so that it is not lit at the start of the game.

- Select the **campfire** object in the **Hierarchy**, and in the **Audio Source** component in the **Inspector**, deselect the **Play On Awake** parameter.
- Select the **FireSystem** child object of the campfire, and in the **Particle Emitter** component, deselect the **Emit** parameter.
- Select the **SmokeSystem** child object of the campfire, and in the **Particle Emitter** component, deselect the **Emit** parameter.

Now we need to create the collection of matches and an interface display of the fact we have matches. To do this, we'll need to do the following:

- Add the **matchbox** model downloaded earlier to the outpost, making it the goal of gaining entry.
- Make a GUI Texture using a texture in the **Fire feature** folder, and save this as a prefab.
- Add to the existing **PlayerCollisions** script, building in collision detection for the matchbox in order to destroy it and instantiate the matchbox GUI prefab.

Adding the matches

Select the **matchbox** model in the **Fire feature** folder of the **Project** panel, drag this over to the **Hierarchy**, and drop it onto the **outpost** object, making it a child object. This will make it easier to position.

In the **Transform** component for the matchbox in the **Inspector**, set the **Position** values to (**0, 3.5, 0**). Now set all the values for **Scale** in the same component to **5**.

As we need to collect this object, it will need a collider in order to detect collisions between it and the player. With the **matchbox** still selected, go to **Component | Physics | Box Collider**, and click on **Add** when presented with the **Losing Prefab** dialog window. To avoid the player bumping into the object, we'll put this collider into trigger mode. To do this, simply select the box next to the **Is Trigger** setting in the **Box Collider** component of the **Inspector**.

To make this object more obviously a collectable item, we'll add the script we used to rotate the batteries in our game. Go to **Component | Scripts | Rotate Object**. Then, in the newly added script component in the **Inspector**, set the **Rotation Amount** variable to **2**.

Creating the Matches GUI

Select the **MatchGUI** texture file in the **Fire feature** folder in the **Project** panel. Go to **GameObject | Create Other | GUITexture**. We needn't position this texture on screen as this can be done when we instantiate it as a prefab.

Select the **Fire feature** folder in the **Project** panel, and from the **Create** button, select **Prefab**. Rename this prefab to **MatchGUIprefab** and then drag-and-drop the **MatchGUI** object from the **Hierarchy** onto this empty prefab in the **Project** panel.

Finally, select the original **MatchGUI** object in the **Hierarchy** again, and remove it from the scene by pressing *Command + Backspace* (Mac) or *Delete* (PC).

Collecting the matches

From the **Scripts** folder in the Project panel, open the script called **PlayerCollisions**. To remember whether we have collected the matches or not, we'll add a boolean variable to the script, which will be set to `true` once the matches are collected. Add the following line to the top of the script:

```
private var haveMatches : boolean = false;
```

We will also need a public member variable to represent the prefab of the Matches GUI Texture so that we can instantiate it when the player collects the matchbox. Add the following variable to the top of the script:

```
var matchGUI : GameObject;
```

Now scroll down to the `OnTriggerEnter()` function of the script, and beneath the existing one, add in the following `if` statement:

```
if(collisionInfo.gameObject.name == "matchbox"){
    Destroy(collisionInfo.gameObject);
    haveMatches=true;
    audio.PlayOneShot(batteryCollect);
    var matchGUIobj = Instantiate(matchGUI, Vector3(0.15,0.1,0),
transform.rotation);
        matchGUIobj.name = matchGUI;
}
```

Here we are checking our existing `collisionInfo` parameter, which registers any objects collided with. We are checking whether `collisionInfo` contains an object called `matchbox` by using `gameObject.name` and comparing it to the string of text `"matchbox"`. If this is the case, then we perform the following commands:

- Destroy the `matchbox` object, by referring to the current `gameObject` in `collisionInfo`.

- Set the `haveMatches` variable to `true`.

- Play an audio clip assigned to our `batteryCollect` variable. As the player is already used to this sound for collecting objects, it makes sense to re-use it.

- Instantiate an instance of the game object assigned to public member variable `matchGUI`, at screen position (0.15, 0.1, 0), bearing in mind that the z axis in 2D objects is simply for layering, hence the value of 0. We have also used the command `transform.rotation` to inherit rotation from the parent object as rotation is irrelevant in 2D objects.

- Name the newly instantiated object by using the variable `matchGUIobj`, which we create in the instantiation line. This will be used later when removing the GUI from the screen.

Go to **File | Save** in the script editor now and switch back to Unity. Press the **Play** button and ensure that upon entering the outpost, you can pick up the matches by walking into them. The texture of the matches should also appear in the lower left of the screen. Now we will use the `haveMatches` variable to decide whether the fire can be lit or not.

Setting fire

In order to light the fire at all, we need to check for collisions between the player and the campfire object. For this, return to the script editor to alter the **Player Collisions** script, or if you have closed it, re-open it from the **Scripts** folder of the **Project** panel.

Locate the `OnControllerColliderHit()` function opening line:

```
function OnControllerColliderHit(hit: ControllerColliderHit){
```

then move down to the line below it.

Add the following `if` statement:

```
if(hit.collider.gameObject == GameObject.Find("campfire")){


}
```

This will check that we have hit the **campfire** object. However, we need to perform another check as to whether the player is carrying matches, so inside that `if` statement, place the following:

```
if(haveMatches){
    haveMatches = false;
    lightFire();
}else{
    TextHints.textOn=true;
    TextHints.message = "I'll need some matches to light this
camp fire..";
}
```

Here we are checking if the `haveMatches` variable is set to `true`, and if not (`else`), we are using the `TextHints` script to switch on our `TextHint` GUI and display a suggestion to the player on screen.

If `haveMatches` is `true`, we are calling a function called `lightFire()`, which we will need to write next in order to switch on the audio and particle systems. Scroll to the bottom of the script, and add the following function before the `@script` line:

```
function lightFire(){
    var campfire : GameObject = GameObject.Find("campfire");
    var campSound : AudioSource = campfire.GetComponent(AudioSource);
        campSound.Play();

    var flames : GameObject = GameObject.Find("FireSystem");
```

```
    var flameEmitter : ParticleEmitter = flames.GetComponent(ParticleE
mitter);
        flameEmitter.emit = true;

    var smoke : GameObject = GameObject.Find("SmokeSystem");
    var smokeEmitter : ParticleEmitter = smoke.GetComponent(ParticleEm
itter);
        smokeEmitter.emit = true;

        Destroy(GameObject.Find("matchGUI"));
}
```

In this function, we had to perform four operations:

- Starting the audio loop for the fire
- Switching on the Fire particle system
- Switching on the Smoke particle system
- Removing the on screen Matches GUI to suggest that matches have been "used"

In the first three operations, we needed to address the object by creating a variable to represent it, for example:

```
var campfire : GameObject = GameObject.Find("campfire");
```

So here we've named the variable, set its data type to `GameObject`, and set it equal to a game object called `campfire` using the `Find` command.

Next we addressed the specific component of that object by using the variable just established, and the `GetComponent` command:

```
var campSound : AudioSource = campfire.GetComponent(AudioSource);
```

Again, we're establishing a new variable to represent the component, setting the data type to `AudioSource`, and finally we use this variable to call a command:

```
campSound.Play();
```

As the `Play` command is a specific command to `Audio Source` components, Unity knows exactly what to do and simply plays the sound clip assigned in the **Inspector**.

This approach is repeated in the second and third operation, except this time, we address the `emit` parameter of the **Particle Emitter** component, for example:

```
flameEmitter.emit = true;
```

The last operation in this function is the `Destroy()` command, which simply finds the GUI object displaying the matches, which is named `matchGUI` upon instantiation (refer to the **Collecting the matches** section).

Go to **File | Save** in the script editor now, and switch back to Unity.

As we have created a public member variable for the **MatchGUIprefab** in the **PlayerCollisions** script, it will need assigning. In the **Hierarchy**, collapse up any expanded parent objects by clicking on their gray arrow, then select the **First Person Controller** object to see its list of components in the **Inspector**.

Find the **Player Collisions (script)** component and then drag the **MatchGUIprefab** asset from the **Fire feature** folder in the **Project** panel, and drop it onto the unassigned public member variable called **Match GUI**.

Congratulations! Your fire lighting element is now complete. Go to **File | Save Scene** in Unity to ensure that your project is up to date.

Testing and confirming

As with any new feature of your game, testing is crucial. In Chapter 9, we'll look at optimizing your game and ensuring that test builds work as they are expected to, along with various options for delivering your game.

For now, you should ensure that your game functions properly so far. Even if you have no errors showing in the console part of Unity (*Command* + *Shift* + *C* shows this panel on Mac, *Ctrl* + *Shift* + *C* on PC), you should still make sure that as you play through the game, no errors occur as the player uses each part of the game.

Press the **Play** button and play through the battery collection, coconut shy game, match collection, and fire lighting to ensure that all elements currently work. If any errors occur, then refer back to your scripting and check that everything matches the code listings in this book.

If you encounter errors while testing, the **Pause** button at the top of the Unity editor will allow you to pause, play, and look at the error listed in the console. When encountering an error, simply double-click on it in the **Console**, and you'll be taken to the line of the script which contains the error—or at least to where the script encounters a problem.

From here, you can diagnose the error or check your script against the Unity scripting reference to make sure that you have the correct approach. If you are still stuck with errors, ask for help on the Unity community forums or in the IRC channel. For more information, visit the following page:

`http://unity3d.com/support/community`

Summary

In this chapter, we have looked at the use of particles to give a more dynamic feel to our game. Particles are used in a wide array of different game situations, from car and spaceship exhausts to guns and air-vent steam, and the best way to reinforce what we have just learned is to experiment. There are a lot of parameters to play with and, as such, the best results are found by taking some time out of a project just to see what kind of effects you can achieve.

In the next chapter, we will take a look at making menus for your game, and this will involve scripting with Unity's GUI class, as well as using GUI Skin assets to style and create behaviors for your interfaces. The GUI class is a specific part of the Unity engine, which is used specifically for making menus, HUDs (Heads Up Displays), and when used in conjunction with GUI Skin assets, becomes completely visually customizable and re-usable. This is because Skin assets can be applied to as many GUI class scripts as you like, creating a consistent design style throughout your Unity projects.

8
Menu Design

In order to create a rounded example game, in this chapter, we will look at creating a separate scene to our existing island scene to act as a menu. Menu design in Unity can be achieved in a number of ways using a combination of built-in behaviors and 2D texture rendering.

Game titles you introduce should be added using GUI Textures, such as a splash screen with developer logos or loading screen. However, when adding interactive menus, you need to consider two different approaches, one using GUI Textures—an area we've already explored when implementing our Matches GUI in the previous chapter and the crosshair in Chapter 6, and the other utilizing UnityGUI classes, incorporating GUI skin assets.

In this chapter, you will learn the following:

- Creation of two different approaches to interface design
- Control of GUI Texture components with scripted mouse events
- Writing a basic UnityGUI script
- Settings for GUI skin assets
- Loading scenes to navigate menus and loading the game level

We will learn two approaches for adding interactive menus:

- **Approach 1**: GUI Textures and mouse event scripting

  The first approach will involve creating GUI Texture objects, and with scripting based on mouse events—mouse over, mouse down, and mouse up—for example, swapping the textures used by these objects. With this approach, less scripting is required to create the buttons themselves, but all actions must be controlled and listened to through scripts.

- **Approach 2**: UnityGUI class scripting and GUI skins

  The second approach will take a more script-intensive methodology and involve generating our entire menu using scripts, as opposed to creating individual game objects for menu items in approach 1.

  With this approach, more scripting is required to create menu elements initially, but GUI skin assets can be created to style the appearance and assign behavior through the **Inspector** for mouse events.

The latter approach is generally the more accepted method of creating full game menus, as it gives the developer more flexibility. The menu items themselves are established in the script, but styled using GUI skins in an approach comparable to HTML and CSS development in web design—the **CSS** (**Cascading Style Sheets**) controlling the form with the HTML providing the content.

While working with GUI skins, you'll also notice a few conventions of CSS cropping up, such as margins, padding, and justification. This will be helpful if you have any experience of web development, but do not worry if this is not the case—GUI skin settings are designed, like most Unity features, to require minimal prior knowledge.

Interfaces and menus

Menus are most commonly used to set up controls and to adjust game settings, such as graphics and sound, or to load saved game states. In any given game, it is crucial that the accompanying menu does not hinder access to the game or any of its settings. When we think of a great game, we always remember it for the actual game itself, rather than the menus—unless they were especially entertaining, or especially badly designed.

Many games seek to tie the menu of their game with the game's design or themes. For example, in 2D Boy's excellent *World Of Goo*, the cursor is changed to the form of a goo ball with a trail that follows it in the menus and game, tying the game's visual concept with the game interface. This is a good example, as the game itself is already giving the player something to toy with as they navigate through the opening menu.

In Media Molecule's *LittleBigPlanet*, this concept is taken to another level by giving the player a menu that requires them to learn how to control the player character before they navigate through the game menu.

As with any design, consistency is the key, and in our example, we'll be ensuring that we maintain a set of house colors and consistent use of typography. You may have encountered poorly designed games in the past and noticed that they use too many fonts, or clashing colors, which—given that the game menu is the first thing a player will see—is a terribly off-putting factor in making the game enjoyable and commercially viable.

The textures to be used in the menu creation are available in the code bundle provided on packtpub.com (`www.packtpub.com/files/code/8181_Code.zip`). Locate the file called `Menu.unitypackage` from the extracted files and then return to Unity. Go to **Assets | Import package**, and introduce the assets by browsing and choosing the package you have extracted.

Post import, you should see that you have added a folder called **Menu** to the **Project** panel. In this folder, you will find the following:

- Textures for a main game title and three buttons—**Play**, **Instructions**, and **Quit**
- An audio clip of an interface beep for the buttons

Making the main menu

In this section, we'll take our existing design work of the island itself and use it as a backdrop for our menus. This gives players a sneak preview of the kind of environment they'll be exploring and sets a visual context for the game.

By duplicating our existing island, viewed from a distance using a remote camera, we'll overlay 2D interface elements using the two previously mentioned approaches.

Creating the scene

For our menu, we'll aim to make use of the island environment we've already created. By placing the island in the background of our menu, we're effectively teasing the player with the environment they can explore, if they start playing the game. Visual incentives such as these might seem minor, but they can work well as a way of subliminally encouraging the player to try the game.

Visual example

Here is what our menu will look like when it is complete. This example is taken from approach 1; approach 2's menu items will look different:

Duplicating the island

To begin, we'll reuse our **Island Level** scene that we have created so far. To make things easier to manage, we'll group together the essential environment assets to keep them separate from objects we don't need, such as the outpost and batteries. This way, when it comes to duplicating the level, we can simply remove everything but the group we are about to make. Grouping in Unity is as easy as nesting objects as children under an empty parent object.

Grouping the environment objects

- Go to **Game Object | Create Empty**.
- This makes a new object called simply **GameObject**, so rename this as **Environment** now.
- In the **Hierarchy** panel, drag-and-drop the **Directional Light**, **Daylight**, **Simple Water**, and **Terrain** objects onto the **Environment** empty object. Now we are ready to duplicate this level to create our menu in a separate scene.

Duplicating the scene

Follow these steps to duplicate the scene:

1. Ensure that the **Island Level** scene is saved by going to **File | Save Scene**, and then select the **Island Level** asset in the **Project** panel.

2. Go to **Edit | Duplicate**, or use keyboard shortcut *Command + D* (Mac) or *Ctrl + D* (PC). When duplicating, Unity simply increments object/asset names with a number, so your duplicate will be named **Island Level 1**—ensure that the duplicate is selected in the **Project** panel and rename this to **Menu** now.

3. Load this scene to begin working on it by double-clicking on it in the **Project** panel.

4. With the **Menu** scene open, we can now remove any objects we do not need. If you are on a Mac, then hold down the *Command* key, or if on PC, then hold down the *Ctrl* key and select all objects in the **Hierarchy** except for the **Environment** group by clicking on them one-by-one.

5. Now delete them from this scene by using keyboard shortcuts *Command + Backspace* on Mac, or *Shift + Delete* on PC.

As shown in the previous screenshot, our menu will be a shot of the island from afar—positioned in the lower-right of the screen, with the title and menu superimposed over the top in empty space, such as the sky and the sea. To achieve this, we will need to introduce a new camera to the scene, as previously the only camera was the one attached to the **First Person Controller**. As there is currently no camera in the scene, the **Game** view should now be completely blank, as there is no viewport on our 3D world.

To create a camera, go to **GameObject | Create Other | Camera**. Ensuring that this new **Camera** object is selected in the **Hierarchy**, enter the following **Position** into the **Transform** component in the **Inspector**—**(150, 250, -650)**.

Cancelling mip mapping

Mip mapping is a way of generating smaller versions of textures to save performance when they are viewed from afar in a game engine. This can improve performance by up to 33 percent in the Unity engine. However, this applies only to textures that are part of the 3D world—not those used as 2D textures such as those we are about to use for our title and three menu buttons. We need to switch off this feature in the **Import** settings for each asset.

Begin by selecting the **MainTitle** texture file inside the **Menu** folder in the **Project** panel. You will now see the **Import** settings for this texture in the **Inspector**, so simply deselect the checkbox for **Generate Mip Maps**. This saves performance because Unity will no longer generate smaller versions at runtime.

Repeat this step for the other textures inside the **Menu** folder:

- **InstructionsBtn**
- **InstructionsBtnOver**
- **PlayBtn**
- **PlayBtnOver**
- **QuitBtn**
- **QuitBtnOver**

Adding titling

Next we need a logo for our game. The easiest way to add this is with a texture you have designed, which is set up in Unity as a GUI Texture.

GUI Texture formats

In the **Project** panel's **Menu** folder, select the texture named **MainTitle**. This texture, designed in Photoshop, is saved as a **TIFF** (**Tagged Image File Format**). This is a good format to use for any textures you intend to use as a GUI Texture. It provides high quality uncompressed transparency and can avoid some problems with white outlines, which you may see when using other formats, such as **GIF** (**Graphics Interchange Format**) or **PNG** (**Portable Network Graphics**).

Object creation

With this texture selected, create a new GUI Texture-based object by going to **GameObject | Create Other | GUI Texture**. This automatically reads the dimensions of the selected texture and sets it as the texture to use in the new object, as discussed previously. You will now find an object called **MainTitle** in the **Hierarchy**, as the object would have taken the name from the file you had selected during its creation.

Positioning

As most computers nowadays can handle resolutions at or above 1024x768 pixels, we'll choose this as a standard to test our menu and ensure that it works in other resolutions by using the `Screen` class to ascertain dynamic positions. In the upper-left of the **Game** view, you'll see a drop-down menu (refer to the next screenshot). This menu will allow you to specify different screen ratios or resolutions. From this drop-down menu, select **Standalone (1024x768)** to switch to a preview of that size.

Bear in mind that if your own computer's resolution is running close to this size, then the **Game** view will not show an accurate representation of this, as it may make up a smaller part of the Unity interface.

To toggle the **Game** view (and any of the interface panels) into fullscreen mode, you can hover over it with the mouse and tap the *Space* bar. As we position GUI elements in this chapter, use this method to preview what the interface will look like in the finished game.

By default, all GUI Textures begin with their position at (0.5, 0.5, 0), which—given that 2D elements work in screen coordinates from 0 to 1—is in the middle of the screen.

In the **Transform** component for the **MainTitle** object in the **Hierarchy**, set the position to **(0.5, 0.8, 0)**. This places the logo in the upper-center of the screen. Now that we have added the main title logo of the game, we'll need to add three buttons using further GUI Texture objects.

Creating the menu—approach 1

In this first approach, we'll create a menu that uses a transparent background texture as a GUI Texture, in the same way as we have just done with our main title logo.

We will then need to write a script in order to make the texture receive mouse events for mouse enter, mouse exit, and mouse down/up.

Adding the play button

In the **Menu** folder in the **Project** panel, select the texture called **PlayBtn**. Go to **GameObject | Create Other | GUI Texture**. Select the **PlayBtn** object in the **Hierarchy** that you have just made. In the **Inspector**, set its **Transform** position to (**0.5, 0.6, 0**).

GUI Texture button script

This is the first of our three buttons, and because they all have common functions, we will now write a script that can be used on all of the three buttons, using public member variables to adjust settings. For example, each button will:

- Play a sound when clicked on
- Load a different level (or **Scene** in Unity terms) when clicked on
- Swap texture when the mouse is over them to highlight them

Select the **Scripts** folder in the **Project** panel, and from the **Create** button drop-down menu, select **JavaScript**. Rename the **NewBehaviorScript** to **MainMenuBtns**, and then double-click its icon to launch it in the script editor.

Begin by establishing four public member variables at the top of the script, as shown in the following code snippet:

```
var levelToLoad : String;
var normalTexture : Texture2D;
var rollOverTexture : Texture2D;
var beep : AudioClip;
```

The first variable we will use to store the name of the level to be loaded when the button this script is applied to is clicked. By placing this information into a variable, we are able to apply this script to all three buttons, and simply use the variable name to load the level.

The second and third variables are declared as `Texture2D` type variables, but not set to a specific asset so that the textures can be assigned using drag-and-drop in the **Inspector**.

Finally, an `AudioClip` type variable is established, which will be played when the mouse is clicked.

Now add the following function to set the texture used by the GUI Texture component when the mouse enters the area that the texture occupies. This is usually referred to as a hover or rollover state:

```
function OnMouseEnter(){
  guiTexture.texture = rollOverTexture;
}
```

In the Menu pack that you imported, you are provided with a normal and over state for each button texture. This first OnMouseEnter() function simply sets the texture field used by the component to whatever has been assigned to the public member variable rollOverTexture in the **Inspector**. In order to know when the mouse moves away or exits the boundary of this texture, add the following function:

```
function OnMouseExit(){
  guiTexture.texture = normalTexture;
}
```

If this was not present, the rollOverTexture would simply stay on—appearing to the player as if that specific menu option was still highlighted.

Now, to handle the sound and loading of the appropriate scene, add the following function:

```
function OnMouseUp(){
  audio.PlayOneShot(beep);
  yield new WaitForSeconds(0.35);
  Application.LoadLevel(levelToLoad);
}
```

We are playing the sound as the first command to ensure that it plays before the next scene is loaded, and that it is not cut off. By placing a yield command in between the script for playing the sound and loading the next scene, we are able to halt the script for the defined number of seconds. Using yields in scripting is a quick way of creating a delay without having to write a timer.

Here we are simply creating a delay with a yield, but they can also be used to carry out an entire set of instructions before carrying out the next line of code. This is known as a **coroutine**, as **routine** is a blanket term for the instructions being carried out in programming terms.

After the yield, our game will load the scene using the Application.LoadLevel() command, taking whatever text we write into the levelToLoad public member variable in the **Inspector** and using that to find the relevant scene file.

 When creating interfaces, it is usually advised to place actions into a mouse up event, rather than a mouse down event. This gives the player a chance to move their cursor away if they have selected the wrong item.

Finally, as we are playing a sound, ensure that your object has an `AudioSource` component by adding the following `RequireComponent` line to the bottom of your script:

```
@script RequireComponent (AudioSource)
```

Go to **File | Save** in the script editor and return to Unity now. Select the **PlayBtn** object in the **Hierarchy**, and go to **Component | Scripts | Main Menu Btns** to apply the script you have just written. It should then appear in the **Inspector** list of components for the **PlayBtn** object. As a result of the `RequireComponent` line, you will also have an **Audio Source** component on your object.

Assigning public member variables

As you will see, the public member variables will need to be assigned before this script can function. In the **Level To Load** variable, type in the name **Island Level** in order to ensure that it is loaded when the button is clicked on. Then drag the **PlayBtn** and **PlayBtnOver** textures from the **Menu** folder in the **Project** panel to the **Normal Texture** and **Roll Over Texture** variables respectively. Finally, drag the **menu_beep** audio clip from the same folder to the **Beep** variable. When finished, your component should look like this:

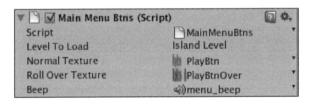

Testing the button

Now press the **Play** button to test the scene. When you move your mouse cursor over the **Play Game** button, it should swap texture to the **PlayBtnOver** texture, which is colored and has a flame motif to the right. When moving the cursor away from the texture, it should switch back.

Now try clicking the button. At the bottom of the screen, you will see an error in the console, which is the bar at the bottom of the screen saying:

Level Island Level couldn't be loaded because it is not added to the build settings.

This is Unity's way of ensuring that you do not forget to add all included levels to the **Build Settings**. Build settings are effectively the export settings of your game (in game development terms, a finished or test product is referred to as a build). The build settings in Unity must list all scenes included in your game. To rectify this, make sure you press **Play** to stop testing the game, and then go to **File | Build Settings**.

With the **Build Settings** panel open, beneath the **Scenes to build** section, click on the **Add Current** button to add the Menu scene we are working on. Scenes in the build settings list have an order, represented by the number to the right of the scene name, and you should make sure that the first scene you need to load is always in position **0**.

Drag-and-drop the **Island Level** from the **Project** panel, and drop it onto the current list of scenes so that it is listed beneath **Menu.unity**, as shown in the following screenshot:

Be aware that there is no confirmation or save settings button on the **Build Settings** dialog, so simply close it and then retest the game. Press **Play** in Unity and then try clicking on your **Play Game** button—the **Island Level** should load after the **menu_beep** sound effect is played. Now press **Play** again to stop testing, and you will return to the **Menu** scene.

Adding the instructions button

To add the second button in our menu, simply select the **InstructionsBtn** texture in the **Menu** folder in the **Project** panel, and go to **GameObject | Create Other | GUI Texture**. This creates an object also called **InstructionsBtn** in the **Hierarchy**. In the **Transform** component of this object, set the **Position** values to **(0.5, 0.5, 0)**.

As the scripting is already done, simply go to **Component | Scripts | Main Menu Btns** to add the script to this button, and then assign the appropriate textures and **menu_beep** in the same manner as we did in the *Assigning public member variables* section previously. As we have not made the instructions scene in Unity yet, simply fill in the name **Instructions** in the `levelToLoad` variable, and we will ensure that our scene is named this later.

Adding the quit button

This button works in a similar manner to the first two, but does not load a scene. Instead it calls upon the build's **Application** class, using the **Quit()** command to terminate the game as an application so that your operating system closes it down.

This means that we'll need to modify our `MainMenuBtns` script to account for this change. Double-click this script in the **Scripts** folder of the **Project** panel to launch it in the script editor.

Begin by adding the following boolean public member variable to the top of the script:

```
var QuitButton : boolean = false;
```

This we will use as a toggle—if it is set to `true`, then it will cause the click of the button —the `OnMouseUp()` function—to run the `quit()` command. If it is `false` (that is, its default state), then it will load the level applied to the `levelToLoad` variable as normal.

To implement this, restructure your `OnMouseUp()` function with an `if else` statement, as shown in the following code snippet:

```
function OnMouseUp(){
  audio.PlayOneShot(beep);
  yield new WaitForSeconds(0.35);
  if(QuitButton){
    Application.Quit();
  }
  else{
    Application.LoadLevel(levelToLoad);
  }
}
```

Here we have simply modified the function to play the sound and pause (`yield`), regardless of what kind of button this is. However, we have to choose between two options—if `QuitButton` is `true`, then the `Application.Quit()` command is called, otherwise (`else`), the level is loaded as normal.

Go to **File | Save** in the script editor, and switch back to Unity.

Select the **QuitBtn** texture in the **Menu** folder in the **Project** panel, and go to **GameObject | Create Other | GUI Texture**. This creates an object called **QuitBtn** in the **Hierarchy**. In the **Transform** component for this object, set the **Position** values to (**0.5, 0.4, 0**).

With **QuitBtn** still selected in the **Hierarchy**, go to **Component | Scripts | Main Menu Btns** to add the script. In the **Inspector**, fill in the public member variables as before, but this time leave **Level To Load** blank, and select the box next to the newly added **Quit Button** variable.

To double-check your script, here it is in full:

```
var levelToLoad : String;
var normalTexture : Texture2D;
var rollOverTexture : Texture2D;
var beep : AudioClip;
var QuitButton : boolean = false;
function OnMouseEnter(){
  guiTexture.texture = rollOverTexture;
}
function OnMouseExit(){
  guiTexture.texture = normalTexture;
}
function OnMouseUp(){
  audio.PlayOneShot(beep);
  yield new WaitForSeconds(0.35);
  if(QuitButton){
    Application.Quit();
  }
  else{
    Application.LoadLevel(levelToLoad);
  }
}
@script RequireComponent(AudioSource)
```

Now go to **File | Save Scene** to update the project, and then press **Play** to test the menu. Pressing the **Play Game** menu button should load the Island Level. The **Instructions** button will cause the 'level could not be loaded' error we saw previously, as we have not created it yet. The **Quit Game** button will not cause an error but will also not preview in the Unity editor, so we will not be able to test this until we create a build later.

Remember to press **Play** again to finish testing. As the first approach at making a menu creation is now complete, we'll now take a look at another method of creating a functional menu in Unity, using the **OnGUI()** function, referred to in Unity as part of the GUI 2.0 system because it was introduced with Unity version 2.0.

Using debug commands to check scripts

Despite the `Application.Quit()` command not previewing in the Unity Editor, we should ensure that the **Quit** button does work, rather than assuming that this is the case. In order to test any part of a script, you can simply place in a debug command. This will send a message to the console part of Unity, which is previewed at the bottom of the interface.

Let's try this out now. Return to your **MainMenuBtns** script in the script editor, and locate the `QuitButton` part of the code:

```
if(QuitButton){
   Application.Quit();
}
```

A debug read-out can be logged in a list with others of its kind along with errors in the console. They normally look like this:

```
Debug.Log("This part works!");
```

By writing this line of code to where you expect the script to execute, you can discover whether or not particular parts of your script are working. In our example, we would place this command after the `Application.Quit()`, as this would prove that the command had been executed without a problem. Add this in so that it looks like the following code snippet:

```
if(QuitButton){
   Application.Quit();
   Debug.Log("This part works!");
}
```

Save the script by going to **File | Save** in the script editor, and return to Unity. Now test your menu scene again by pressing the **Play** button, and you will see the debug command printing at the bottom of the Unity interface. If you open the **Console** part of Unity (*Command + Shift + C* on Mac, *Ctrl+Shift + C* on PC), then you'll see this listed there also, as shown in the following screenshot:

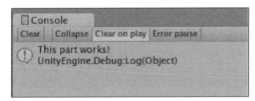

This technique can prove very useful when diagnosing script issues or even when designing parts of a theoretical script for which you don't have commands to fill out yet.

Creating the menu—approach 2

As we already have a working menu, rather than removing it from our scene, we will temporarily disable the objects that make it up. By doing this, you can choose which menu you prefer later and reinstate as necessary.

Disabling Game Objects

One at a time, select the **PlayBtn**, the **InstructionsBtn**, and the **QuitBtn** in the **Hierarchy**, and deactivate them by doing the following:

- In the **Inspector**, deselect the checkbox to the left of the name of the object
- Ensure that this has turned the text of the object to light gray in the **Hierarchy** and that the element itself has disappeared from the **Game** view preview

Writing an OnGUI() script for a simple menu

Now, create a new empty object by going to **GameObject** | **Create Empty**. This makes a new object in the **Hierarchy** called **GameObject** with only a **Transform** component attached. This will be the holder object for our GUI 2.0 menu. This is because the script we are going to write will need to be attached as a component in order to function. It makes sense to have an object dedicated to it for the sake of organization.

As the position of OnGUI elements is handled through scripting, the transform position of this object is irrelevant, so we will not need to adjust this. Simply rename the object from its default name to **Menu2** in the usual manner.

Select the **Scripts** folder in the **Project** panel and click on the **Create** button, choosing **JavaScript** as the type of asset to create. Rename this script to **MainMenuGUI2** and then double-click its icon to launch it in the script editor.

Fixed versus layout

For this example, we'll be using Unity's GUI Layout class, something that is more flexible for positioning as opposed to the GUI class, which has a fixed layout.

GUI Layout is favored by many developers as it automatically positions elements, such as forms and buttons, below one another. It allows the developer to spend more time styling their layout with a GUI skin asset, which when applied to an `OnGUI()` script, functions in a similar way to stylesheets for web design.

Public member variables

Begin your script by establishing four public member variables:

```
var beep : AudioClip;
var menuSkin : GUISkin;
var areaWidth : float;
var areaHeight : float;
```

Here we're creating the same beep audio clip as seen in our first approach script, then a slot for a GUI skin to be applied and two numerical variables, which we can use to define the overall size of our GUI's area.

The OnGUI() function

Next, establish the following function in your script:

```
function OnGUI(){
  GUI.skin = menuSkin;
}
```

This establishes the `OnGUI()` function, and sets up some crucial elements. First we apply the skin asset represented by the `menuSkin` variable. This means that any GUI elements placed into this function, such as buttons, forms, and so on will be governed by the style of the skin applied to this variable. This makes it easy to swap out skins, and thus completely restyle your GUIs in one go.

Flexible positioning for GUIs

Next we need to establish an area for the buttons that we need to be drawn in. We already have `areaWidth` and `areaHeight` variables waiting to be used, but we need to make sure that the area where we draw the rectangular space for our GUI is going to be flexible, depending upon what screen resolution the game is being run at.

If we did not do this and gave specific measurements, then the GUI would look different on different resolutions and would seem unprofessional. To counter this, we will create some private variables within our `OnGUI()` function, which will store a center point on the screen. We need not use the `private` prefix as we are establishing the variables inside the function. Therefore, they are inherently private.

After the `GUI.skin` line you just added, establish the following two variables:

```
var ScreenX = ((Screen.width * 0.5) - (areaWidth * 0.5));
var ScreenY = ((Screen.height * 0.5) - (areaHeight * 0.5));
```

Here we are creating two variables that are equal to a sum. The sum itself has two parts:

```
((Screen.width * 0.5) - (areaWidth * 0.5));
```

In the above line, `(Screen.width * 0.5)` uses the `Screen` class's `width` parameter to acquire the current width of the game screen. We divide this by two to find the center point.

 Note that here we are replacing "/2" with `* 0.5`. This is because multiplication requires fewer CPU cycles than division—around 100—when finding values in Unity.

We then see `(areaWidth * 0.5)`, which takes our GUI area's width and finds the center point of that by dividing by two. So why do we subtract this from the center point of the screen? This is because GUI areas are always drawn from their lefthand edge, so finding the center point of the screen and drawing from there would have resulted in an off-center rendering, as shown in the following image:

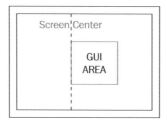

By subtracting half of the width of the GUI area, we will achieve a central position, as shown in the following image:

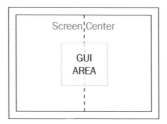

The two parts of the sum are placed within their own brackets so that they are treated as a single sum, which the variable receives as a value. We then repeat this process for a second variable, `ScreenY`, to get the vertical position for our GUI area.

Areas are crucial for GUILayout — without them OnGUI () assumes that you wish to draw a menu using the entire screen space, starting from the top-left. By establishing an area with BeginArea(), we are able to specify four parameters:

```
GUILayout.BeginArea(Rect( distance from left of screen, distance
    from top of screen, width, height ));
```

The Rect() command simply establishes a rectangular area for the BeginArea() command to use, so by using private variables ScreenX and ScreenY, we will be able to provide a position for the rectangular area to be drawn. For the width and height, we will use the public member variables established at the top of the script.

Let's add this code to our OnGUI() function now beneath the two private variables you just established:

```
GUILayout.BeginArea (Rect (ScreenX,ScreenY, areaWidth,
    areaHeight));
```

The area must also be closed with an EndArea() command. As this closes our area, the rest of our GUI code must be placed before this line in the function. Add the following line to close the GUI area and then move this line down so that you have space to write in the code before it:

```
GUILayout.EndArea();
```

Adding UnityGUI buttons

Before the EndArea() line, add the following lines to establish the first button:

```
if(GUILayout.Button ("Play")){
  OpenLevel("Island Level");
}
```

This establishes a new GUILayout.Button with the word **Play** on it. By placing this into an if statement, we are not only creating it, but telling Unity what to do when the button is pressed. The instruction we are giving it is to call a custom function named OpenLevel() with a single parameter — our level name. We will write the OpenLevel() function after finishing the OnGUI() function.

Next, add the following two if statements to create the other two buttons:

```
if(GUILayout.Button ("Instructions")){
  OpenLevel("Instructions");
}
if(GUILayout.Button ("Quit")){
  Application.Quit();
}
```

With the second `if` statement button we are calling the same custom `OpenLevel()` function, but this time we are sending a different string to its only parameter—the name of the still-to-be-created `Instructions` level.

The third `if` statement button does not load a level, but simply calls the `Application.Quit()` command instead, as seen in our approach 1 GUI.

Opening scenes with custom functions

Now, we need to write a custom function that can be called to load a specified level. Beneath the closing right curly brace of the `OnGUI()` function, establish the function as follows:

```
function OpenLevel(level : String){
}
```

Here we are creating a function with a parameter called `level`, which is given the data type of `String`—meaning that as long as we pass a string of text to it when calling the function, we can use the word level to represent whatever text is passed to it. In the `OnGUI()` function, we just added this call:

```
OpenLevel("Island Level");
```

In this example the words `"Island Level"` are being passed to the `level` parameter of the `OpenLevel()` function. Note that we do not need to say `level = "Island Level"` as it automatically knows to apply this text to the parameter it finds in the `OpenLevel()` function. If we did not include the correct data type here, for example passing a number or a variable name, we would receive an error, as this would not be appropriate for our `level` parameter.

As a result of using this parameter to send a string of text to, wherever the level parameter is used, the code will read in the string sent to it.

Now within this function, place the following three commands:

```
audio.PlayOneShot(beep);
yield new WaitForSeconds(0.35);
Application.LoadLevel(level);
```

We have used these commands in approach 1. Refer to them if you need to, but the key difference to note here is our use of the `level` parameter to pass the string into `Application.LoadLevel()`. To complete the script, ensure that our sound file will play by adding the usual `RequireComponent` line at the bottom of the script:

```
@script RequireComponent(AudioSource)
```

Go to **File** | **Save** in the script editor now, and switch back to Unity.

To double-check your script, here it is in full:

```
var beep : AudioClip;
var menuSkin : GUISkin;
var areaWidth : float;
var areaHeight : float;
function OnGUI(){
  GUI.skin = menuSkin;
  var ScreenX = ((Screen.width * 0.5) - (areaWidth * 0.5));
  var ScreenY = ((Screen.height * 0.5) - (areaHeight * 0.5));
  GUILayout.BeginArea (Rect (ScreenX,ScreenY, areaWidth,
    areaHeight));
  if(GUILayout.Button ("Play")){
    OpenLevel("Island Level");
  }
  if(GUILayout.Button ("Instructions")){
    OpenLevel("Instructions");
  }
  if(GUILayout.Button ("Quit")){
    Application.Quit();
  }
  GUILayout.EndArea();
}
function OpenLevel(level : String){
  audio.PlayOneShot(beep);
  yield new WaitForSeconds(0.35);
  Application.LoadLevel(level);
}
@script RequireComponent(AudioSource)
```

Applying and styling

Back in Unity, select your empty game object **Menu2** in the **Hierarchy** panel. Go to **Component** | **Scripts** | **Main Menu GUI2** to add the script to your object.

Drag the **menu_beep** audio clip from the **Menu** folder in the **Project** panel to the **Beep** public member variable in this script in order to assign it. Now fill in **Area Width** and **Area Height** with a value of **200**.

Press the **Play** button to view the menu. Because the GUI class is compiled from a script, it will only render when the game is tested. Currently the menu we have created through script looks a little dull, as shown in the following screenshot:

So we will need to apply a style to it to make it look a little neater, which is where **GUI skins** come in.

The menuSkin variable needs to have a GUI skin asset assigning to it, so we must create one now. Select the Menu folder in the **Project** panel, and then click on the **Create** button at the top of the **Project** panel. From the drop-down menu, select **GUI Skin**. This makes a new asset called **New GUISkin**, simply rename this to **MainMenu**.

GUI skin settings

GUI skins offer settings for every element in the GUI class:

- Boxes
- Buttons
- Toggles
- Labels
- Text fields and areas
- Sliders, scrollbars, and scrollviews

The first parameter—**Font**—is universal to all elements governed by the skin. So, begin by taking the font you introduced to the game (which was **Sugo**, if you followed what I did), and drop it from the **Project** panel onto this parameter.

We will be using this skin to style button elements. Ensure that you have the **Button** section of the **GUISkin** expanded in the **Inspector** by clicking on the gray arrow to the left of it so that you can see its settings, as shown in the following screenshot:

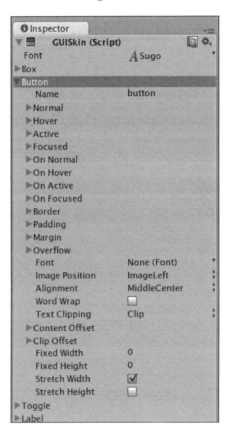

Expand **Normal**, **Hover**, and **Active** so that you can see the **Background** and **Text Color** of each, as shown in the next screenshot. The **Background** parameter sets a texture for the background of the button—by default, Unity provides a professional looking rounded-edge graphic with highlighted states for **Hover** and **Active**. We will stick with these for this book. However, when creating a menu for your own games, this is definitely something you should experiment with. For now, click on each **Text Color** block, and use the color picker that appears to choose a color for the **Normal**, **Hover**, and **Active** (mouse pressed down) states of the button:

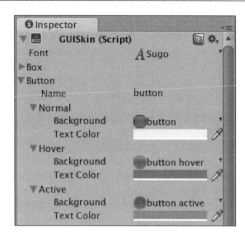

Next, expand the settings for **Padding** and set the **Top** and **Bottom** values both to **6**. This will give us more room inside the button above and below the text itself, just like padding does in CSS.

To keep our buttons spaced vertically further apart, we'll need to increase the bottom margin. Expand the **Margin** parameter, and set the **Bottom** value to **10**.

We have now made the adjustments to the skin and are ready to apply it to our GUI script. Select the **Menu2** object in the **Hierarchy** panel, and in the **Main Menu GUI2** script component, assign the **Menu Skin** public member variable by dragging and dropping the **MainMenu** skin you have just made from the **Project** panel to the variable slot.

Now test that your skin is applied by pressing the **Play** button to see the GUI script render. It should look like this:

This looks more professional. As we have used the game's main font, it ties in better with the game logo. The finished fullscreen should now look like this:

Press the **Play** button again to stop testing the game, and go to **File** | **Save scene** in Unity.

Decision time

Now it's your turn to take some creative control! Choose the approach whose look you prefer. Based on what you learned in the *Disabling game objects* section previously, either keep the second approach and leave the three GUI Texture game objects disabled, or disable **Menu2** and reinstate them using the checkboxes at the top of the **Inspector**.

However, it is recommended that you continue to work with the second approach, using UnityGUI, as it has many uses in addition to simple menus—providing statistics presentation during testing, for example, or building settings for the player to adjust. These more advanced topics are something you're likely to encounter when you progress from this book.

Summary

In this chapter, we have looked at the two core ways of creating interface elements in Unity—GUI scripting and GUI Textures. By now you should have a good understanding of how to implement either approach to build interfaces. While there are many more things you can do with GUI scripting, the techniques for establishing elements that we have covered here are the essentials you'll need each time you write a GUI script.

We are still to produce the **Instructions** scene containing information for the player, but don't worry, we'll be creating this as we look at some new techniques for animation in the next chapter, among other finishing touches for the game itself.

9
Finishing Touches

In this chapter, we will take our game from a simple example to something we can deploy, by adding some finishing touches to the island. As we have looked at various new skills throughout this book, we have added a single example at a time. In this chapter, we'll reinforce some of the skills we have learned so far, and also look in more detail at some final effects that we can add that aren't crucial to the gameplay—which is why it is best to leave them until the end of the development cycle.

When building any game, mechanics are crucial—the physical working elements of the game must be in place before additional artwork and environmental flair can be introduced. As in most cases, when building a game, deadlines will be set either by yourself, as part of an independent developer discipline, or by a publisher you are working for. By keeping the finishing touches at the end of the development cycle, you'll ensure that you have not lost any time working on getting the most important element—gameplay—just right.

For the purposes of the book, we'll assume that our game mechanics are complete and working as expected. Now, turn to what we can add to our island environment and game in general to add some finishing flair.

For this, we'll be adding the following to our game in this chapter:

- A particle system inside the volcano part of the terrain
- Proximity-based sound of the volcano rumbling
- Light trails for our coconut shy minigame to show coconut trajectory
- Fog to add realism to the line of sight
- An animated **Instructions** scene to explain the goal of the game to the player
- Fade-in transition for the **Island Level** using a GUI Texture and Alpha scripting
- A game win message to the player

We'll finish by building and looking at different issues for testing your game, as well as opportunities for taking your game to the market via independent developer channels.

First, let's get started with our finishing touches by making our volcano more dynamic.

Volcano!

For this next step, ensure that you have the **Island Level** scene open in Unity. If you have not, then open it now either by double-clicking on the **Scene** file in the **Project** panel, or by going to **File | Open Scene** and then selecting it from the **Assets** folder. Scene files are easy to spot, as they use the same icon as the Unity editor itself—the Unity logo.

In Chapter 2, we built an island terrain with the terrain editor, including a corner of the island dedicated to a volcano mouth. To make this volcano seem a little more realistic, we'll add a plume of smoke and a mono-clip audio source to create a proximity-based sound of the volcano bubbling with molten lava. By adding both the audio and visual element, we'll hopefully achieve a more dynamic and realistic feel to the island and maintain player immersion in our game.

Begin by creating a new particle system in Unity by going to **GameObject | Create Other | Particle System**. This creates a new particle system called **Particle System** in the **Hierarchy**. Ensure that this is selected now, and rename it **Volcano Particles**.

Positioning the particle system

As our volcano is simply part of the terrain object itself and not an independent object, positioning our particles in relative terms is not possible in the usual manner. Ordinarily, to relatively position an object, we would make the new object a child of the object we wish it to be near and reset its local position to (0, 0, 0).

In this instance however, we'll need to take advantage of the **Scene** panel's view gizmo. Begin by clicking on the **Y-axis** (green handle) of the gizmo to change from a perspective view to a top-down or bird's eye view of the island. If done correctly, the gizmo then shows the word **Top** beneath it:

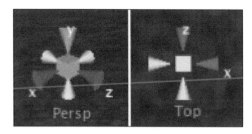

Then to see where your particle system is located, ensure it is selected in the **Hierarchy** panel, and then select the **Transform** tool (Shortcut key: *W*) to see its axes in the Scene.

As the new particle system will be created in the center of your current **Scene** view, we'll need to reposition it inside the volcano using this **Top** view. Make sure you can see both the particle system's axes and the volcano itself—you may simply need to zoom out to see both on screen. To do this, switch to the view tool (Shortcut key: *Q*), and holding the *Command* key (Mac) or *Ctrl* key (PC), drag the mouse to the left to zoom out, then switch back to the Transform tool (*W*) to see your object's axis handles again.

Now using the **Transform** tool, drag the **X** (red) and **Z** (blue) axis handles independently until you have positioned your particle system in the center of the volcano mouth from this perspective, as shown in the following screenshot:

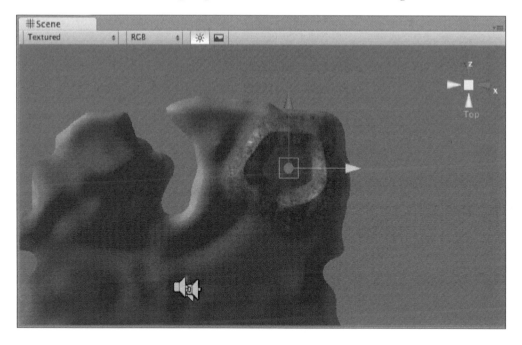

Do not be confused by the handles highlighting in yellow when you have them selected — you still have the correct handle!

Now click on the red **X**-axis handle of the **Scene Gizmo**, in order to give you a side-on view of the island. Now use this view, along with the **Transform** tool, to drag the **Y**-axis handle (green) of your particle system, in order to get it to a position in the centre of the volcano, as shown in the following screenshot:

Note that in the image, the green handle is currently selected and thus is highlighted in yellow. Finally, switch back to Perspective view by clicking on the **white cube** in the center of the **Scene Gizmo**.

Downloading assets

Next, we'll need to add some assets to our project to complete the volcano. The assets are available in the code bundle provided on packtpub.com (www.packtpub. com/files/code/8181_Code.zip). Locate the package called volcanoPack. unitypackage from our extracted files, and then switch back to Unity.

Go to **Assets | Import Package**, navigate to the file you just downloaded on your computer, and choose it as the package to import. Confirm this when you are shown a list of the assets included, and you will find that you have added a **Volcano** folder to your project. In this folder, you will find:

- A texture for the smoke of the volcano
- A sound file to represent the rumbling lava of the volcano
- A texture file called `white`, which we will use later for our level fade-in

Making the smoke material

Now that we have imported the relevant assets, we'll need to make a material for our volcano smoke texture. To keep things neat, we'll create this inside the **Volcano** folder. Select the **Volcano** folder in the **Project** panel, and then click on the **Create** button, selecting **Material** from the drop-down menu.

Rename this new material **Volcano Smoke Material**, and ensure that it is selected in the **Project** panel to see its settings in the **Inspector**. From the **Shader** drop–down menu, choose **Particles | Multiply**. This will set the rendering style for the material to one suitable for particles—**Multiply** will show the particle textures' transparent background and softened edges. Drag-and-drop the **volcano_smoke** texture file from the **Volcano** folder onto the empty slot to the right of the **Particle Texture** setting, leaving the **Tiling** and **Offset** parameters at their defaults.

Now drag the **Volcano Smoke Material** from the **Volcano** folder in the **Project** panel, and drop it onto the **Volcano Smoke** particle system in the **Hierarchy** to apply it.

Particle system settings

As with any visual effect, especially regarding particle systems—a lot of experimentation is necessary to achieve an effect that you personally feel looks good. With this in mind, I recommend you to simply use the settings I suggest here as a guide, and then take some time out to try adjusting a few settings by yourself to achieve an effect that:

- You like the look of
- Works well with the style of volcano mouth you created on your terrain.

Note that settings listed here are only the ones that have been adjusted from the default.

Ellipsoid Particle Emitter settings

- Min Size: 40
- Max Size: 60
- Min Energy: 10
- Max Energy: 40
- Min Emission: 2
- Max Emission: 8
- World Velocity Y axis: 30

Particle Animator settings

- Color Animation[0]: Orange color, 5% Alpha
- Color Animation[1]: Red color, 25% Alpha
- Color Animation[2]: Mid Grey color, 40% Alpha
- Color Animation[3]: Darker Grey color, 25% Alpha
- Color Animation[4]: Black color, 5% Alpha
- Size Grow: 0.15
- Rnd Force: (25, 0, 25)
- Force: (1, 0, 1)

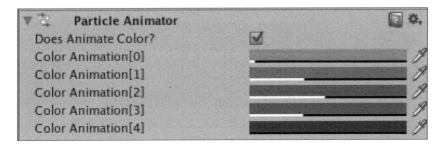

Now take some time to adjust these settings to make the particles suit your terrain a little better.

Adding audio to the volcano

To complete the effect of a genuine volcano, we'll add a sound source now with our volcanic audio loop playing on it.

As noted previously, our volcano is not an actual game object, so in this instance also, we cannot add a component to it because of this fact. However, we do now have an object at the center point of our volcano—the particle system. This means that we can use that object as the one to add our audio component to.

Ensure that the **Volcano Smoke** object is selected in the **Hierarchy** and then go to **Component | Audio | Audio Source**.

This adds an audio source component to the bottom of the list of components in the **Inspector**. As the particle system already has several components making it work, you may need to scroll down in the **Inspector** to find the **Audio Source**.

Assign the **volcano_rumble** audio clip from the **Volcano** folder to the **Audio Clip** parameter, and ensure that **Play On Awake** is selected—this ensures that the sound will not need triggering, but simply plays when the scene is loaded. Set the **Volume** and **Max Volume** parameters both to 200. This will ensure that:

- The sound of the volcano is loud enough to overpower the stereo sound of hillside ambience applied to the terrain
- The sound reaches this level when the player is near the audio source, that is, stands next to the volcano

We'll leave the **Min Volume** on **0** as this means the sound can completely fade away if the player is far enough from the volcano.

Next, we can define how far away the player must be in order for the sound to fade out, by adjusting the **Rolloff Factor** setting. On my terrain, a setting of **0.025** is a good amount—with this setting, the higher the value, the closer the player must be to the source before hearing it—so by using a low value, as I have, this sound carries for a long distance, as you'd expect the sound of a rumbling volcano to do. Start with this value, and try different settings when you play test the game shortly. Finally, select the box for **Loop** to ensure that the sound continues to play indefinitely.

Volcano testing

Now that our volcano is complete, we should test its effectiveness. Firstly, go to **File | Save Scene** to ensure that we do not lose any unsaved progress. Then press the **Play** button, and try walking from the current location of your player, towards the volcano. The particles should be rising into the air. As you approach the volcano, the volume of the volcano's sound should become louder. If it is not loud enough, simply tweak the values in the **Volume** fields, or if the sound does not carry far enough, then lower the value for **Rolloff Factor** in the **Audio Source** component.

 Remember that any changes made using the **Inspector** during play testing will be undone as soon as you hit the **Play** button again to stop testing. Simply use this as a literal testing period, and ensure that you place the values you settle upon in the **Inspector** again when you have stopped testing the game.

It is worth noting that for testing purposes, you may wish to increase the speed of the **First Person Controller** to allow you to walk around your island more quickly. To do this, while you are play testing, select the **First Person Controller** object in the **Hierarchy**. Set the **Speed** public member variable of the **FPSWalker(script)** component to your desired value—remember this is simply for testing, so unrealistic speeds are fine! Because you are doing this during testing, this **Hierarchy** setting will revert back once you press the **Play** button again to stop the test—meaning you will not lose your original intended speed.

Coconut trails

Next we'll add some flair to our coconut shy game by adding light trails to our coconut prefabs. By doing this, when the player throws them, they'll see a trail of light following the trajectory of the projectile, which should give a nice visual effect.

Editing the Prefab

To implement this change, we'll need to return to our coconut prefab from Chapter 6, as the **Trail Renderer** component we will use must be attached to this object. Open the **Prefabs** folder in the **Project** panel, and locate the **Coconut Prefab** asset. Drag it into the scene so that we can work on it—assets can be worked on directly from their location in the **Project** panel, but in order to preview and test the effect we're creating, it is best to drag them to the scene, and see what we're doing "in action". Remember that by pressing *F* with your cursor over the **Scene** view, you can zoom straight to the location of the selected object.

Trail Renderer component

To add the component, ensure that the **Coconut Prefab** is still selected in the **Hierarchy** panel, and go to **Component | Particles | Trail Renderer**. You will be prompted, explaining that you are losing the connection with the prefab, simply continue at this point—we will update the prefab once we have finished making our trail.

This component simply draws an arcing vector line by plotting a series of points behind an object, as it moves through the 3D world. By specifying the length, material, and start/end widths of the line, we'll be able to achieve the effect we want. To see the default setting of the trail renderer, press the **Play** button now, and watch the coconut fall to the ground, leaving a trail behind it. You should see a nasty wide black line being rendered—not good!

Firstly we'll address some performance issues—for Unity Pro version users, the ability to use dynamic shadows comes as standard; however, as we do not need the line to cast or receive any shadows, deselect the first two parameters on the component in the **Inspector**. Shadows are generally expensive, and as the trail renderer itself is adding to the strain put on the processing power of the player's computer, anything we can do to reduce the strain is definitely a good idea.

Next expand the **Materials** parameter to see the **Size** and **Element 0** settings. Here we can assign a texture to use for the trail. As we have already made a flame material, we'll re-use that because it uses an appropriate shader type for a trail—Additive (soft). Open the **Fire Feature** folder in the **Project** panel, and locate the **Flame** material, then drag-and-drop it onto the **Element 0** setting for the **Trail Renderer** component in the **Inspector**.

Now, to ensure the trail is not overly long, set the **Time** parameter to a value of **1**. This means that the trail is one second long—points at the end of the trail are deleted after they have existed for this amount of time.

Now set the **Start Width** to **0.25** and the **End Width** to **0.15**—these define the width of the rendered material at either end of the trail, and, generally speaking, it makes sense to make the start wider than the end in order to taper the trail.

Finally, expand the **Colors** parameter so that you can see each box for color. With this, we can animate the appearance of the trail through color and also visibility, using the alpha settings. As we have color in our flame texture, we'll leave the colors of these settings, but simply make the trail fade towards its end. Click on each **Color** block in turn. By using the **A** (Alpha) value, set value from 80 percent down to 0 percent over the course of each of them:

Continue entering these settings until you have something like that shown below:

The remaining settings can be left at their defaults—**Min Vertex Distance** simply defines what the shortest distance between two points in the line can be—the more points present, the more detailed the line is, but also the more costly it is processing wise. **Autodestruct** needn't be enabled either, as the object itself has a script handling removal of these prefabs from the world—the **Coconut Tidy** script we wrote in Chapter 6.

Updating the prefab

As we are effectively working on an instance of the prefab that has lost its connection with the original asset—hence the warning when we added the trail renderer—we'll need to apply the changes we've made to the original asset in order to have all new instances of the prefab to feature this trail.

To do this, you have two options: either select the **Coconut Prefab** in the **Hierarchy** and go to **GameObject | Apply Changes to Prefab**, or use the **Apply** button at the top of the **Inspector** for this object:

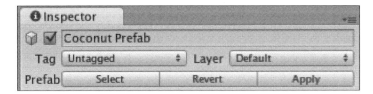

Now that you have updated the original prefab asset, we no longer need the instance in the scene. So we simply select it and remove it using the keyboard shortcut *Command + Backspace* (Mac) or *Shift + Delete* (PC).

To see the effect, play test the game now, and try out the coconut shy minigame. You should see flaming trails following each coconut you throw!

Performance tweaks

In this section we will look at ways in which you can boost the performance of your game as an end product. Also known as optimization, this process is crucial to do once you have ensured that your game works as expected.

Camera Clip Planes and fog

To add a nicer visual appearance to our island, we'll enable fog. In Unity, fog can be enabled very simply and can be used in conjunction with the Camera's **Far Clip Plane** setting to adjust draw distance—causing objects beyond a certain distance to not be rendered. This will improve performance. By including fog, you will be able to mask the cut-off of rendering distant objects—giving a less clunky feel to exploring the island. We discussed **Far Clip Plane** settings in Chapter 3 when we deconstructed the First Person Controller. Now, let's adjust the value of the far plane to improve performance by cutting down the distance at which objects are still rendered by the camera.

- Expand the **First Person Controller** parent group by clicking its gray arrow to the left of its name in the **Hierarchy** panel.

- Select the child object called **Main Camera.**

- In the **Inspector**, find the **Camera** component, and set the **Far Clip Plane** value to **600**. This is a shorter distance, described in meters, and although it cuts down the visual distance of our player's view, this will be masked by the fog we are about to add.

Go to **Edit | Render Settings**. This brings up **Render Settings** in place of the **Inspector**. Simply select the box for **Fog** here, and then click on the **Color** block to the right of **Fog Color** to open the settings for Color and Alpha. Set the Alpha value (A) to around 60%, as shown below, and then set the **Fog Density** value to **0.004**:

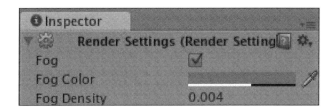

We are setting the **Fog Color** alpha and **Fog Density** to a lower value, as the default and higher values mask the view so well that the particles from the volcano would become invisible until the player stands quite close to the volcano.

Ambient lighting

In **Render Settings**, you can also set the **Ambient Light** of the scene. While our **Directional Light** handles the main lighting—acting as the sun in this example—the ambient light will allow you to set a general overall brightness, meaning you can create scenes that look like a certain time of night or day. Try adjusting this setting now by clicking on the color block to the right of the setting and experimenting with the color picker.

Instructions scene

To finish our game, we'll complete the menu we made in Chapter 8 by creating the **Instructions** scene for the user to read. In this, we'll implement some animation using scripting, and we'll learn a new command that we haven't utilized yet called **linear interpolation**, or **lerp** for short.

As our **Instructions** scene should mimic the rest of the menu, we'll start with the **Menu** scene as a basis. Before we do this, however, ensure that the **Island Level** scene is saved by going to **File | Save Scene**. Duplicate the **Menu** scene by selecting it in the **Project** panel and using the keyboard shortcut *Command + D* (Mac) or *Ctrl + D* (PC).

This will duplicate the **Menu** scene, and give it the name **Menu 1**, rename this **Instructions**, and open it by double-clicking on its icon now.

Adding screen text

We'll need to write our instructions for the player on this screen, so we'll utilize a GUI Text object for this purpose. Go to **GameObject | Create Other | GUI Text**. This creates a new object with a GUI Text component called **GUI Text** in the **Hierarchy**. Select it and rename it **Instruction Text**.

Next, to maintain consistency, assign the font you've used thus far in your game as the font for the GUI Texture to use. I've been using the free to download font, **Sugo**, so I have simply dragged it from the **Project** panel over to the **Font** field in the **GUI Text** component.

Next write in a short paragraph explaining the aim of the game to the player. They need to light the campfire with the matches in order to survive, so I have written:

"You have been stranded on a desert island and need to keep warm! Find the campfire and find a way of lighting it, or you'll surely freeze come nightfall..."

To write in text on multiple lines in the **Text** field of this component, simply finish your line, and move to the next line by using keyboard shortcut *Alt + Enter* (Mac and PC).

Finally, position this text by placing the following values in the **Transform's** position field—**(0.5, 0.55, 0)**. I have chosen to place my text on three lines so that it visually lines up with the logo at the top of the screen, which looks like this:

Text Animation using Linear Interpolation (Lerp)

Next we'll animate this text using a script, so select the **Menu** folder in the **Project** panel and click on **Create**, selecting **Javascript** from the drop-down menu.

Rename the **NewBehaviorScript** you have created, calling it **Animator**. Now double-click the script's icon to launch it in the script editor.

We'll begin by establishing some public member variables we can use in the **Inspector** to control the behavior of our text animation. Add the following to the top of your script:

```
var startPosition : float = -1.0;
var endPosition : float = 0.5;
var speed : float = 1.0;
private var StartTime : float;
```

We will use these variables in the next part of the script, but we've named them based on what they do—the start and end position variables are in charge of the position in screen coordinates (hence the default start position of -1, meaning off screen). Given that they are public member variables, we'll be able to adjust them in the **Inspector**. The speed variable will simply be used to multiply the speed of the animation over time, so the default is 1.

Finally, we include a variable called StartTime, a floating point variable which is only used within the script and is therefore declared as private. We will use this variable to store the default value of time when the scene is loaded. If we do not do this, after the first loading of this scene, any return visits to the instructions screen will show the instructions already on screen, as the value of time in Unity we are about to use counts from the first load of the game.

Next, to set up our assignment of this variable, we'll capture Unity's time command when the scene loads, by adding the following function:

```
function Start(){
    StartTime = Time.time;
}
```

Now when the scene loads, StartTime captures that value. We will use this when establishing the animation.

Now, move the closing curly brace of the Update() function down by a couple of lines so that you can add some code to the function. Add the following line:

```
transform.position.x = Mathf.Lerp(startPosition, endPosition, (Time.
time-StartTime)*speed);
```

Here we are picking a specific axis of the position values of the transform component, therefore:

```
transform.position.x
```

Then we are setting this to equal a Maths Function—Mathf—called Lerp, which is a function that linearly interpolates—travels directly—between two values. The values we are sending this function are defined by our startPosition and endPosition variables, so the Lerp function will provide a number for the X axis position between those two numbers.

The third parameter for the Lerp function is the amount to interpolate—a value of 1 would mean the value returned travels completely from the start to end value, and a value of 0 would mean no change. We want this interpolation to occur over time here, so instead of a single value, we are using Unity's built in Time.time command to count up and subtracting the value of StartTime we set earlier—effectively resetting its value so that it can count from 0. Finally, we are altering the time by multiplying by our speed variable. Currently the speed variable is set to 1.0, so no change will be made, but any value over 1 will increase the speed, and values lower than 1 will decrease it.

This command must be done in the Update() function, as it requires incremental change—which our lerp provides—each frame, so placing this in a Start() function, for example, would not work.

To double-check your script, here it is completed:

```
var startPosition : float = -1.0;
var endPosition : float = 0.5;
var speed : float = 1.0;
private var StartTime : float;

function Start(){
   StartTime = Time.time;
}
function Update () {
   transform.position.x = Mathf.Lerp(startPosition, endPosition,
(Time.time-StartTime)*speed);
}
```

Go to **File | Save** in the script editor now, and switch back to Unity.

Now we'll apply the script and adjust settings of the public member variables in the **Inspector** to ensure that it is doing what we want. Select the **Instructions Text** object in the **Hierarchy** panel, and go to **Component | Scripts | Animator**.

This adds the script as a component. In the settings of the public member variables, you should see the default values established in the script you just wrote:

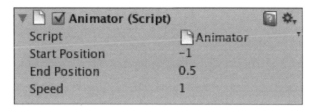

To see this effect in action, we'll need to play the scene, but first, we should remove the menu that has been carried over from duplicating the original menu scene. If you opted for the GUI Texture-based menu, then you'll need to check all three button objects. If you are using the GUI-scripted menu, then simply check the object which has that script as a component. To remind yourself about deactivating, see the previous chapter.

Once you have deactivated the menu, return to the **Instructions Text** object. In the **GUI Text** component, set **Anchor** to **Middle Center** and **Alignment** to **Left**. Now press the **Play** button to see the animation effect. Your text should move in the **X** axis from off-screen left to a central position of **0.5**. Press **Play** again to end your test before continuing.

If you would like the animation to occur from off-screen right, then you could change the **Start Position** public member variable to a number higher than `1.0`—as this is the right edge of the screen. However, if you wanted animation to occur in the Y axis, you'd need to return to your script, and change the effect axis there. For example, `transform.position.y = Mathf(...)`

Menu return

As we are working on a scene that is separate to our menu, we'll need to include a button to return the user to the **Menu** scene itself. Otherwise they will be stuck on the **Instructions** screen!

For this, we will use the GUI scripting technique discussed in the previous chapter and save some time by duplicating some of the existing work we've already done. In the **Scripts** folder of the **Project** panel, locate the script **MainMenuGUI2**, and duplicate it using keyboard shortcut *Command + D* (Mac) or *Ctrl + D* (PC). As Unity numbers objects and assets that it generates, your duplicate will be called **MainMenuGUI3**, so rename this **BackButtonGUI**. Then double-click its icon to launch it in the script editor.

In the first `if` statement of the `OnGUI()` function, adjust the text on the button to say `Back` instead of `Play`. In the call to the `OpenLevel()` function, set the string to say `Menu`, instead of `Island Level`. It should look like this:

```
if (GUILayout.Button ("Back")) {
    OpenLevel ("Menu");
}
```

As we only want this script to generate one button, delete the other two `if` statements, leaving you with just the single one to go back to the `Menu` scene. The only other issue here is the positioning of the button. As we are using the `ScreenY` variable from our **MainMenuGUI2** script – this places our GUI area to draw the button in the center of the screen. As our text will be in the way of this, we ideally need to render the button lower down. To get around this, simply amend the `ScreenY` variable establishment to use a slightly lower value:

```
var ScreenY = ((Screen.height / 1.7) - (areaHeight / 2));
```

This will place the button lower than the instructional text.

The completed **BackButtonGUI** script should look like this:

```
var beep : AudioClip;
var menuSkin : GUISkin;
var areaWidth : float;
var areaHeight : float;

function OnGUI () {

    GUI.skin = menuSkin;

    var ScreenX = ((Screen.width / 2) - (areaWidth / 2));
    var ScreenY = ((Screen.height / 1.7) - (areaHeight / 2));

    GUILayout.BeginArea (Rect (ScreenX, ScreenY,
                         areaWidth, areaHeight));

    if (GUILayout.Button ("Back")) {
        OpenLevel ("Menu");
    }

    GUILayout.EndArea ();
}

function OpenLevel (level : String) {
        audio.PlayOneShot (beep);
```

```
        yield new WaitForSeconds(0.35);

        Application.LoadLevel(level);
}
@script RequireComponent(AudioSource)
```

Go to **File | Save** in the script editor, and switch back to Unity now.

As with all GUI-scripted interface elements, we need to attach the script to an object in order for this button to appear. Create a new empty game object to house this script by going to **GameObject | Create Empty**. With the new object selected in the **Hierarchy**, rename it **Back Button**. Attach the script we just made by going to **Component | Scripts | Back Button GUI**. As you'll notice, the public member variables of the script need assigning, so you'll need to do the following:

- Drag the audio clip **menu_beep** from the **Menu** folder in the **Project** panel to the **Beep** member variable

- Drag the **Main Menu skin** asset from the **Menu** folder to the **Menu Skin** variable

- Set the **Area Width** variable to **200**

- Set the **Area Height** variable to **75**, as we only have a single button this time

Now that our **Back** button is complete, we can test the entire menu. But first we need to add the **Instructions** scene to the project's **Build Settings**, in order for Unity to load it during testing. Go to **File | Build Settings**, and click on the **Add Current** button. Your list of levels in the **Build Settings** should now look like this:

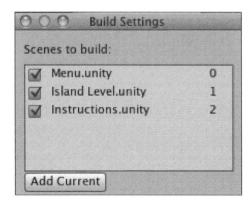

Close the **Build Settings** dialog, and you're ready to test. Press the **Play** button to test the scene—the **Back** button should appear, and the text should animate in. Click the **Back** button, and you should be taken to the **Menu** scene. If any of this does not work, then double-check that your script matches the changes listed above.

Your instructions screen should look something like this:

Now stop testing the scene, and go to **File | Save Scene** to update it.

Island level fade-in

In order to ease the player into the environment when they enter the game, we'll create a fade-in at the start of our actual game level using a GUI texture that covers the screen and is faded out over time using the Lerp technique we have just learned.

Double-click the icon of the **Island Level** to open that scene. Now, in the **Volcano** folder you imported earlier, you'll find a texture file called **white**. This texture, a flat white color created in Photoshop, is of size 64x64 pixels; this may sound rather small to cover the screen but as it is simply a flat color, it needn't be large—we will simply stretch it to the size of the screen.

Select the texture now and in the **Inspector**, deselect **Generate Mip Maps** in the **Texture Importer** component to stop Unity from rendering smaller versions of it for 3D use—then press the **Apply** button at the bottom to confirm the change. We will use this texture with further UnityGUI and Lerp scripting to stretch it to full screen and fade it out when the scene launches—this will make the game view fade in from white.

Select the **Scripts** folder, and click on the **Create** button, selecting **Javascript** from the drop-down menu. Rename this script **FadeTexture**. Double-click the script's icon to launch it in the script editor.

Begin by establishing two variables, one a public member and the other a private variable:

```
var theTexture : Texture2D;
private var StartTime : float;
```

The first variable here will hold the white texture asset ready to be stretched over the screen, and the second is a floating-point number which we will use to store a value of time.

Next, capture the value of `Time.time` in the `StartTime` variable when the level loads by adding the following function to your script beneath the variables you just added:

```
function OnLevelWasLoaded(){
    StartTime = Time.time;
}
```

We need to use this variable to capture the current amount of time elapsed, because `Time.time` starts from when the first scene is loaded—that is, the menu. Because the player will view the menu first, we know that `Time.time` will not equal 0 when the **Island Level** scene is loaded. We will use this variable shortly to subtract from the current reading of time and thereby get a point to count from.

Now in the `Update()` function, place in the following code:

```
if(Time.time-StartTime >= 3){
    Destroy(gameObject);
}
```

This `if` statement checks the value of `Time.time`, minus the time it was at when the current scene loaded — `StartTime` — and if it is more than or equal to 3, then we destroy the game object this script is attached to. This simply removes the game object we will attach this script to after three seconds — as after the fade effect occurs, we no longer need the object in the scene.

UnityGUI texture rendering

Establish a new `OnGUI()` function in your script, and place in the following lines of code:

```
function OnGUI(){
    GUI.color = Color.white;
    GUI.color.a = Mathf.Lerp(1.0, 0.0, (Time.time-StartTime));
    GUI.DrawTexture(Rect( 0, 0, Screen.width,
                                 Screen.height ), theTexture);
}
```

Here we are addressing the GUI class directly. In the first line, we address the color parameter, setting it to an in-built reference of the Color class called "white".

Then with this color set, we address its `alpha` parameter — its visibility — by saying `GUI.color.a`. We use the same `Mathf.Lerp` command we used to animate our GUI Text object earlier, interpolating the alpha from `1.0` (fully visible) to `0.0` (invisible). The third parameter in the loop is the amount to interpolate — because we are using `Time.time-StartTime` here, we are effectively starting a counter from 0.0 which will increase as time passes, so the Lerp occurs over time, creating the fade.

The third line actually renders the texture itself, using the `DrawTexture` command of the GUI class. By specifying a `Rect` (rectangular space) for this to be drawn, starting at `0,0` — the top left of the screen — we make sure that this texture stretches to fill the screen by using `Screen.width` and `Screen.height`. This makes the fade work in whichever resolution the player runs the game at, as it automates the size of the texture on screen.

Go to **File | Save** in the script editor, and return to Unity now.

Back in Unity, go to **GameObject | Create Empty**. This creates a new object in the **Hierarchy** called **GameObject**. Rename this to **Fader** now. Add the script you have just written by going to **Component | Scripts | Fade Texture**. This adds the script as a component. Now, simply drag-and-drop the **white** texture from the **Volcano** folder in the **Project** panel to the public member variable **theTexture** in the **Inspector**.

Now press the **Play** button, and you should see that the screen fades in from white and that the **white** game object in the **Hierarchy** is removed after three seconds. Stop testing, and go to **File | Save Scene** to update the project now.

Game win notification

As a final finishing touch, we'll tell the player that they have successfully won the game when the fire has been lit, as this is the goal of our game.

Open the **PlayerCollisions** script in the **Scripts** folder of the **Project** panel, and scroll to the bottom. The last function in the script is lightFire() and into this we'll add some more commands before its terminating right curly brace. Move down a couple of lines from the current last line:

```
Destroy(GameObject.Find("matchGUI"));
```

And place in the following commands:

```
        TextHints.textOn=true;
        TextHints.message = "You Lit the Fire, you'll survive, well
done!";

        yield new WaitForSeconds(5);

        Application.LoadLevel("Menu");
```

Here we're switching back on our TextHints GUI from earlier, and sending the message "You Lit the Fire..." as the string of text to display on screen. We then use a yield command to halt the script for 5 seconds, and then load the Menu level of the game, so that the player may play again.

Now press the **Play** button, and play through the whole game. You should be able to collect three batteries, win the fourth battery from the coconut shy minigame, enter the outpost, collect the matches, and light the fire. When the fire is lit, you should be notified, and taken to the main menu screen.

Once you have verified this, stop testing, and go to **File | Save scene** to update the project.

Summary

In this chapter, we have looked at the various finishing touches for your game. The visual effects, lighting, and animation discussed here only scratches the surface of what you can do with Unity, but while Unity makes it easy to add these polishing features to make your game really stand out, it is crucial to keep in mind that they should only be considered once your project's gameplay is honed—finishing touches are a great way to complete your project, but the playability should always come first.

Now that we have completed the game, we'll spend the next chapter looking at building, testing, and rebuilding, and the implications of deploying your game. We'll also take a look at further optimizations for your game and discuss getting your game seen as an independent developer.

10
Building and Sharing

In order to take our game from a simple example to something we can share with play testers, we need to consider the various platforms of deployment and how we can adapt the game to be exported to the Web. The best method for you as a developer is to share your work. Unity allows for various scales of the final build of your game and will compress textures and various other assets as appropriate for you. You should also be aware of platform detection for web builds in order to adjust certain settings when deploying online, as opposed to a full standalone desktop build.

The standard Indie and Pro releases of Unity offer you the chance to build for Mac desktop, Windows desktop, as a Widget for Mac OS X's **'Dashboard'** facility, and as a web browser plugin.

In this final chapter, we'll look at how to customize assets to create a web build and a standalone desktop build. We will cover the following topics:

- Working with **Build Settings** to export your game
- Building a web and standalone version of your game
- Platform detection to remove elements from web builds
- Ways in which you can share your games with others and get further help with your Unity development

Build Settings

In Unity, go to **File | Build Settings** now, and take a look at the options you have. You should see the various options mentioned previously:

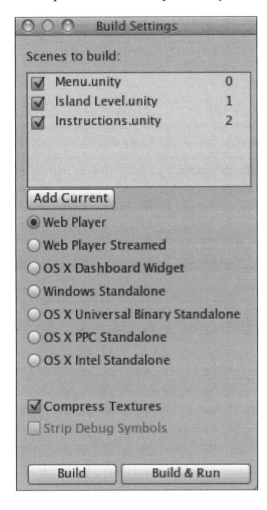

In the **Build Settings**, Mac builds are marked by the prefix **OS X** – the current generation of operating system. The Mac builds also give you various options, as there are different generations of Mac computer to consider – the older generation, running on the **PowerPC** processor, and the current generation built around **Intel** processors. The **Universal Binary** setting will build an OS X binary that runs on both the older PowerPC systems as well as the new Intel systems. This results in a larger file, as you are effectively including two copies of your game in one application.

In our example, the **Build Settings** show the list of scenes we have added to our project so far, beginning with the **Menu** scene. It is important to have the first scene you'd like your player to see as the first item in the **Scenes to build** list. If your menu or first scene is not first in the list, then you can simply drag the names of the scenes to reorder them.

Let's begin by looking at the different options in more depth and what you would get by building each option.

Web Player

When placing any plugin-based content onto the Web, it must be included as an object which calls the installed plugin. Viewers of Unity's web builds will be required to download the plugin for their browser in much the same way as Adobe Flash content requires users to download Flash Player. Web player builds create a game file with the extension `.unity3d`, which calls the Unity Web Player plugin, along with an accompanying HTML file containing the necessary embedding code. This embedding HTML can then be taken along with the game file and embedded into a web page of your own design.

Player Settings

As web players rely on the browser software to load the HTML containing the call to a plugin, any computer running your game as a web player is already using up processing power on the browser. With this in mind, it can help to provide your game at a lower resolution than you would for a desktop build. We designed our game to an entry-level desktop resolution of 1024x768 pixels. However, when deploying into a web build, the screen size should be reduced to something smaller, such as 640x480. This makes the load on the CPU less intensive as smaller frames are being drawn, thus giving better performance.

To adjust settings such as this, we'll need to look at the **Player Settings**. Go to **Edit | Project Settings | Player** now to switch the **Inspector** panel to show settings for the project. When you build your game, you're effectively placing your finished project into a **Player**—on the Web, the player file calling the plugin itself. In **Player Settings**, you can specify certain elements—such as screen size—for the player to use.

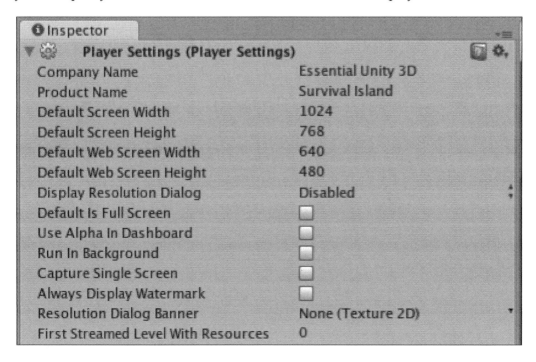

On this screen, you should begin by filling in the details for your project. Add in **Company Name** and **Product Name,** which at this stage need not be anything formal. Then fill in the **Default Screen Width** and **Height** with the **1024x768** we originally designed for.

Now fill in **Default Web Screen Width** and **Height** with **640** and **480** respectively, as shown in the previous screenshot. The only other setting relevant to our web player deployment is the setting for **First Streamed Level With Resources**, which allows you to choose the first level in your build list which has a set of assets to load in. With this you can create splash screens, which segway into your game. If that were the case, then you'd use this setting to choose the particular level which first features assets by stating its number in the order of the build list.

In our game, the first menu screen contains assets—the island—and we can happily leave this default setting on **0**. We'll return to the **Player Settings** shortly when we look at desktop builds.

Web Player Streamed

Web Player Streamed—a separate build option on the list—allows you to build a web deployment that does not force the player to wait too long for a loading bar to complete.

When encountering any wait online, it is characteristic for users to be impatient, and it is important that you restrict waiting times as much as possible when creating web builds of your game. Using **Web Player Streamed** means that your game can start being played before the entirety of its assets are loaded—then as the player interacts with the first scene, the rest of the game's assets continue to load.

This factor is absolutely crucial when submitting your game to games portal sites, such as `www.shockwave.com`, `www.wooglie.com`, or `www.blurst.com`. Sites such as these expect your game to be playable after around 1MB of data has been downloaded, and by adhering to these guidelines, you're more likely to be able to get your game onto such sites, giving you exposure for your work. For more information on this, visit the Unity web site.

OS X Dashboard Widget

Mac operating systems (version 10.4 onwards) have a feature called the Dashboard. It is a set of simple tools and applications known as **Widgets**, which can be brought up at any time as an overlay over the screen. Unity can publish your game as a Widget, and this is simply another way for you to provide your game to people. If you're making a simple puzzle or timewaster game, this could be appropriate as a deployment method. However, with a game such as our first person walkaround, the Dashboard is less appropriate.

Here is what our game looks like as part of the Mac Dashboard:

Ideally, games deployed as Widgets should be basic because it is best to avoid loading masses of data into a Dashboard Widget, as this has to stay resident in the computer's memory so that the game can continue when the Dashboard is activated and deactivated.

OS X/Windows Standalone

Standalone or desktop builds are fully-fledged applications that can be delivered in the same way as a commercial game.

Building your game for Mac OS X standalone will build a single application file with all required assets bundled inside, while building for Windows PC standalone will create a folder containing a .exe (executable) and assets required to run the game.

Building a standalone is the best way to ensure maximum performance from your game as the files are stored locally, not online, and are not already using processing power by running a browser or the OS X Dashboard.

Building the game

Now that we are ready to build the game, you need to consider the varying deployment methods discussed previously, and adapt the project to be built for the Web as well as a standalone game.

Adapting for web build

In Unity, the 3D world you work with is fully scaled by the engine to be presented in whatever resolution you specify in the **Player Settings**. We have also designed the menus in this book to be scalable in different resolutions by utilizing the `Screen` class to position GUIs based on current resolution. However, in order to learn about platform detection we will remove an element we don't want to be seen in our web version—the **Quit** button. In the `Scripts` folder in the **Project** panel, double-click the icon for `MainMenuGUI2` to launch it in the script editor now.

Quit button platform automation

As this is a web build, the **Quit** button we have added to the menu is meaningless. This is because `Application.Quit()` commands do not function when a Unity game is played through a browser—instead, players simply close the tab containing the game or navigate away when they are finished playing. We need to exclude this button from our web menu, but we do not want to delete it from our script because we still want the script to render the **Quit** button in a standalone build.

To solve this problem, we'll utilize another part of the `Application` class called `platform`, which we can use to detect what kind of deployment (desktop, web, or Dashboard) the game is being built as.

We will do this by writing the following `if` statement:

```
if(Application.platform == RuntimePlatform.OSXWebPlayer ||
    Application.platform == RuntimePlatform.WindowsWebPlayer)
```

Here we are simply checking the `platform` parameter of `Application`, as to whether it is being run on an `OSXWebPlayer` (Mac) or `WindowsWebPlayer` (PC)—the symbol `||` between the two simply means 'OR'. So here we are saying, if this is being run on a web player, then do something! Now we simply need to combine this with an `else` statement, because we really want to make a condition for when the game is not deployed for the web, and render the **Quit** button.

In the OnGUI() function, locate the if statement in charge of creating the **Quit** button, it should look like this:

```
if(GUILayout.Button ("Quit")){
  Application.Quit();
}
```

Now add in the following if else structure, placing the original **Quit** button's if statement above into the else section. It should now look like this:

```
if(Application.platform == RuntimePlatform.OSXWebPlayer ||
  Application.platform == RuntimePlatform.WindowsWebPlayer){
}
else{
  if(GUILayout.Button ("Quit")){
    Application.Quit();
  }
}
```

Notice here that we have simply left an empty line for the if condition being met, and placed the **Quit** button piece of code in the else part, so that it will only be drawn if the game is not detected as being played on the Web.

Now locate the two if statements that render the **Play** and **Instructions** buttons:

```
if(GUILayout.Button ("Play")){
  OpenLevel("Island Level");
}
if(GUILayout.Button ("Instructions")){
  OpenLevel("Instructions");
}
```

Place these into the if part of the statement we just added, so that you have this:

```
if (Application.platform == RuntimePlatform.OSXWebPlayer ||
  Application.platform == RuntimePlatform.WindowsWebPlayer){
    if(GUILayout.Button ("Play")){
      OpenLevel("Island Level");
    }
    if(GUILayout.Button ("Instructions")){
      OpenLevel("Instructions");
    }
}
else{
  if(GUILayout.Button ("Quit")){
    Application.Quit();
  }
}
```

Now, your initial platform detection `if` statement will render the **Play** and **Instructions** buttons if it detects being run online, and the **Quit** button if it is not online.

But wait! We need **Play** and **Instructions** buttons for the standalone build too right? Of course—copy/paste the code for the **Play** and **Instructions** buttons into the `else` statement too. Your final platform detection statement should look like this:

```
if (Application.platform == RuntimePlatform.OSXWebPlayer ||
   Application.platform == RuntimePlatform.WindowsWebPlayer){
   if(GUILayout.Button ("Play")){
      OpenLevel("Island Level");
   }
   if(GUILayout.Button ("Instructions")){
      OpenLevel("Instructions");
   }
}
else{
   if(GUILayout.Button ("Play")){
      OpenLevel("Island Level");
   }
   if(GUILayout.Button ("Instructions")){
      OpenLevel("Instructions");
   }
   if(GUILayout.Button ("Quit")){
      Application.Quit();
   }
}
```

Here you can see that we have only `Play` and `Instructions` in the `if` condition and `Play`, `Instructions`, and `Quit` in the `else`. Go to **File** | **Save** in the script editor, and then switch back to Unity. This has now automated the project to only render the **Quit** button if it is not being played on the Web.

Now thanks to the `Application` class automation we've implemented. You now have a set of scene assets that can be placed in the **Build Settings** list along with the **Island Level** and built as a **Web Player** or **Web Player Streamed**.

Now let's take a look at building both the web and standalone versions of the game.

Texture compression and debug stripping

When building for any platform, you'll have two additional settings at the bottom of the **Build Settings** window—**Compress Textures** and **Strip Debug Symbols**.

Put simply, Unity handles the compression of texture assets used in your game for you based on their import settings, and all you need to do is ensure that this box is selected when building your game. You should also select the box for **Strip Debug Symbols** in most instances when your game is complete enough to build. This makes Unity remove any unwanted Debug class code from your scripts, such as the Debug. Log command we discussed in Chapter 8.

Building standalone

Standalone builds of your game by default launch with a splash page allowing users to customize the resolution at which your game should be played. Known in Unity as the **Resolution Dialog**, this window also lets your player customize **Input** settings and **Graphics Quality**. As a developer, you can brand this dialog window with a banner image.

Here is what our **Resolution Dialog** window will look like without any customization (Mac version shown):

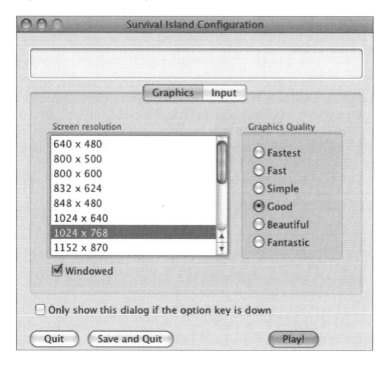

Most developers prefer to keep this screen enabled, as it allows the player to specify their chosen resolution and levels of graphic quality that suit their computer's specification. However, it can be disabled if you'd like to force users to play at a particular resolution.

In order to disable this, you can go to **Edit | Project Settings | Player** and change the setting of **Display Resolution Dialog** to **Disabled**. Lastly, you can select the box for **Default is Full Screen** here, to force your computer to play the game in fullscreen mode, unless you wish the game to open in a window, which is the default setting. Bear in mind that players that receive builds where the **Resolution Dialog** window is disabled can force it to appear by holding the *Alt* key (also known as *Option* on Mac) when launching the build—this can be useful when sending out test builds.

> To design a banner graphic to decorate the upper box part of the resolution dialog, design and save an image file in your project of size 432x163 pixels, and select it from the **Resolution Dialog Banner** drop-down menu on the **Player Settings** screen.

Now go to **File | Build Settings**, and ensure that your three scene files are listed in the **Scenes to build** area:

- **Menu.unity**
- **Island Level.unity**
- **Instructions.unity**

> If any scenes do not appear in the list, remember that they can be dragged and dropped from the **Project** panel to the **Build Settings** list.

It is important that **Menu** is the first scene in the list as we need this to load this first, so make sure it is at position **0**.

Compress Textures is selected by default and this should be kept that way, as it will ensure that your textures are compressed in order to load the game more quickly. The first time you build your game can take longer than ensuing builds, as the textures are compressed for the first time.

Now simply select which format you'd like to build for, either Windows, which will create a build to work on Windows XP, Vista, and 7+, or Mac—taking into account either PowerPC, Intel, or both (**universal binary**).

Click on the **Build** button at the bottom of this dialog window, and you'll be prompted for a location to save your game. Navigate to your desired location and name your built game in the **Save As** field. Then press the **Save** button to confirm.

Wait while Unity constructs your game! You'll be shown progress bars showing assets being compressed, followed by a loading bar as each level is added to the build. Once building is complete, your game build will be opened in an operating system window to show you that it is ready.

On Mac, double-click the application to launch it, or on PC, open the folder containing the game and double-click the .exe file to launch your game. Bear in mind that if you build a PC version on a Mac or vice versa, they cannot be tested natively.

Indie versus Pro

When building your game with Unity Indie version, you should be aware that your player will be shown a **Powered by Unity** splash screen before your game loads. This watermark is not present when building with the more expensive Pro version of Unity:

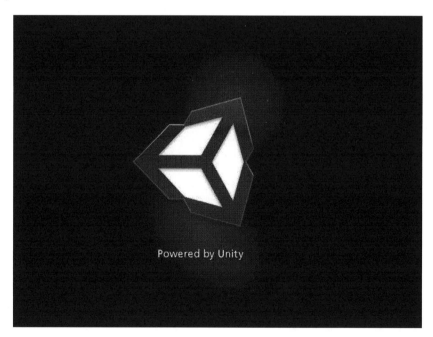

Other Indie versus Pro differences, such as the lack of dynamic shadows in Indie, can be found in a full table at the following URL:

```
http://unity3d.com/unity/licenses.html
```

Building for the Web

In Unity, open the **Build Settings** by going to **File | Build Settings**, and choose **Web Player** from the radio button list of types to build, and then simply click on **Build**. Unity will handle the relevant conversions and compressions necessary to create a build that will run well on the Web, and that's just one of its many charms!

You'll be prompted to specify a name and location to save the file. So enter this and then press the **Save** button at the bottom to confirm.

When complete, the operating system will switch to the window your build is saved in, showing you the two files that make the web build work—the game itself (a .unityweb extension file), and an HTML file containing the embedding code and JavaScript required to load or prompt download of the Unity Web Player plugin.

To play the game, open the HTML file in a web browser of your choice, and this will launch the game.

Adapting web player builds

As the default Unity build provides you with the necessary HTML/JavaScript code to include the .unityweb file in a web page, should you want to place this into your own HTML/CSS web pages, you'll simply need to take the code from the <head> and <body> areas of the page to place this build into your own design.

Detection script—<HEAD>

Open the build's accompanying HTML page in the script editor that comes with Unity or your favored HTML editor, for example, Dreamweaver, SciTE, TextMate, and TextWrangler. Select all code from the <head> part of the HTML—from the opening <script> to closing </script> tag, and copy this to a new JavaScript document, saving it as UnityDetect.js.

Then you can save this file to the same folder as your web pages and include this JavaScript by calling it in the <head> of your own page with the following line of HTML:

```
<script type="text/javascript" src="UnityDetect.js"></script>
```

Object embed—<BODY>

Then, take the embedding of the object itself by copying everything in the <body> of the page from the opening <script> tag, down to the closing </noscript> tag. Take this chunk of HTML and place it into your own web page in order to call the Unity player.

Remember that in order for this to work, this code assumes that the .unityweb file is in the same directory as the HTML which calls it.

Quality Settings

When exporting from Unity, you are not restricted to any single level of quality. You have a lot of control over the quality of your output, which comes in the form of the **Quality Settings**. Open this now in the **Inspector** part of the interface by going to **Edit | Project Settings | Quality**.

Here you'll find the ability to set your three different builds to one of the six different quality presets—**Fastest**, **Fast**, **Simple**, **Good**, **Beautiful**, and **Fantastic**. You can then edit these presets yourself to achieve precise results as you need to. As you are just starting out with Unity, let's take a look at the opposite ends of the scale, comparing **Fastest** with **Fantastic**:

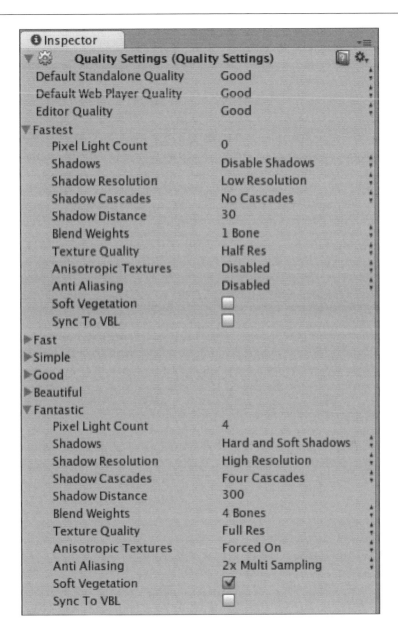

As you can see from the previous screenshot, the settings are vastly different from each end of the scale, so let's take a look at what the individual settings do:

- **Pixel Light Count**: The number of pixel lights that can be used in your scene. Lights in Unity are rendered as a pixel or vertex, pixel looking better but being more expensive processing-wise. With this setting, you can allow a certain number of pixel lights, with the rest being rendered as vertex lights. This is why the low end of the scale **Fastest** preset has the **Pixel Light Count** set to **0** by default.

- **Shadows**: This feature is available only in a Unity Pro version and allows you to specify no dynamic shadows, hard shadows only, or hard and soft shadows (the two levels of shadow quality).

- **Shadow Resolution**: Again this applies to Unity Pro only, and this setting allows you to choose a quality setting specifically for the shadows being rendered. This can be useful to save performance when having multiple objects with dynamic shadows in your scene—setting them to a low resolution could mean the difference between switching them off and keeping shadows entirely during optimization.

- **Shadow Cascades**: Unity Pro can take advantage of **Cascaded Shadow Maps**, which can improve the appearance of shadows on directional lights in your scene. By drawing the same shadow map over progressively larger expanses dependent upon proximity—closer to the player's camera gets more shadow map pixel detail, improving quality.

- **Shadow Distance**: Similar to the optimization of restricting the camera's far clip plane, this is another level of detail tweak. It can be used to simply set a distance after which shadows are not rendered.

- **Blend Weights**: This setting is used for rigged characters with a boned skeleton, and controls the number of weights (levels) of animation that can be blended between. Unity Technologies recommend two bones as a good trade-off between performance and appearance.

- **Texture Quality**: Exactly as it sounds, the amount to which Unity will compress your textures.

- **Anisotropic Textures**: **Anisotropic filtering** can help improve the appearance of textures when viewed at a steep angle, like hills, but is costly in terms of performance. Bear in mind that you can also set up this filtering on an individual-texture basis in the **Import Settings** for assets.

- **Anti Aliasing**: This setting softens the edges of 3D elements, making your game look a lot better. However, as with other filters, it comes at a cost of performance.

- **Soft Vegetation**: This allows Unity terrain elements, such as vegetation and trees to use **alpha blending,** which vastly improves the appearance of transparent areas of textures used to create the vegetation.

- **Sync to VBL**: This forces your game to be synchronized to the refresh rate of the player's monitor. This generally degrades the performance, but will avoid 'tearing' of elements in your game — the appearance of a misalignment of vertices where textures appear 'torn' from each other.

You should use these presets to set options that will benefit the player, as they will have the ability to choose from them in the **Resolution Dialog** window (see the *Building Standalone* section previously) when launching your game as a standalone, unless you have disabled this. However, it is fairly safe in most instances to use Unity's own presets as a guide, and simply tweak specific settings when you need to.

Player Input settings

While the **Resolution Dialog** window gives the standalone build player the ability to adjust the input controls of your game in the **Input** tab (see the following screenshot), it is important to know that you can specify your own defaults for the control of your game in the **Player Input settings**. This is especially useful for web builds, as the player has no ability to change control settings when they load the game. Therefore, it is best that you set them up sensibly and provide information to the player through your in-game GUI.

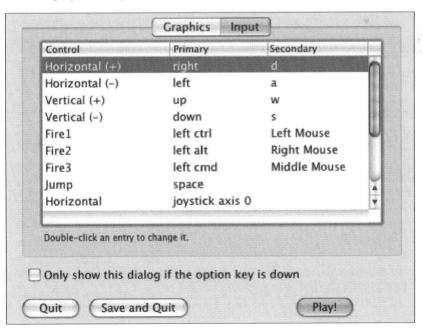

In Unity, go to **Edit | Project Settings | Input** to open the input settings in the **Inspector** part of the interface. You will then be presented with the existing axes of control in Unity. The **Size** value simply states how many controls exist. By increasing this value, you can build in your own controls, or alternatively you can simply expand any of the existing ones by clicking on the gray arrow to the left of their name and adjusting the values therein.

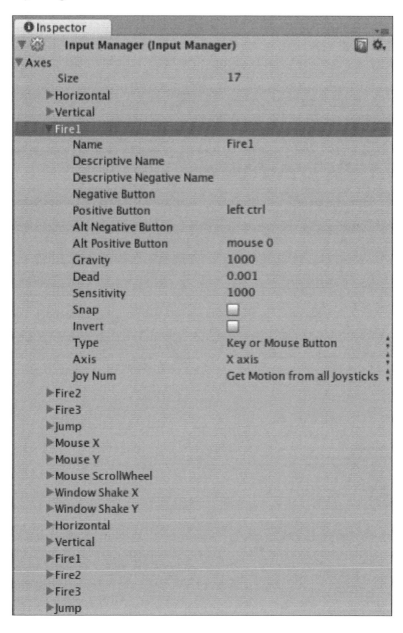

You can see how this ties together with the code we wrote earlier; when looking at the `CoconutThrow` script we wrote:

```
if(Input.GetButtonUp("Fire1")
```

Here, the `Fire1` axis is referenced by its name. By changing the **Name** parameter in the input settings, you can define what needs to be written in scripting. For more information on the keys you can bind to in these settings, refer to the **Input** page of the Unity manual at the following address:

```
http://unity3d.com/support/documentation/Manual/Input.html
```

Sharing your work

In addition to placing your web player build into your own web site, there are also several independent game portal sites available that act as a community for developers sharing their work.

Here are some recommended sites you should visit once you are ready to share your work with the online community:

- `www.shockwave.com`
- `www.wooglie.com`
- `www.blurst.com`
- `www.tigsource.com` (The Independent Gaming source)
- `www.thegameslist.com`
- `http://forum.unity3d.com` (Showcase area)
- `www.todaysfreegame.com`
- `www.learnUnity3d.com`

It is important that you share your work with others not only to show off your development skills but also to get feedback on your game and allow members of the public with no prior knowledge of your project to test how it works.

This kind of unbiased feedback is crucial as it allows you to weed out bugs and troubleshoot unintuitive parts of your game that may make sense to you but baffle the ordinary player.

Also, be aware that some sites may not be able to host your game in `.unityweb` format but will be willing to link to your own blog with the game embedded or host a standalone version for download.

Summary

In this chapter, we've looked at how you can export your game to the Web and as a standalone project. In the conclusion, we'll look back at what you have learned over the course of this book and suggest ways in which you can progress further with the existing skills you have developed and where to look for continued assistance with your Unity development.

11
Testing and Further Study

Over the course of this book, we have covered the essential topics to get you started in development with the Unity game engine. In working with Unity, you'll discover that with each new game element you develop, new avenues of possibility open up in your knowledge. Fresh ideas and game concepts will come more easily as you add further scripting knowledge to your skillset. In this chapter, we'll conclude your introduction to Unity by looking at:

- Approaches to testing and finalizing your work
- Measuring frame rates from test users
- Where to go for help with Unity and what to study next

With this in mind, when looking ahead to where to continue extending your skills, you should take time to expand your knowledge of the following areas:

- Scripting
- Scripting
- Scripting

That's right, it's no joke—while Unity prides itself on providing an intuitive toolset for developing in a visual manner and using the Editor's GUI to build scenes and game objects, there is no substitute for learning the classes and commands that make up the Unity engine itself.

By reading through the Unity manual, followed by the Component Reference and Script Reference—available both online and as part of your Unity software installation—you'll begin to understand how best to create all types of game elements, which may not apply to your current project but should flesh out your understanding to help you work more efficiently in the long term:

- Component Reference (`http://www.unity3d.com/support/documentation/Components/`)

- Scripting Reference (`http://www.unity3d.com/support/documentation/ScriptReference/`)

- Unity Manual (`http://www.unity3d.com/support/documentation/Manual/`)

Testing and finalizing

When considering game development, you should be very aware of the importance of testing your game amongst users who have no preconceptions of it whatsoever. When working on any creative project, you should be aware that to maintain creative objectivity, you need to be open to criticism and that testing is just as much part of that as it is a technical necessity. It is all too easy to become used to your game's narrative or mechanics, and often unable to see "the wood for the trees" in terms of how the player will respond to it.

Public testing

When looking to test your game, try and send test builds to a range of users who can provide test feedback for you with the following variations:

- Computer specification: Ensure that you test on a number of differently powered machines, and get feedback on performance

- Format: Try sending a build for both Mac and PC where possible

- Language: Do your test users all speak the same language as you? Can they tell you if you explain elements of the game in the interfaces?

When handing your game over to a collection of public testers, you are handing them what is referred to as a **beta** test of your game — **alpha** being a test version you and other developers test. By formalizing the process, you can make the feedback you get about your game as useful as possible — draw up a questionnaire that poses the same questions to all testers while asking not only questions about their responses to the game, but also information about them as a player. In this way, you can begin to make assertions about your game, such as:

"Players aged 18 to 24 liked the mechanic and understood the game but players of 45+ did not understand it without reading the instructions."

in addition to technical information such as:

"Players with computers under 2.4ghz processing speed found the game to respond sluggishly."

Frame rate feedback

In order to provide testers of your game with a means of providing specific feedback on technicalities such as frame rate (speed at which game frames are drawn during play), you can provide your test build with a GUI element telling them the current frame rate.

To add this to any scene, let's take a look at a practical example. Open the scene you wish to add a frame rate screen overlay to, and create a new GUI Text object to display the information — go to **GameObject | Create Other | GUI Text**. Rename this object **FPS displayer**, and then in the **GUI Text** component of the **Inspector,** set the **Anchor** to **upper center**, and the **Alignment** to **center**.

Now create a new script in your **Project** by selecting a folder you'd like to create it in, and then click **Create**, and select **Javascript** from the drop-down menu. Rename your script **FPSdisplay**, then double-click its icon to launch it in the script editor.

Because the frame rate your game runs at is variable depending upon hardware and software configuration, we need to perform a sum which takes into account how many frames were rendered within the game's time scale each second. We'll start by establishing the following variables at the top of the script:

```
private var updatePeriod = 0.5;
private var nextUpdate : float = 0;
private var frames : float = 0;
private var fps : float = 0;
```

We establish these four variables here for the following reasons:

- `updatePeriod`: how often in seconds we would like the GUI text to update, and therefore the period in which we sample the amount of frames rendered. We have set this to `0.5` in order to show a new reading every half a second, making it easy for the test user to read—setting this value any lower would result in numbers updating too often to read easily. Setting any higher—for example one second—would result in a less accurate reading, as the frame rate may vary within the second.

- `nextUpdate`: this is a number to store the point in time at which we should check and update the frames per second.

- `frames`: a number incremented each frame, therefore storing the amount of frames rendered.

- `fps`: a number to store the frames per second, which will be assigned the current fps value by taking the value of the `frames` variable and dividing it by the `updatePeriod` variable.

Now, in the `Update()` function, place the following code:

```
frames++;

if(Time.time > nextUpdate){

    fps = Mathf.Round(frames / updatePeriod);
        guiText.text = "Frames Per Second: " + fps;
        nextUpdate = Time.time + updatePeriod;
        frames = 0;
}
```

Here we do the following:

- Increment the `frames` variable by 1 each time the `Update()` function occurs (after each frame).

- Wait for `Time.time`—a real-time counter that counts from the start of the game—to reach a value beyond the value of the `nextUpdate` variable. As `nextUpdate` begins the game at a value of `0`, this occurs immediately when the scene this script is in loads.

- This `if` statement then sets the `fps` variable to equal a rounded value of the count of frames, divided by the `updatePeriod`, in order to give us a whole number of how many frames per second, rather than half a second—the `0.5` value of `updatePeriod`.

- We address the `guiText` component's `text` parameter, and set it to a string saying `"Frames Per Second :"`, and add the number in the `fps` variable to the end.

- Crucially, we then set the `nextUpdate` to the current value of `time`, plus `updatePeriod`, meaning this `if` statement will re-trigger in half a second's time.
- Finally, we reset the frames count so that sampling may continue from zero.

Now, after the closing of the `Update` function, ensure that you include the following line to make sure that you're adding this to an object with a GUI Text component:

```
@script RequireComponent(GUIText)
```

Go to **File | Save** in the script editor, and switch back to Unity. Ensure that the **FPS displayer** object is still selected in the **Hierarchy** and then go to **Component | Scripts | FPS display**. Now test your scene, and you will see the GUI Text displaying the frame rate at the top of the screen.

Your game will perform differently outside of the Unity editor. As such, readings from this FPS displayer should only be noted once the game is built and run either as a web player or standalone version; ask your test users to note the lowest and highest frame rates to give you a range of readings to consider, and if there are particularly demanding parts of your game, for example complex animation or particle effects, then it could be worth asking for readings from these times separately.

Because the game performs differently outside of the Unity editor, the values from this frame rate display will be different from those given in the in-built **Stats** tab of the **Game** view:

Boosting performance

Improving the performance of your game as a result of testing is easily an entire field of study in itself. However, to improve your future development, you'll need to be aware of basic economizing in the following ways:

- Polygon counts: When introducing 3D models, they should be designed with low polygon counts in mind. So try and simplify your models as much as possible to improve performance.

- Draw distance: Consider reducing the distance of your Far Clip Plane in your cameras to cut down the amount of scenery the game must render.

- Texture sizes: Including higher resolution textures can improve the visual clarity of your game, but they also make the engine work harder. So try and reduce texture sizes as much as possible, using both your image editing software and using the Import settings of your texture assets.

- Script efficiently: As there are many approaches to differing solutions in scripting, try and find more efficient ways to write your scripts. Start by reading the Unity guide to efficient scripting online (`http://unity3d. com/support/documentation/ScriptReference/index.Performance_ Optimization.html`)

- Watch the Performance Optimization presentation by Joachim Ante, lead programmer at Unity Technologies (`http://unity3d.com/support/ resources/unite-presentations/performance-optimization`)

Approaches to learning

As you progress from this book, you will need to develop an approach to further study, which keeps a balance between personal perseverance and the need to ask for help from more experienced Unity developers. Follow the advice laid out below, and you should be well on your way to helping other community members as you expand your knowledge.

Cover as many bases as possible

When learning any new software package/programming language, it is often the case that you are working to a deadline, be it as part of your job or as a freelancer. This can often lead to a "take only what you need" approach to learning. While this can often be a necessity due to working demands, it can often be detrimental to your learning, as you may develop bad habits that stay with you throughout your time working with the software—eventually leading to inefficient approaches.

Taking this on board, I recommend that you take time to read through the official documentation whenever you can—even if you're stuck on a specific development problem, it can often help to take your mind away from what you're stuck with. Go and read up on an unrelated scenario, and return with a fresh perspective.

If you don't know, just ask!

Another useful approach to learning is, of course, to look at how others approach each new game element you attempt to create. In game development, what you'll discover is that often there are many approaches to the same problem—as we learned in Chapter 5, when making our character open the outpost door. As a result, it is often tempting to recycle skills learned solving a previous problem—but I recommend always double-checking that your approach is the most efficient way.

By asking in the Unity forum or on the IRC (Internet Relay Chat) channel, you'll be able to gain a consensus on the most efficient way to perform a development task—and more often than not, discover that the way you first thought of approaching your problem was more complicated than it needed to be!

When asking questions in either of the previously mentioned places, always remember to include the following points whenever possible:

- What are you trying to achieve?
- What do you think is the right approach?
- What have you tried so far?

This will give others the best shot at helping you out—by giving as much information as possible, even if you think it may not be relevant, you will give yourself the best chance of achieving your development.

The great thing about the Unity community is that it encourages learning by example. Third party Wiki-based site (`www.unifycommunity.com/wiki`) has wide ranging examples of everything from scripts to plugins, to tutorials, and more. There you'll find useful free-to-use code snippets to supplement the examples of scripted elements within the script reference and even information on how to implement it with example downloadable projects.

Summary

In this chapter, we have discussed ways that you should move on from this book, and how you can gather information from test users to improve your game.

All that remains is to wish you the best of luck with your future game development in Unity. From myself and everyone involved with this book, thanks for reading, and I hope you enjoyed the ride—it's only just the beginning!

Index

Q

Quality Settings
about 270
anisotropic textures 272
anti aliasing 273
blend weights 272
pixel light count 272
shadow cascades 272
shadow distance 272
shadow resolution 272
shadows 272
soft vegetation 273
sync to VBL 273
texture quality 272
quit button, menu
adding 218
OnGUI() function 219
Play Game menu button 219
QuitBtn texture 218
Quit() command 218
Quit Game button 219
Quit Button variable 219
Quit() command 218
Quit Game button 219

R

Raise Height tool 31
ray casting
about 99-102
frame miss 102
predictive collision detection 102, 103
ray casting, outpost opening
about 123
collision detection disabling, comments
used 124
door collider, resetting 124
ray, adding 125, 126
refresh tree 29
RequireComponent 226
rigid bodies
about 154
force 154
Rigidbody component 154
Rigidbody component, parameters 155
Rigidbody component
about 154

parameters 155
Rigidbody component, parameters
angular drag 155
drag 155
freeze rotation 155
interpolate 155
is kinematic 155
mass 155
use gravity 155
Rigid Body physics 12
Rnd Force parameter 194
rollOverTexture 215
Rotate() command 130
Rotate tool [E] 18
rotationAmount 130

S

Scale tool [R] 18
scene, menu
creating 209
duplicating 211
environment objects, grouping 210
island, duplicating 210
visual example 210
scenes 15
Scene window
about 18
Hand tool [Q] 18
Rotate tool [E] 18
Scale tool [R] 18
Translate tool [W] 18
script assignment, minigame 166, 167, 176
scripting
about 81
commands 81, 82
comments 89
dot syntax 88
functions 84
globals 88
globals defining, static used 88
If-else statements 86, 87
variable data types 82
variables 82
scripting reference 278
scripts 16
shader 12

---
[293]

W

web player builds
adapting 269
Detection script-<HEAD> 269
Object embed-<BODY> 270
Web Player, Build Settings
about 259
Player Settings 259, 260
Web Player Streamed, Build settings 261
Widgets 261
work
sharing, with online community 275
world space
versus local space 10

X

X-axis 75, 249

Y

Y-axis 57, 75, 94

Z

Z-axis 9

About Packt Publishing

Packt, pronounced 'packed', published its first book *"Mastering phpMyAdmin for Effective MySQL Management"* in April 2004 and subsequently continued to specialize in publishing highly focused books on specific technologies and solutions.

Our books and publications share the experiences of your fellow IT professionals in adapting and customizing today's systems, applications, and frameworks. Our solution based books give you the knowledge and power to customize the software and technologies you're using to get the job done. Packt books are more specific and less general than the IT books you have seen in the past. Our unique business model allows us to bring you more focused information, giving you more of what you need to know, and less of what you don't.

Packt is a modern, yet unique publishing company, which focuses on producing quality, cutting-edge books for communities of developers, administrators, and newbies alike. For more information, please visit our website: www.packtpub.com.

Writing for Packt

We welcome all inquiries from people who are interested in authoring. Book proposals should be sent to author@packtpub.com. If your book idea is still at an early stage and you would like to discuss it first before writing a formal book proposal, contact us; one of our commissioning editors will get in touch with you.

We're not just looking for published authors; if you have strong technical skills but no writing experience, our experienced editors can help you develop a writing career, or simply get some additional reward for your expertise.

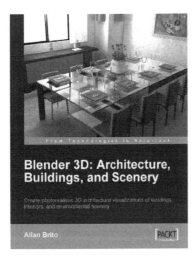

**Blender 3D: Architecture,
Buildings, and Scenery**

Allan Brito

Blender 3D Architecture,
Buildings, and Scenery

ISBN: 978-1-847193-67-4   Paperback: 332 pages

Create photorealistic 3D architectural visualizations
of buildings, interiors, and environmental scenery

1. Turn your architectural plans into a model

2. Study modeling, materials, textures, and light
   basics in Blender

3. Create photo-realistic images in detail

4. Create realistic virtual tours of buildings and
   scenes

Papervision3D Essentials

Paul Tondeur   Jeff Winder

Papervision3D Essentials

ISBN: 978-1-847195-72-2   Paperback: 428 pages

Create interactive Papervision 3D applications with
stunning effects and powerful animations

1. Build stunning, interactive Papervision3D
   applications from scratch

2. Export and import 3D models from
   Autodesk 3ds Max, SketchUp and Blender to
   Papervision3D

3. In-depth coverage of important 3D concepts
   with demo applications, screenshots and
   example code.

4. Step-by-step guide for beginners and
   professionals with tips and tricks based on the
   authors' practical experience

Please check **www.PacktPub.com** for information on our titles

3D Game Development with Microsoft Silverlight 3: Beginner's Guide

ISBN: 978-1-847198-92-1   Paperback: 452 pages

A practical guide to creating real-time responsive online 3D games in Silverlight 3 using C#, XBAP WPF, XAML, Balder, and Farseer Physics Engine

1. Develop online interactive 3D games and scenes in Microsoft Silverlight 3 and XBAP WPF

2. Integrate Balder 3D engine 1.0, Farseer Physics Engine 2.1, and advanced object-oriented techniques to simplify the game development process

Flash with Drupal

ISBN: 978-1-847197-58-0   Paperback: 380 pages

Build dynamic, content-rich Flash CS3 and CS4 applications for Drupal 6

1. Learn to integrate Flash applications with Drupal CMS

2. Explore a new approach where Flash and HTML components are intermixed to provide a hybrid Flash-Drupal architecture

3. Build a custom audio and video player in Flash and link it to Drupal

4. Build a Flash driven 5-star voting system for Drupal at the end of the book

Please check **www.PacktPub.com** for information on our titles